ZVI
THE MIRACULOUS
STORY OF TRIUMPH
OVER THE HOLOCAUST

ZVI

THE MIRACULOUS STORY OF TRIUMPH OVER THE HOLOCAUST

ELWOOD McQUAID

The Friends of Israel Gospel Ministry, Inc.
P. O. Box 908, Bellmawr, NJ 08099

This book was originally published as two books:
ZVI
Elwood McQuaid
Copyright © 1978 by The Friends of Israel Gospel Ministry, Inc.
Library of Congress Catalog Card Number: 78-56149
ISBN 0-915540-23-1

ZVI AND THE NEXT GENERATION
Elwood McQuaid
Copyright © 1988 by The Friends of Israel Gospel Ministry, Inc.
Bellmawr, NJ 08099
Library of Congress Catalog Card Number: 88-80875
ISBN 0-915540-43-6

ZVI THE MIRACULOUS STORY OF TRIUMPH OVER THE HOLOCAUST

Elwood McQuaid

Copyright © 2000 by The Friends of Israel Gospel Ministry, Inc.
Bellmawr, NJ 08099

Ninth Printing 2013

Library of Congress Catalog Card Number: 00130954
ISBN 13: 978-0-915540-66-2

Cover by Left Coast Designs, Portland, OR

Visit our website at www.foi.org.

*When my father and my mother forsake me,
then the LORD will take me up.*

PSALM 27:10

And he brought him forth abroad, and said, Look now toward heaven, and count the stars, if thou be able to number them: and he said unto him, So shall thy seed be.

GENESIS 15:5

from Mom

PUBLISHER'S NOTE

When this book was first published, we felt it
incumbent on us to change many of the names
of the people involved to protect their privacy.
Since that need no longer exists, we would like
our readers to know that Zvi Weichert is, in fact,
our beloved Zvi Kalisher, whose column has
appeared in *Israel My Glory* magazine since 1959
and will continue to appear there until the Lord
calls him home.

TABLE OF CONTENTS

1967–1973

1973–1982

1982–1986

1986–

INTRODUCTION

*Z*vi is the biography of a man who, like his nation, Israel, defies explanation apart from God. His story, in the early stages, is reminiscent of the book of Esther in the Bible—God is not consciously represented, yet He is obviously present and at work.

People and events touch Zvi's life at strategic points in ways that cannot be coincidental. Over the tortuous course he followed in his fight for survival, a clear pattern of divine provision emerges.

Unlike many of the stories told today, this true-life epic has a satisfying climax. How Zvi survived the Holocaust, found his way to the shores of Israel, and experienced a life-transforming encounter with the Messiah is a story one can ill afford to pass by. It is a story of triumph, miracles, and hope, and dramatically reveals the lengths to which a loving God will go to bring one soul safely home.

E. McQ.

1 9 3 9 — 1 9 4 5

CHAPTER ONE

NOW YOU ARE A MAN

He stood at the window looking out for a long time. In the courtyard below, he could see small children playing games. The gate through which his mother had left the orphanage seemed disproportionately large against the gathering darkness. At ten years of age, Henryk Weichert found himself alone. He did not know why. Nor could this frail Jewish lad begin to comprehend the maelstrom of carnage and outrage into which he and Europe were passing. The Poland of his carefree childhood was gone, and life would never be the same again.

Prior to 1939 Warsaw had been a happy place for a young boy to grow up. Oh, there had been guarded conversations among adults and occasional talk of war, but in the world of a small child, such things meant very little. Then the Germans came and introduced Henryk to the demented world of Adolph Hitler.

After a while an attendant came and led the boy down a long corridor to the room he would occupy with other parentless children. He slowly placed the few belongings he had brought along into the drawer assigned to him. Then he walked to the cot he was to sleep on and sat down. Thoughts of the last frantic weeks rushed through his head in confused patterns. A child's mind could not assimilate the great changes that were taking place—changes destined to menace the world and alter the face of Europe.

For months Hitler had been attempting to use political sleight of hand to veil his true designs for Poland from the French and British. He hoped to lull them into inaction at least long enough to implement his program for armed annexation.

On August 23, 1939, the German Führer announced that the Fatherland had signed a nonaggression pact with Russia. A secret clause in this agreement between predators called for the partition of Poland: part of the country would go to Russia, the other part to Germany. The Vistula, Narew, and Sans Rivers would be the dividing line between the occupying forces.

September's first days saw German panzer divisions streaming across the border, while Luftwaffe aircraft simultaneously devastated Polish cities from the skies. The Polish people were determined to resist the onslaught, but their efforts could not stay the German advance. By September 9 the Fourth Panzer Division was positioned on the outskirts of Warsaw and was preparing to enter the city. A counterattack by Polish forces forestalled the inevitable briefly, but the weight of German armor and continuous assaults by dive-bombers eventually prevailed.

On September 27 Warsaw surrendered, and effective resistance was crushed throughout the country. Poland became a slave-state, bled jointly by Nazis and Communists.

Hitler's plan for Poland called for annexing a portion of the country outright and forging it into the Reich as a part of Germany proper. A second area, which included Warsaw, Krakow, and Lubin, was to be incorporated under German administration as the Generalgovernment. But it was Hitler's long-range program that told the story. In a move of calculated duplicity, it would stab the sword of aggression firmly in the back of his Russian allies (June 22, 1941) in an attempt to extend the Nazi utopia to Moscow and the hinterlands beyond.

This situation prevailed when ten-year-old Henryk Weichert had entered his home in the suburbs of Warsaw some months earlier. Despite the concentrated bombing of the city, the area where the Weicherts lived bore no obvious marks of war. The tree-shaded street, now taking on the colors of fall, was deceptively calm. The serenity was broken only when the boy entered the kitchen and found both of his parents in tears.

"What is wrong?" Henryk asked.

"We have lost the war," his father replied. "The Germans have come to Warsaw. Go sit in the other room. I must talk to your mother."

He entered the adjacent room and sat down with his three older brothers and sister. The air seemed heavy as he listened to the hushed conversation that passed between the boys. Arthur, the eldest, was telling them about the things he had heard from some neighbors earlier in the day. Tanks by the hundreds and soldiers—too many to count—had entered Warsaw. Many people had been killed. Everywhere there was fear about what would happen next. They must prepare for the worst.

Mendel and Ruth Weichert were strong people. He was a quiet, reserved sort of man who was seldom known to display his emotions. Today it was different. As he tried to explain the current situation to the children, he found it necessary to pause frequently in order to regain his composure.

"Life will be changed for us now," he said solemnly. "You will no longer be free to come and go as you once did. From now on, stay close to home. If you should see German soldiers, get out of their way. We can only hope that they will soon be driven from our land. Until then, we must be strong."

At that time they could not begin to realize just how strong they would have to be. Poland and her people were entering a period of trauma that had seldom been equaled on this planet. Hitler would pursue with rabid dedication his carefully crafted scheme for the "Aryanization" of Europe. Those who did not fit the mold were doomed.

The Nazi program for the conquered Poles was direct and brutal. Thousands were summarily executed. Thousands more were sent to Germany to be used as slave labor. Others were driven from their lands in the annexed territory and their property given to settlers being transported to the area from Germany. Displaced farmers and other "undesirables" throughout Poland were forcibly exiled into the Generalgovernment area, which was initially viewed by the Germans as a dumping ground for deportees. Consequently, the population of Warsaw swelled due to the tide of refugees flooding the city. Already crippled by the ravages of war, Warsaw was ill-prepared to face the challenge of resettling large numbers of people.

Hard on the heels of the soldiers came a dreaded breed of political police known as Einstzgruppen. Their function was to serve as a strike force dedicated to hunting down and eliminating people suspected of being disloyal to the ideals of National Socialism. A reign of fear quickly spread across the country, producing a perpetual cloud of anxiety, suspicion, and terror that hung ominously over the people of Poland.

The pursuit of life in Warsaw became a grim business. Scowling, helmeted conscripts of the Third Reich were everywhere, and it was soon evident that physical survival would become the primary occupation of the victims of the Nazi conquest. News of arrests and imprisonment became routine. Neighbors suddenly disappeared without notice or explanation. Then, as if these horrors were not enough, hunger descended like a plague.

A situation that was bad for the average Polish citizen became insufferable for the members of the Jewish community. They were earmarked as special objects of Nazi enmity. Hitler's charted course for "a final solution to the Jewish problem" involved successive stages: First, Jews were to be isolated and vilified. Jewish citizens were required to wear identifying armbands; their travel and activities were restricted and their properties and persons subjected to seizure at a moment's whim. Synagogues were destroyed and thousands of executions carried out. Jews were not allowed to have as much food as their Polish neighbors. Shopkeepers were dragged from their stores and beaten in the streets. Windows were broken and anti-Jewish slogans plastered on the walls of buildings. Jewish girls and women became the objects of cruel and violent public humiliation. Consequently, they kept more and more to their homes.

After several months of this type of calculated harassment, the Jewish people were forced to move into specially constructed ghetto areas. Streets were cordoned off and later walled, penning them up inside like animals. The first such ghetto was built in Lodz in May of 1940. Warsaw received her infamous counterpart in November of the same year. Ghettos often contained small industries where the inhabitants were expected to work as their contribution to the war effort, while being systematically starved to death.

The final step on Hitler's road to a Jewless world involved the establishment of death camps and the destruction of the ghettos. It was to be the terminal phase. Six annihilation centers dotted the area Poland occupied prior to the war. Auschwitz, Belzec, Treblinka, and the other camps received what seemed to be an endless stream of wasted Jews who were hustled off the boxcars into which they had been shoved, prodded, and herded worse than cattle, then hurried through the gates for "processing." By the middle of 1942, at Treblinka alone, more than three hundred thousand Jewish people had made the one-way trip to the incinerators.

Destruction of the ghettos began late in 1942. The enclave at Warsaw came under fire in April of 1943. There beleaguered Jews, many little more than boys and girls, mounted a heroic resistance. Somehow they managed to stave off the Nazis onslaught for six weeks. On May 10, 1943, the futile struggle ended; the ghetto and all those inside were annihilated.

Before the war began, 3.3 million Jews had made Poland their home. By the end of the war, 3 million had perished.

These events cast the cauldron into which little Henryk and his family were thrown.

The first rude intrusion into their lives entered when a black-booted representative of the new regime called at the Weichert home one winter afternoon. After a crisp introduction, the man stated his business. "On Monday morning you will bring your three oldest sons to the railroad station in Warsaw. They will be taken to Germany for training, then put to work in an industrial plant.

"You needn't worry about them. They will be well treated. When the war is over, you will see them again."

There was no time for discussion or rebuttal. The matter had been settled by the authorities. Arthur, Hersh, and Jacob would be taken from their midst to serve their captors.

A pall of apprehension hung over the household for the remainder of the week. It was as though the Weicherts were grasping some precious thing that was slipping irretrievably from their fingers. All seemed to be well aware that what they had known all of their lives was passing from them. Would they ever be together as a family again? It was a question none could answer, and a situation over which none had control.

Monday was a dismal day. The weather was bad, the mood depressing. Arthur made a few feeble attempts to cheer the family spirit. It was a vain effort.

The depot was teeming with activity. People were jammed into the terminal, jostling their way to or from the trains. Dozens of families, many of whom were friends or acquaintances of the Weicherts, had come on the same mission. Teenaged boys stood, bags in hand, ready to be ushered aboard the train for the long ride to Germany. Tema and Henryk clutched their parents' clothing during the tearful farewells. Then the boys boarded the train and were gone.

Henryk thought the house seemed larger without his brothers; it was certainly quieter. He and his sister now spent more time playing with one another and the neighborhood children than they had before. After a time most of the older boys had disappeared from the community, and only the small ones remained.

In the months that followed, Mendel increasingly spent long periods of time locked in silence. When the children spoke to him, the words did not appear to penetrate. It seemed that his thoughts were as far away as Henryk's brothers. When he came home in the evenings, he and Ruth would send the children into another part of the house while they talked quietly. It seemed like hours before Tema and Henryk were allowed into the room. Frequently following these conversations, Ruth wore a worried expression. The children could often see that she had been weeping.

One night the news was unusually bad. Mendel told his wife that the rumors they had heard were now confirmed. All Jewish families were to be relocated within a designated area in the city of Warsaw. Official notification of the order would arrive soon.

"But what will become of our home?" Ruth asked, distraught.

"It will be used for housing German soldiers. At least, that is what I'm told they plan to do with most of the dwellings confiscated from Jews."

"And the children, Mendel, what will become of our children?" Her tone carried a pleading burst of consternation that had been building for months.

"I have been giving much thought to that question," her husband replied softly. "Tema must come with us. But I see no future in the ghetto for Henryk. I feel it would be best to do what we can to conceal his identity as a Jew and place him in an orphanage."

Ruth was stunned but receptive. "I've seen what has happened to the others. It can't be worse for him in an orphanage. At least we will be in the same city. Perhaps this way he has a chance."

So the decision was made. In a few days Ruth would take the boy to a home for orphans.

The day came quickly. Soon a mother and her son walked hand in hand through the streets of Warsaw. Ruth proceeded hesitantly, a small valise in her left hand. Somehow she wished they could walk past the orphanage into a world free from death and trouble. But it was not to be. Soon an austere gray building, which stood behind a low stone wall, appeared before them. Ruth quickened the pace as they passed the gate and climbed the steps toward the entrance.

Once inside, there was a brief exchange of introductions before the committal papers were filled out. After this was completed, Ruth asked for a few moments to be alone with her son. One hand gripped his arm tightly; the fingers of the other passed repeatedly through his hair.

Henryk looked into his mother's face. What he saw there would remain etched in his memory for life. She appeared much older than she had looked just weeks ago. Her eyes possessed a strange, frightened expression he had never seen in them before. Still, he thought, she was a very beautiful woman. Small, blond, and round-faced, she represented all that a mother could properly personify to a son. And when he looked at her, he saw all the affection, strength, and attention a boy could ever desire.

She spoke in carefully measured tones. "Henryk, I want you to make a promise, one that you must always carry with you—a promise you must never forget. Do not tell anyone that you are a Jew."

"But mother, why?"

"Because they don't like Jews here. You must watch your words. Be careful what you say, and always remember what I have told you.

"My son, you must learn to be strong. From now on you are no longer my child—now you are a man."

He could feel her body quiver as she embraced him. Rising quickly, she paused for a moment to assure him. "Remember, be strong. I will come often to see you." Then turning away, she left the room. When he could no longer hear her footsteps in the hallway, he walked to the window and looked out. He saw his mother cross the courtyard and pass through the gate.

For a time Henryk spent hours at the window watching for his mother to visit him—or better still, to take him home and put an end to this bad dream. On holidays and weekends he searched the faces of those who arrived to see relatives, eagerly hoping to find someone who was familiar to him. But it was always the same; a disappointed boy would return to his room to await another day in the hope that it would bring his mother back to him. By this time, however, his parents, along with so many other Jewish families, were enduring the rigors of their trial.

Soon things at the orphanage began to change. German teachers arrived to instruct the children in the German language. Along with their language studies, the youngsters were carefully exposed to Nazi political indoctrination. They were, after all, prime prospects for the Hitler Youth movement the Nazis were developing in Poland. Before long the children found themselves joining heartily in the songs of the Fatherland, many of which were packed with anti-Jewish lyrics. Children could often be seen in the courtyard imitating the goosestep of the soldiers of the Third Reich and raising stiffened arms in salutes to the Führer. After a full year of concentrated brainwashing, the boys had indeed become very German. Henryk was no exception. He was now conversant in German and harbored the same ambition as all the other boys—to become a soldier and fight for Deutschland.

One day an announcement was made at a special assembly: "You will be happy to know that you are going to take a long journey. Tomorrow morning you will board a train bound for Berlin. For the first time, you will see the Fatherland. Along the way, you will tour the country and get a good look at the land of the Führer. Who knows, you may even see him."

Everyone was ecstatic over the news. To ride a train so far! It was the opportunity of a lifetime—and to go to Germany. What more could one ask?

Henryk was not so sure. This would mean leaving Warsaw. If his mother should come for him, he would be gone. He was disturbed even more when he learned that after their departure, the orphanage would be closed permanently. How could she find him if he went so far away? He didn't sleep much that night. His mother's words kept running through his mind: "Be strong . . . I will come back to see you . . ." There in the darkness of the room, it seemed as though he could reach out and touch her face. He was almost certain he could feel the grip of her hand on his arm. Surely she would come for him. Finally sleep enveloped little Henryk and brought quiet to his troubled mind.

In the morning he came to a decision: What will be, will be. Germany lay ahead of him. He would go there as a man—he would be strong.

Several days on the rails provided plenty of mental diversion for the boy traveler. The countryside was beautiful. Deep ravines, with their picturesque rambling streams, passed frequently beneath the wheels of the train. They journeyed through hamlets and cities, where people always seemed to be in a great hurry to get where they were going—and always there were soldiers. Sometimes they stretched out in long columns, marching along the roads. At every railroad station, one could see them walking slowly, with rifles strung over their shoulders.

The Germans kept their promise to show these Polish boys the heartland of the Third Reich. The train rumbled through many of the major cities in eastern and southern Germany. Dresden, Frankfort on the Oder, Stargart, and Brandenburg all moved slowly past the windows of the train before it swung north toward its final destination. As the train approached the city of Berlin, it slowed and moved onto a siding near a railroad station. "Everybody out!" cried one of the men who accompanied the boys. "Take all of your belongings. Leave nothing on the train."

It was good to be off the train and out in the fresh air again. They waited about thirty minutes before a gleaming black car drove up to the station house and stopped. Several uniformed Germans got out and approached the man who was in charge of the children. "Move them inside and line them up according to size," one of the officers ordered.

The boys were herded into a large room and lined up according to the instructions. An officer stepped forward to address the group.

"Welcome to the Fatherland. I bring you greetings in the name of the Führer.

"Your group will now be divided into two units. Those who are largest and strongest will be placed in a group that will proceed to Berlin. The rest of you will return to Poland."

The soldiers then hustled them through a line where the final selection was being made. Henryk found himself standing before an angular officer.

"Well, young man, what do you want to be when you are grown?" the soldier asked.

"I want to be an officer in the German army and fight for Deutschland," Henryk replied.

The German threw back his head and laughed. "Such courage in one so small," he said.

"But I am not too small to fight! You will see," the boy challenged.

The officer smiled down at him. "Yes, you will fight, but not now. You are too small. Go back to Poland and drink as much milk as you can. Then you will come back and serve the Reich."

Tickets and food rations were issued to those who were not selected to continue. Soon they were on the train for the return trip to Poland. For the boy, it was a great disappointment; but in terms of survival, being too small probably saved his life.

Henryk did some hard thinking on the journey home. What would he do now? He could not return to the orphanage. But where would he go? More than ever, he wanted to see his family. That was it! If his parents could not come to him, he would go to them. He would return to Warsaw and go back to his home.

It took some time to find the old neighborhood. Things had changed. As Henryk neared his home, however, the surroundings appeared reassuringly familiar. Finally the homestead came into view. He began to run excitedly toward the house. At long last he would be reunited with his parents and Tema. How good it was to be home again.

As he turned onto the walkway to his house, the front door opened and a woman stepped out. It was not his mother. This woman wore a German uniform. She stood before him on the sidewalk with a frozen expression. "What do you want?" she snapped. "If it's food you are after, you will find none here. Go away."

The stunned eleven-year-old spun on his heel and walked quickly into the street. Once he was beyond the woman's view, he stopped. Fresh questions now flooded his mind. What, he wondered, could have happened? Where were his parents? Would he ever see them again? How could he find them?

As he struggled with his thoughts, a boy walked toward him. Henryk paid little attention to him at first. But then he realized that the lad was Janusz, a neighbor with whom he had spent many hours at play before his days at the orphanage. Henryk called out to him and rushed forward. The boy's face registered instant recognition, but just as quickly, his features became rigid with fear. The youth sped up his pace and brushed by without a word. As Henryk turned to pursue him, the boy turned in at his house, slamming the door behind him.

Henryk's small fists frantically assailed the door through which his former playmate had darted. He had to find the answer. Someone must tell him where his parents had gone. At last the door opened a crack, and Henryk recognized the boy's father. Before he could say a word, the man was speaking. "Go away from this place, please; go quickly."

By now the boy was weeping openly. "But why? What has happened?"

There was a brief silence. Then the door was thrown open and the man stepped out. His eyes were apprehensive as they swept the street. Pushing Henryk inside, he said: "All right, I will tell you where they are, but then you must go. The Germans have forbidden us to take Jews into our homes. To do so means death for the whole family. Even to speak to you places me in grave danger.

"Your family has been taken to the ghetto. There are no more Jews living in this neighborhood. I will tell you a place where you might find them—it is in the Jewish quarter. The wall outside is heavily guarded. I don't know if you will be able to get in.

"Now please, leave by the back door—hurry—tell no one you were here."

CHAPTER TWO

LIKE A CAT ON THE WALL

Darkness was falling by the time Henryk reached the ghetto. Janusz's father had been right. Guards wearing heavy military coats that nearly dragged the ground were stationed at frequent intervals along the wall. As he stood pondering the problem of entry, several shadowy forms moved into the alley he had chosen for an observation post. Their approach startled him at first, but as they neared, he could see they were boys his own age. They came abreast of him and stopped. One of the boys, with a sturdy frame and close-cropped hair, asked what he was doing there.

"I am looking for a way to get into the ghetto," Henryk replied.

"And why do you want to get inside? There is only death and misery beyond that wall."

Henryk responded, "I have come with a message for some friends of my parents. But there are so many guards, it seems impossible to get in."

"No," replied the boy confidently, "it is very simple to get in, if one knows how and where to enter. We do it all the time."

"But with all the soldiers and police, how do you do it?"

"Sometimes we go over the wall at places where there are fewer guards, or those who have little heart to see Jews starved to death. Tonight we will enter through the sewers. You can come along, if you are willing to carry a sack of potatoes on your back."

This chance meeting was Henryk's introduction to Warsaw's famous boy smugglers, who by night dug up potatoes from the fields surrounding the city then sold them to the Jews confined behind the walls. These children were credited with saving or prolonging the lives of many Jewish people during the days before the Nazis finally destroyed the ghetto. His acquaintance, Peter, was the leader of a band of these Polish lads who were themselves caught up in the quest for self-preservation.

After darkness had cast a thick blanket over the city, the boys took up their sacks and moved toward the entrance of the sewer complex that carried away Warsaw's refuse. They crept quietly along the streets, just beyond the vision of the men whose business it was to keep the Jews penned up to die.

As the boys descended into the sewer, it was immediately apparent that Peter knew the subterranean passages very well. For Henryk, it was an unpleasant initiation into the smuggling business. The strong stench from the new environment seemed to immobilize his lungs, and for a moment, he drew quick, reluctant breaths. Weighed down by the potatoes, his feet sank deeply into the heavy, wet slime underfoot. Rats loitered nearby. His first impulse was to retreat quickly into the freshness of the night air. But his longing to be reunited with his family overshadowed his revulsion and compelled him to push forward toward his destination.

Finally the boys and their cargo ascended to street level and pushed their way out into the darkness. They emerged inside the Warsaw Ghetto. For a time they sat in the street, drawing deep breaths of nontoxic air. Peter gave orders to his comrades to stay put until he returned. Turning to Henryk, he said, "Follow me and I will show you a place where you can spend the night." He led him to a niche beneath a porch at the rear of one of the buildings. "I sometimes sleep here myself. It will do for shelter until morning; then you can search for your friends. Good luck!" Peter's form melted quickly into the murk as he left to go about his business.

Henryk awakened the next morning to find a bright sun penetrating the ghetto. Now he would begin to look for his parents. Striding quickly from between the buildings, he entered the street. The sights that accosted him were beyond belief. Never had he seen so many people in so small an area. Even at this early hour, people seemed to swarm in the street like flies.

Over one-half million Jews had been driven into the Warsaw Ghetto. One hundred fifty thousand of them were refugees who, like Henryk's parents, had been forced to relocate there. They lived everywhere. Schools, deserted buildings, alleys, and streets all quartered the gaunt, decaying masses.

Starvation and disease reigned supreme. Henryk winced at the sight of emaciated, ragged children with outstretched hands pleading, "I am hungry. Please, give me bread."

Scattered here and there, close to the buildings, huddled the elderly and the very young, their frail, brittle bodies inching laboriously toward death. Some waited for it silently, while others lifted feeble hands and uttered pitiful entreaties for death to remove them from their horrible existence. Now and then Henryk could hear mumbled prayers for the Messiah to come quickly and bring deliverance.

Scores of those who walked the streets bore the ravages of disease on their faces. According to estimates, as many as 150,000 people in the ghetto suffered with typhus. Tuberculosis, dysentery, and a host of related maladies added to the misery.

Also obvious were the vacant stares of those who had been psychologically scarred beyond recall. Their accumulated suffering and torment had so overloaded their mental sensibilities that they finally went mad. All that remained now were the pathetic physical remnants of once vital people who could do no more now than be led about by loved ones or wander aimlessly, waiting for death.

Henryk stood mesmerized by the variegated smells, sights, and sounds assaulting his senses. Suddenly he became aware of a clattering sound coming slowly up the street. He looked around to see a pushcart attended by two men with handkerchiefs over their faces. Human remains lay stacked on the carts like cordwood, as these members of the death crew gathered the bodies of those who had expired during the night. Arms and legs protruded in grotesque gestures amid expressionless faces that stared open-mouthed into the autumn sky. For them, their arduous sojourn in the Warsaw Ghetto was over. Others, however, would live to see the dying continue.

All that day Henryk walked the streets searching faces of passers-by in hopes of finding a familiar figure. Occasionally he paused to inquire about his parents. Some people shook their heads and walked on without so much as a word. One man stopped to listen patiently to the anxious boy. "I have never heard of such a one," the man said. "Maybe they are all dead, like so many of the others." His answer did not satisfy Henryk. It couldn't be, he thought. Not all three of them. That night he retreated to his little haven, discouraged but determined to continue looking until he found them.

It was nearly noon of the following day when he saw a familiar face. It was Mordecai Friedman, a wealthy Jewish man who had lived a few doors from them in the old neighborhood. Determined to catch the man before he became lost in the press of people, the boy ran after his one-time neighbor. The man stopped as the lad called to him. "Mr. Friedman, wait, wait! I must talk to you."

For a moment the old man's brow furrowed. Then his face lit up as he recognized his small pursuer. "Henryk, Henryk Weichert. Can it be you? The last I knew of you, you had been sent off to an orphanage. Now you are here in the ghetto. Come, let us sit down on this step. You must tell me how you have come to be in this place."

The boy and the elderly gentleman sat down together and began to talk of other days. Henryk related his experiences to his friend, who listened with great interest. It was strange that these two, who had barely known each other except by name and face, were now so completely bound together by the thread of the past. It seemed that even recalling the memories of better times was a balm that fleetingly turned minds from their current stresses. When the lad paused, the old man asked about his parents. "Mendel and Ruth, Henryk—are you with them here?"

"No," the boy replied, "I am searching for them. Can you tell me where they are?"

"I am afraid not," came the disappointing reply. "They came here at the same time I did, but I have long since lost track of them."

Henryk asked him if he knew of the address that Janusz's father had given him. "Yes, I know the place, and I will tell you how to get there. But you must know that there are now no addresses in this place. Those who lived as one family in a small flat now have ten families living there. It is virtually impossible to find anyone here. If you have good luck, you may run across them. If not, perhaps they are dead.

"Henryk, let me give you some advice before we part. Don't spend too much time looking for them. You are a boy, and still strong. If you stay here in the ghetto, soon you will grow weak like the rest. Don't die here. Do everything you can to save yourself.

"And now, my young friend, good-bye. Let us hope the next time we meet will be a better day for both of us." He thrust out a bony hand and patted Henryk's shoulder in a parting gesture, then ambled off down the street.

Henryk knew the old man had given him sound advice. Still, he did not feel he could leave until he was certain there was no hope of finding his family. The address he had been given did not lead him to his parents or provide any further clue to their whereabouts. Always the answer was the same: "So many have died; perhaps they are gone too."

After a few more days of searching, with only starvation rations to eat, the boy began to feel the effects of the lack of food. Friedman's words came back to him. He must not stay here and die. But he did not wish to give up the search either. After weighing his options, he decided to leave the ghetto and dig some potatoes for himself. He would then set up a business as a smuggler and sell food to the people in the ghetto. It was a dangerous occupation, but no other avenue seemed logically open to him. He would go over the wall that night and hunt for food. Henryk had little trouble getting out of the ghetto. He was quick and agile—like a cat on the wall.

In addition to stamina and agility, however, this hazardous occupation required either a supreme sense of self-confidence or the drive of sheer desperation. Henryk had a measure of both. He was quite willing to take the chances involved, trusting his wits and agility to get him past the guards and back again. Hunger and the conviction that he must live long enough to see his family stoked the fire that provided the mental impetus to go on.

Once he was out of the city, he had but a short distance to go before he came to a small village. Outside the town lay several fields with potatoes enough to serve his purpose. Henryk burrowed along the rows until he had unearthed a sufficient quantity to fill both his stomach and the sack he carried. Slinging the lumpy load over his shoulder, he made for the city and the ghetto in search of a customer for his first transaction. The next morning it did not take long to find an interested party.

The man was tall and haggard. Several children clustered about him looking hungrily at Henryk's treasure. "Wait just a moment until I get a box," the man instructed. Within moments he returned carrying a small container. As the boy began to transfer the precious potatoes to the box, the man and the children began knocking them away. No sooner had they hit the ground than the children scooped them up and thrust them into their ragged pockets; few of them reached their intended destination. The man hefted the box and balanced it for a moment. "It looks like you have about eight pounds here," he said.

Henryk was livid with anger. "It is more like twenty," he thundered.

"No, I will pay you for eight pounds of potatoes."

"But I risked my life to bring them to the ghetto. Now you are trying to steal them from me."

The man spoke tersely. "If you don't like it, take them elsewhere."

His impulse to assault the people who were cheating him was almost overwhelming. Then he looked into their faces, and the rage drained from him. How could he bring himself to fight against these bags of bones? With a weak nod of the head, he held out his hand. The man dropped in a few coins and departed.

Henryk's career as a smuggler was over almost as soon as it had begun. This first encounter soured him on being a ghetto trader. He would wait until nightfall and go over the wall.

While it was still daylight, the boy took a careful survey in order to find the most appropriate place from which to make his escape. The wall was about eight feet high, so it was advantageous to pick a spot where the ground below was relatively soft. Henryk selected a likely-looking place, then retreated to await darkness.

A cold rain, which began falling late in the afternoon, was coming down in torrents as he lithely mounted the top of the wall. He perched there for a moment, peering into impenetrable darkness so thick that he could not see the ground below him. He listened intently for a few seconds—nothing stirred. Fleetingly he thought, what will be, will be; and he flung his small body into the darkness. Henryk landed with a soggy thud. To his dismay, he had come down squarely between two guards who were standing close to the wall in an effort to keep dry. His sudden arrival momentarily startled them, and they froze. The boy hit the ground, running as fast as his scrawny legs could carry him. When the flustered guards regained their wits, they began to cry into the rain-swept evening: "Halt! Halt at once!" Their guns began spitting small darts of flame toward the sound of the youngster's splashing feet. He could hear the shots and the whine of bullets speeding past him. It was as though the shouts and the bullets had issued a new order for him to hasten his departure. His legs seemed to fly as he scrambled toward the safety of some bombed-out buildings that stood a short distance from the wall. He managed to reach them before the bullets found him. Diving into the rubble, the young escapee lay listening. Breath came in painful gasps, and his heart raced as though it were completely out of control. A few yards away he could hear the guards groping through the ruined houses in search of their quarry. He pressed his frail body against the debris and waited. In due time the men gave up the hunt and returned to their posts. With their departure, Henryk was up and running again. When he had gone what he considered a safe distance, he sought shelter and waited for the rain to stop.

Now the question was what to do. He was cold, wet, and hungry. Something must be found to eat. After that, he would seek shelter. The rain had stopped when Henryk stepped out into one of Warsaw's lighted boulevards. Shoppers, delayed because of the rains, were out late. Consequently, many people were on the street. A storeowner eyed the hungry youth suspiciously as Henryk paused to browse in front of his shop. Small baskets of fat red apples sat lusciously beside other fruits and vegetables along the sidewalk.

Henryk formulated his plan. The money he had received for the potatoes was of no use to him here. It was currency issued specifically for the ghetto. To offer it to anyone outside the wall would surely betray his identity. Desperation drove him to a decision. He would wait until the proprietor was distracted, then steal something and make his escape. Henryk wandered slowly to the front of the next shop up the street and feigned interest in the goods displayed in the store window. Soon a woman arrived and ordered some cherries. As the owner turned aside to measure out the purchase, the youngster dashed in, snatched up a basket of apples, and ran up the street. Not far behind, the storeowner charged after him, shouting at the top of his lungs, "Stop thief! Someone stop the thief!"

People along the boulevard saw what was happening. But rather than help apprehend the boy, they stood aside and let him pass. They had no stomach for contributing to the prolonged hunger of one of Warsaw's waifs. Soon the man gave up his futile chase. Leaving the lighted area, Henryk searched until he found what appeared to be a short tunnel that ran beneath some of the bombed-out buildings. It was partially filled with rubble but was relatively warm. At least it would be a safe place to pass the night.

The small boy sat alone in the dark and munched his apples. Well, he thought, now I am assured of living to see tomorrow.

The next morning the boy whose mother had told him to be a man awakened to a scene that severely strained his youthful powers of manly self-control. Scattered amid the debris choking the tunnel where he had slept lay the grisly skeletons of people who had been killed during the German bombing of the city in 1939. Henryk had spent the night in the company of the dead. As the horrified child fled, it was almost as if something dreadfully symbolic were being projected: For years to come, this little Jewish lad would constantly be fleeing from the presence of death.

For the next few weeks, Henryk attempted to squeeze out a living by carrying heavy bags for travelers who passed through the central train station. This was not much more rewarding than selling potatoes. The police and adult baggage handlers repeatedly chased him and the other boys his age from the station. Tiring of the kicks and threats of his hide-and-seek existence, he decided to leave the city.

With his future a bleak question mark, Henryk took to the roads away from Warsaw seeking a means to sustain the frail thread of life.

CHAPTER THREE

THE FÜHRER'S SHEPHERD

T he countryside around Warsaw was speckled with small farms. A few animals meandered in the fields around ramshackle barns, creating a pastoral picture book effect. Bright winter sun chased the frost from the surface of the dirt roads, causing mud to ooze beneath Henryk's feet as he walked. All in all, it was good to be away from the city. The air was fresh and crisp, there were not so many people, and one saw fewer soldiers. As he tramped along, there was a new feeling about his situation. Perhaps now he could forget some of the things that had befallen him.

Before the day was out, however, his old problems were back again: finding shelter and obtaining food. This, he felt, should not be so difficult here in the country. "I will offer myself to one of the farms to work for them. With so many young men gone to the war, surely there will be a place for me," he thought.

Before he made his approach to the first house, Henryk looked himself over. Confessedly, what he saw was somewhat less than impressive. His clothes were dirty and rumpled. It had been days since he had taken them off or taken a bath. His stature, to be sure, was not one of his best selling points. He had always been shorter and smaller than other boys his age. Even his heavy-soled, ankle-high shoes, which always appeared much too large, would not help elevate him appreciably. He had suffered significant weight loss during his recent ordeal, but his winter clothing made him appear a little more bulky around the middle and in the shoulders.

Carefully tucking in his shirt all the way around, he surveyed his buttons to see that they were in proper order. His blond hair, which always seemed to have a way of falling back down over his forehead, was raked into place with his fingers. In a last effort to become reasonably presentable, he paused at a stream to dash some cold water on his face. On his way up the walk, he made a stab at shaking some of the mud from his shoes. Henryk was ready to apply for a position.

The farmer was heavy-set and did not look too friendly. "What can I do for you?" he asked.

"I am looking for work," the boy replied hopefully.

"You are only a child," the man countered. "You could not do the heavy work on this farm."

"But I can," Henryk fired back. "Yes, I am small. Yet I can do any work you ask of me. You will see. I am a good worker."

The man seemed to soften momentarily. "Where are you from?" he questioned.

"I am from Warsaw, but there is no food for me there now."

"Do you have papers?" the farmer queried.

"No, sir."

"Are you a Jew?"

"No, sir, I am not."

The man stood thoughtfully for a moment. Then he began to shake his head slowly. "No—no," he said. "There is too much risk involved. I cannot take the chance. I have no place for you in my house."

As the disappointed youth left the yard, he murmured to himself. "Why is it such a terrible thing to be a Jew? Mother was right. No one must ever know who I really am."

During this period, people throughout Poland lived in constant fear for their lives. Harboring or being found in the company of a Jew could mean death. But those who collaborated with the Nazis and turned in someone they knew to be Jewish received a reward—bottles of vodka or increased food rations were the usual incentives. To add to the general terror, many who roamed the countryside were notorious thieves or, worse yet, informers who would report their countrymen for the most incidental violations of the rules of the Reich. As a result, Poles had inordinate suspicions about strangers, even very small ones.

Henryk had a marked advantage over most of his Jewish kinsmen. His facial features did not harmonize with the Jewish stereotype. Nor did his cotton-white hair and bright blue eyes. Furthermore, he did not speak with a pronounced Jewish dialect, thanks in part to his days in the orphanage, which had isolated him completely from other Jews. These characteristics did much to disguise his identity and contribute to his survival by allaying suspicions that he might be Jewish.

All that day he heard the same response: "Too small, no papers—sorry, nothing for you here."

Soon an empty stomach began to send its familiar message to his brain. He must look for food. It was, in fact, a simpler and much less hazardous task to obtain sustenance in the country— even if the fare was less than exotic. The fields, where he had once dug up an abundant supply of potatoes, were now frozen, so that source was gone. As he passed a farmhouse, he saw his staple victual being served by a local farmer. The man was throwing potatoes and peelings into his pigpen. Henryk waited until the farmer had returned to the house, then moved in to share the meal. Pushing the reluctant hogs aside, he managed to get a fair portion of the pig slop.

Barns, he found, also contained numerous items waiting to be claimed by those who, like himself, were emboldened by hunger. A few days of this kind of foraging would have the color back in his cheeks and the strength flowing to his muscles.

Sleeping presented a problem of another kind. But the thick woods flanking the roads offered an adequate solution. One could always find a low place and crawl up under a fallen log. Leaves, which covered the ground with a thick blanket, provided insulation enough to ward off the cold of these early winter months if pulled about a body in sufficient quantity.

Eventually he found his way to the door of a rather large and prosperous farm—large, Henryk learned, because it actually comprised several farms confiscated from hapless Poles who were driven from their lands. Their properties had been given to loyal Nazis who managed them for the Fatherland. From the number of livestock in the fields, it appeared that there would be plenty of work to do around the place. An anemic-looking girl answered Henryk's knock and quickly retreated to beckon her father.

When the man appeared in the doorway, Henryk was taken aback. For a moment he thought he had come face to face with the Führer himself. The farmer had a square patch of mustache nestled atop his upper lip. His hair was jet black, parted on the right side, and swept down Hitler-style across the left side of the forehead. He was a large man—obviously strong and charged with energy. Henryk noticed that when he talked, he had a strange way of twitching the thatch beneath his nose. It appeared he was perpetually attempting to adjust it to a comfortable position.

"Do you have work for me here?" Henryk began.

The Führer look-alike eyed the young applicant carefully. "Yes, there is a great deal of work to do here, but you are just a little one," he said.

"Please, at least give me a chance. I will show you that I can be a good worker," the boy pleaded.

"Well, you are big enough to tend the cows and carry water," the farmer said. "How much do you charge?"

Elated, Henryk responded, "Give me food and a place to sleep. If you think I am a good worker, then you can pay me something."

"All right, you can work here for me. But first I must have a look at your papers."

The lad's heart sank. "I have no papers. They have been lost."

The man's face was stern. "Are you a Jew?"

"No, I am not."

"Are you sure you are not lying to me?"

"No, I am Polish."

"Well then, we will not worry about the papers. I can see to it that you get them."

The boy soon learned why his new employer was not overly concerned about the lack of proper identification. As his appearance had indicated, the man was a fanatical Nazi. He was also very influential in the district. His influence easily enabled him to obtain the necessary papers for his young tenant with no questions asked. The man was also in desperate need of help. All six of his sons were in the armed forces serving on the Russian front. He was left with only his fragile daughter at home.

Henryk was feeling much better. At last he had regular employment and a table at which he could eat—although he was not allowed to eat with the family, but at a small table beside the door in the kitchen. This made little difference to the famished boy. The food was what mattered.

Sleeping accommodations were spartan by any standard. He would be allowed to sleep in the barn. It was dirty, but the animals' bodies provided heat to keep him warm. After all he had been through, the place seemed like the Grand Palace Hotel.

His position on the farm was to serve as a shepherd to the forty cows owned by the German. Besides the feeding and milking chores, he was charged with keeping an eye out for the interests of his employer. Many hungry people roamed the countryside, and some indulged in impromptu feasts off quickly slaughtered cows. Others, who had little milk for their children, would manage to secure premature milking sessions in some obscure corner of the pasture. A pair of eyes on the scene throughout the day provided the best deterrent available.

A fringe benefit of Henryk's job was a ready supply of milk to drink. At the table, he was allowed only the residue from the milk after the cream had been removed. In the barn, however, he had a constant source of fresh, whole milk.

The work also gave him the opportunity to meet and establish friendships with Polish people from the neighboring farms. For all of his past difficulties, Henryk remained a very outgoing boy who was constantly on the alert for someone to talk to, particularly someone in a position to teach him something. He had learned through bitter necessity to be wary, cunning, and deceptive. But in the process, he retained an openhearted warmth that people found easy to respond to.

The German was not aware that his young laborer could understand the language of the Fatherland. And Henryk was careful not to betray the secret. Consequently, the farmer addressed him only in Polish. Family conversation, however, was always in German. As a result, the lad learned a great deal about the man's activities as a Nazi from the unguarded talk with the wife and daughter at mealtimes. The man harbored a deep hatred for the Polish people. In the prevailing spirit of National Socialism, he saw them as a permanently inferior class of subhumans who deserved to be erased from the face of the earth. In short, he was an extremely cruel man who amassed all he could for himself while giving as little as possible in return. Henryk would feel the brutal lash of his philosophy on more than one occasion.

With the advent of summer, the young farmer found that his living quarters had been invaded by a new species of inhabitants—lice were everywhere. Before long his body was so thoroughly infested that his head had become a mass of bleeding sores. When he approached the farmer to ask for ten cents to have his head shaved, the man exploded. "You Polish pig!" he shouted. "Do you dare to ask me for money? Get out of my sight before I give you something that will be worse than a few sores on your head."

The boy said nothing. In the months he had been on the farm, he had learned how to hold his tongue while in the volatile presence of his master. Fortunately, he had other hands to help him in time of need. One of the Polish families with whom Henryk had struck up an acquaintance offered immediate assistance to the skinny little fellow. While the husband cut his hair, the woman of the house prepared a kettle of hot water to warm a tub for bathing—a luxury denied him by the Nazi. While Henryk was in the water scrubbing himself, the man burned his infested clothing and brought him a fresh change from the family supply. It felt good to be rid of the crawling, biting pests that had come to regard him as their personal feeding ground.

Cherished hours were passed with this family. Henryk took great pains to show his appreciation for such acts of kindness. In response to their constant complaints that they did not know what was going on around them (Polish people were forbidden radios and allowed only newspapers printed in German) the boy confided that he could read German. Thereafter, he became their private interpreter, holding regular sessions in their home to read aloud the news from the papers the man picked up in the village.

Another face also became familiar during the days of servitude to the mini-Führer. At first it was just a smile and the wave of a hand as the postman passed the road with the mail. But as the months wore on, simple greetings progressed to long conversations. This mailman was a veritable wellspring of information. He knew all about local personalities and the state of national affairs. Henryk learned a great deal from him that was not to be found in the carefully censored publications allowed them by the Germans. He was particularly fascinated by the tall one's running commentary on the progress of the war, along with editorial comments on the ultimate outcome. It was obvious that the lanky carrier, who had several children of his own, had developed a fondness for the boy who served the gruff taskmaster.

This was a man who had abundant troubles of his own. The police, Henryk learned, had him under surveillance as one who might be engaged in dubious activities. Therefore, they were making it difficult for him to augment his meager income, and he was encountering problems providing for his family. The coarse, black bread available to them was hardly fit for human consumption. Milk was a watery variety akin to what the Nazi put on the table for the hired hand. With the approach of winter, fresh vegetables would again become virtually impossible to obtain. The boy's friend was, indeed, a man who could use a helping hand. So Henryk decided to launch a one-man relief operation. The situation was not too big for him to handle.

The mailman was surprised, and profusely grateful, when his young confidant ceremoniously offered him some eggs and two bottles of milk.

"But my friend," the postman protested, "I have nothing with which to pay for these things. And besides, you are placing yourself in great danger by bringing them here to me."

"No," said Henryk, "it is never wrong to steal from a thief. The Germans stole the land from Polish farmers. Then they took the cows and the chickens. None of this belongs to them; it is as much yours and mine as it is theirs. Besides, he will never miss what little I bring to you."

The little fellow did not expect anything in return for what he brought for the family. But one day the postman reached into his bag and brought out a pair of worn but serviceable shoes and handed them to Henryk. On another visit he pressed a coin into his hand. Shortly an exchange program was in full swing. Before his friend arrived with the mail, Henryk would hurry to fill the larder in a hollow tree that had become a prearranged drop place. After the mailman passed, he would return for his gratuity. Trips to the tree became a happy adventure for the youngster. For months the exchange provided the central joy in his life until one afternoon, when it all came to an abrupt end.

The postman approached the house with a somber expression on his long face. Henryk was outside, bringing the cows into the barn for milking. Catching the boy's eye, he shook his head and turned six fingers toward the ground. The message was clear; all six of the farmer's sons had been killed on the Russian front. This news arrived only a few days after the Nazi had learned of the death of his two brothers in the same war sector. The bad tidings would spell trouble for the child shepherd.

CHAPTER FOUR

THAT SWINE WILL DIE

News of the deaths sent the farmer into a frenzy. Henryk had seen him react on other occasions with unreasoning fury against farm animals that had irritated him in some small way. Never, however, had he seen him quite like this. As Henryk passed the house, he could catch glimpses through the window of the man stalking about the room, flailing his arms, and ranting in German. The mustached follower of the Führer was completely beside himself.

Henryk hesitated to enter the house for his meal that evening, but he knew that even a slight delay in his arrival might offer an excuse for the man to vent his anguish on him. The boy went in and sat down at his table just inside the kitchen. In the next room, where the family dined, the Nazi ignored his food in favor of a rambling diatribe against the Russians and their allies, who were resisting Hitler's brand of deliverance. His wife made one or two feeble suggestions that he calm down and eat. But she, too, knew better than to say too much at the wrong time. As he continued, ominous words spewed from his mouth—words that sent a quick shiver through Henryk's mind and body.

"The Russian dogs have killed my brothers and my sons," the farmer stormed. "All I have left is a Polish pig. Why should I make a good life for him while my sons lie dead in the snow? Tonight I will fix it. That Polish swine, too, will learn how it feels to die—I will kill him!"

His wife responded to the irrational outburst: "Do what you wish. I have nothing to say."

With the gruesome objective stated, the man seemed to calm down somewhat.

The youth's first impulse was to flee the house immediately. But a quick mental appraisal of his situation counseled otherwise. He must not, at any cost, betray the fact that he understood what the man had said. He must conduct himself as though he suspected nothing. His mind was racing as he finished his meal, rose, and walked to the door of the dining room. Trying to maintain a casual tone, the boy said, "I am going to sleep now. Good night."

"Yes, sleep well," answered the man who intended to kill him. "You have been working hard. Tomorrow I will give you a free day." His voice sounded almost pleasant.

"Thank you very much," the lad replied. He had no intentions of staying around to taste just what kind of freedom his employer was talking about.

A new snow was falling as Henryk walked the short distance between the house and the barn. He needed to act with haste to make preparations for his departure. Realizing that he faced a night in the cold, he pulled on as much clothing as he could. Henryk picked up a sack and stuffed in several of the choice items he had received from the postman. Everything else would have to be left behind. Alongside the small gifts, he dropped crusts of bread that he had spirited from the kitchen. He stood for a moment peering toward the house through a crack between the barn's siding. Seeing no movement, he slipped quietly through the door. Across the barnyard stood the small building where the family's supply of cured meat was kept. Quickly he shoved a few pieces into the sack. Before bidding farewell to the place he had called home for more than a year, he snatched two roosting chickens from their perch in the hen house. Henryk was now prepared to begin his dash for freedom.

The road under his feet was frozen solid. As he ran through the night, his footfalls tapped rhythmically, compressing the fresh-fallen snow between shoe leather and ice. The melodic cadence seemed to spur him along. During the night he passed through several small villages in an attempt to put as much distance as possible between himself and his Nazi persecutor. The man was widely known throughout the area. He knew he couldn't risk stopping as long as there was a chance of being caught and turned over to him. Each time he was tempted to pause for a while, he could hear the grim words: "The Polish swine will die tonight." No further incentive was necessary. When he slowed to a walk, the cold soon invaded his garments and prompted him to break into a trot again.

As morning neared, exhaustion and cold forced him toward the doors of homes in a village. He was turned away several times before a woman offered him a bit of warm water and a towel to sponge the moisture dripping from his face. But she refused his request to rest there, and he was forced to seek another place of refuge.

Later in the morning he found himself looking into the face of a woman who was asking the inevitable question: "Are you a Jew?"

This time Henryk was prepared. "I am Polish," he replied. He quickly ran his hand into his pocket and produced the identification papers the farmer had obtained for him.

"All right, you may come in and rest for a few hours; but after this you must leave." The woman's words were music to his frigid ears. She gave him food, but first insisted he get out of his clothes, which were saturated by melted snow. While he was undressing, she disappeared momentarily. When she returned, she carried suitable replacements from a supply her own boys had outgrown.

After he had warmed up a bit, she sat him down at a table and served tea and hot food. The tired boy savored the meal. It seemed as though the warmth of the tea began to move perceptibly into his fingers and feet. When he had finished, Henryk arose from the table and walked to the porch to retrieve his bag. Reaching in, he produced a token of his gratitude. The chickens had spent the night in close confinement. Now he triumphantly offered them to his hostess. She eyed him suspiciously. "These chickens are not ours," she said sharply. "Where did you steal them?"

Judging from the tone in her voice, Henryk suspected that if he did not come up with a suitable answer, it would mean a sudden return to the hostile environment he had spent the night fleeing. He decided to gamble on the truth. He told her about his days with the Nazi farmer and the succession of events that forced his hasty departure. As the story unfolded, the corners of her mouth began to turn up in a restrained smile. Finally she interrupted him. "All right. Good, good. To steal from a German or a Jew is acceptable; I will keep your chickens."

She then showed him into a bedroom and told him he could stay there until the next morning. Many months had gone by since Henryk had last slept in a room. It felt strange at first to be in a real bed, devoid of scratchy straw and creeping things. He pulled the covers up to his chin and stretched his tired limbs as far as he could. It was good to be a boy in a house again.

Henryk left the house the next morning refreshed and ready to follow his fortunes. The keen need to remove himself still farther from his former employer set him on a course that took him back briefly to the city of Warsaw. Nothing there had changed. So, with only a look at the ghetto from the outside, he pressed on. For the remainder of the winter he led a vagabond life, moving among the villages southeast of Warsaw.

By the time spring of 1943 threw a green mantle over the Polish landscape, Henryk was thirteen and wise to the ways of the road. He had mastered the subtleties of survival and moved skillfully about the business of making a way for himself. Warm weather was a welcomed change from the bitter months just past. When the fresh, green fruits and vegetables began to reappear in the fields, he felt that he had a new lease on life.

One bright spring day he was tramping along a road that led to the industrial city of Lodz, a city second only to Warsaw in population. As he walked along, a boy whom Henryk judged to be about eleven fell in step alongside him. Henryk had met many such wandering boys during his travels, but the sight of this child flabbergasted him. If someone had taken a pen and written "Jew" in big black letters across his forehead, his identity would not have been more obvious. His features and general appearance were so markedly Jewish that Henryk was amazed he could have gone any appreciable distance on the roads in daylight without having been apprehended.

"Where are you going?" the boy ventured.

"I don't know," Henryk replied. "I'm just going. What about you? Where are you going?"

"I don't know either," he said. "I'm running away from the ghetto."

They were nearing a grove of trees, and Henryk suggested they leave the road and stop there to talk. He was well aware of the risks one ran by traveling the roads in daylight. This boy, he knew, needed some quick, basic instructions in how to stay alive. Henryk listened to the boy's story. His name was Saul Blum, and he had lived in the city of Lodz with his family. Life in the ghetto there was intolerable, as it had been for Henryk in Warsaw. Consequently, several youngsters had decided to escape and go to Warsaw in the hope that things there would be better for them. Together they had traveled at night and had managed to get safely into the ghetto at Warsaw. Saul soon learned, however, that the only choice open to him in either place was where he would prefer to starve to death. So he had left the others to strike out on his own, heading in the general direction of Lodz but not sure where he should go. Finding a sympathetic ear to his troubles, the boy talked on and on. Often tears welled up in his eyes as he described the conditions the Jewish people were being forced to endure and the atrocities they were suffering at the hands of the Nazis and the anti-Semitic Poles. As Saul talked, Henryk looked at him and nearly wept himself. The boy bore all the marks of his agony. Malnutrition had so marred his dark features that his eyes appeared much too large for his face. His clothing was as ragged as his nerves. In fact, the youth was in a state of such complete demoralization that he had thrown caution to the winds and was exposing himself to obvious danger.

Henryk draped an arm around Saul's emaciated shoulders. "I understand all about what you have gone through. Now we must find a way to see to it that you can stay alive until the war is over," he said comfortingly.

"Don't say you understand about the ghetto! They don't lock Polish people up so they will die! You cannot possibly understand how terrible the place is," said the boy, who by now was almost shouting.

"But I am not Polish," Henryk confided. "Like you, I am a Jew. My parents and sister were taken to the ghetto in Warsaw. I, myself, have been there. Believe me when I say I know what it is like."

"You are a Jew? It cannot be. To meet another Jew here, it must be a miracle." He was weeping uncontrollably now.

Henryk allowed him to cry while he did some thinking. This was the first time since leaving his home that he had admitted to anyone that he was Jewish. Now he had confessed it without a moment's hesitation. He felt an immediate sense of kinship and responsibility for the desperate and stressed-out youth—the same responsibility he would feel, he thought, if he suddenly came upon one of his own brothers. He felt, too, that he had someone else to live for. Henryk was going to do everything in his power to keep this boy alive.

The first order of business was a stern warning. "If you will stay close to me and do what I tell you, you will be all right. But you must never show that Jewish face in daylight. There are many Germans around here who would enjoy putting you on the end of a bayonet or using you for target practice. To some Polish people, you are worth one bottle of vodka; and they will turn you in at the drop of a hat to get it."

The boy listened without speaking a word. A spark of hope was beginning to flicker in his eyes. Henryk continued, "For now, you will stay right where you are while I go and look for some food and a place to spend the night." With this understood, he moved off toward a row of houses to seek shelter and a meal. At the first farm he visited, a kindly farmer responded to his request with a gesture toward the barn. "Certainly, you can sleep there. I have plenty of hay inside. It will make you a good soft bed for the night. Wait here at the door and I will get you something to eat." The man returned with bread, milk, and a few potatoes. Henryk thanked him and took them into the barn and left them there. Saul would have a pleasant surprise waiting for him when he came to their lodging place.

Henryk watched in wonder as his companion wolfed down the food he had set before him. It was difficult to believe that a boy this size could consume a meal as ravenously as the eleven-year-old did. When he had finished, Henryk outlined his plans for their future. "We will not travel on the roads in the daylight. When we move, it will be at night so no one will see you. I will seek food and shelter for both of us. Your job will be to stay out of sight."

The system worked well. Saul kept to the woods while his friend foraged. A large grove of fruit trees, supplemented by fresh vegetables gathered at night, supplied their needs abundantly. Before long the boy, who had been little more than a rack of bones, was fleshing out and in much better spirits. The companionship was beneficial to both of the young wanderers. For Henryk, it was good to have someone he could finally talk with openly. Many hours were spent in satisfying conversation, sharing needs and pondering questions.

After several weeks of traveling together, Saul began to show signs of depression. Henryk attempted to cheer him up, but the boy grew progressively worse. The older boy decided it was time to talk the matter out. "I want to return to the ghetto at Lodz and be with my parents," Saul answered in response to Henryk's inquiry.

"You cannot think of going there," his friend objected. "It is too dangerous. There are German soldiers everywhere in Lodz. You will be in great danger of being killed—please, do not do it."

"But my parents live in a house that is close to the wall. Maybe I can go there in the night and see them from the outside. Perhaps I can get their attention and speak to them."

"Listen to me," Henryk said earnestly. "We cannot act as blind fools. When I left the ghetto, I knew I must take my life in my own hands. If my parents are dead, I cannot help them by dying too. Neither can you. Your life is in your hands, and you must save it. Anyway, if you do succeed in getting into the ghetto, what is there for you then? A quick death at the hands of the Germans is better than slow starvation in the ghetto. If you want to die, go to a German and say, 'Look, I am a Jew. Take me and shoot me in the head.'"

But the impassioned speech fell on deaf ears. Saul had already decided what course he would take. To attempt to persuade him any longer was futile. Henryk gave in. "If you must go, I will go with you as far as the outskirts of the city. Then you will be on your own."

The journey to Lodz was uneventful until they came to a village close to the city. "I want to stop here," Saul told Henryk. "My relatives lived here before they were taken to the ghetto. I spent much time with them and came to know this place very well. There is a market here where the owner keeps his money in the open in a box. I will go there and take some money to give to my parents when I see them."

Again Henryk warned him of the danger of being caught. Saul assured him, "I will not be in danger. The owner is old and fat. I will have no trouble getting away from him."

Henryk had reservations, but Saul gave him no choice in the matter. The boys entered the village just as dusk was falling. Saul led them straight to the market, which was located near the center of the town. The establishment had a covered roof but was open on both sides, making access from either street possible. They stopped on the corner in front of the market. Henryk watched as Saul entered the shop and made straight for the cash box. Without hesitating, he thrust in his hand and came up with a fistful of money. Before the startled storeowner could react, Saul ran to the other side of the market and out into the street. Henryk watched in horror as the boy ran squarely into the arms of a German policeman who was coming up the street. The youth, driven by homesickness and a compulsion to help his parents, had had no chance at all. The policeman got a firm grip on the boy as a patrolling German soldier rushed to the scene. The man looked at Saul's face and cursed loudly. "This little _____ is a Jew!" he called to the approaching soldier.

"We know what to do with Jew pigs," the soldier called back.

Henryk felt nauseous as he saw the soldier reach out, squeeze the boy by the throat, and hoist him to eye level. The coins tumbled from Saul's hand. His eyes rolled wildly and his tongue was forced from his mouth by the strangling grip of the soldier's hand. As Henryk turned to leave, the soldier was dragging the boy backward up the street.

For days afterward, Henryk bore the weight of severe depression. Saul had been more than a friend to him. In a sense, he had represented hope. If they could somehow help each other survive until the war was over, they would have contributed to each other's future. For Henryk, who had been so alone for so long, there would have been someone else who had suffered with him and survived—someone who would have known how it really was. But that was not to be.

Instead, the young man who had accumulated so many mental and physical scars would take on yet two more: an enduring memory of the sound of coins striking the pavement and the distorted face of his young friend. To live, to die, it all seemed futile. Maybe the dead were better off than those who continued to exist. Why did he even care to go on? What purpose could possibly be in it? Thankfully, he fell asleep and extinguished, for the moment, the fire of frustration that raged within him.

CHAPTER
FIVE

ALL IN A
DAY'S WORK

Like a hunted rabbit returning to his lair, Henryk was drawn repeatedly back to Warsaw. The magnetism created by the faint possibility that his parents were still alive was irresistible. His experience with Saul rekindled the desire to find some trace of his family. But when he returned in the early days of May 1943, the Jewish compound was in flames. His arrival had brought him on the scene in time to witness the death throes of the Warsaw Ghetto. Flames from the giant funeral pyre leaped toward the sky as entire blocks of buildings and the wretched masses of humanity within them were systematically incinerated.

By mid-July 1942, Heinrich Himmler, who was in charge of implementing Hitler's "Final Solution," had decided that the tenacious Jews in Warsaw were not starving to death fast enough. Consequently, he issued a directive ordering the massive "resettlement" of ghetto Jews. By year's end, approximately 310,000 Jewish people had been "resettled" into the gas chambers at Treblinka. Their remains were then "processed" into fertilizer, soap, hair mattresses, and other ghoulish products masterminded by the intelligentsia of the Third Reich. Only sixty thousand remained in the ghetto at the beginning of 1943.

Those who remained, however, had come to a decision of their own: They would declare war on their tormentors and go to their graves fighting. One ghetto leader called it "the most hopeless declaration of war ever made." Their assessment of the situation was succinctly summarized in the words of another, who observed, "One way or another lies death."

Originally, the ghetto had covered an area approximately two and one-half miles long by one mile wide. Following the major deportations, it was reduced to one thousand yards. Beneath the streets, some of the Jewish people had created a honeycombed concentration of fortifications from which they could direct military operations. For weapons, they used a pitifully meager assortment of pistols, rifles, and a few machine guns that had been smuggled in. The arsenal also contained a supply of homemade Molotov cocktails (firebombs).

In January of the new year, Himmler himself paid a visit to Warsaw and found it intolerable that so many stubborn Jews were still eluding his efforts. S.S. Brigadefüehrer Juergen Stroop was commanded to destroy the ghetto and remove the recalcitrant resisters. General Stroop was a man who fervently shared Adolph Hitler's estimation of Jewry as a species of subhumanity. He needed little encouragement to warm to the task before him.

Stroop took two thousand troops and launched his attack against the determined handful of defenders. The Germans entered the battle armed with all the tools of war available: automatic weapons, flamethrowers, howitzers, antiaircraft artillery, and tanks. He was shocked and infuriated when the resistance mounted a defensive action that would frustrate the German force for weeks. The general settled on burning the ghetto, one block at a time, as the most effective means of terminating the battle. Slowly the Nazis began to flush the Jews from their defensive positions. Even so, many Jewish fighters refused to surrender. Some men and women were seen leaping from burning buildings, then dragging their broken bodies into other places of shelter to keep up the fight. Stroop was dumbfounded at the sight of wounded Jews staggering into the flames to avoid falling into his hands. Toward the end, a group of trapped defenders resorted to a Masada-like mass suicide to avoid being captured.

In the end, of course, these heroes and heroines were out-gunned and overmatched. But they had raised the voice of their pent-up defiance for all the world to hear and remember. For a significant number of them, it was not the end. They disap-peared into the sewers to slip past the German dragnet and join the partisans, who operated against the common foe. They would continue to fight.

Henryk and the citizens of Warsaw stood watching the tragic drama, their faces illuminated by the spectacular blaze of the Holocaust. A resounding explosion ended the episode. As a last act to emphasize their triumph, Stroop's soldiers dynamited the Warsaw synagogue. The ghetto was no longer.

For Henryk, it was one more bitter potion. Once again he turned his back on the city of his childhood. Crossing the Vistula River, he turned north in search of a haven. As if some unseen hand of mercy was moving in to help the buffeted child, a door of friendship readily opened to him. In a village not far from Warsaw, he encountered a Polish family who seemed more concerned about the possibility of his being German than fear-ing that he might be a Jew. A quick look at his identification papers reassured them, and they took him in. The father of the family was a rather elderly man who had married late in life. His wife was much younger than he, but she suffered from a debilitating disease. The couple had two strapping sons, Stanislov and Janek, who were eighteen and twenty-three years of age respectively.

In this household, Henryk was not treated as a servant. Here he was taken in as a full member of the family. He occupied a room with a bed of his own. Often the woman placed addi-tional food before him and admonished him to eat well so he could become big and strong like Stanislov and Janek. The boy eagerly shared the duties around the house and made every contribution that opportunity afforded. The months he spent with the family were indeed a healing time for young Henryk. For the remainder of the year and well into the next, he enjoyed a happy and refreshing interlude.

Trouble, however, constantly stalked Jew and Pole alike during these days, and sooner or later it was bound to step through the door. It entered on a morning when Henryk came downstairs to find that the boys were not at home. His inquiry about where they had gone brought only a vague reference to their being at work somewhere. They had, in fact, fled. Word had come to them that the Germans were sweeping the area to press all able-bodied males into work on a military installation being constructed nearby. When the soldiers came to the house looking for the sons, the father said they had gone to another village to work and that he did not know when they would return. When Henryk returned to the house from his hiding place, he found the man badly beaten. He had not revealed the whereabouts of the boys.

Matters went from bad to worse as military movements through the villages accelerated. The Russians were making life hard for the Germans, and the ultimate outcome of the conflict was now becoming clear. A number of partisan terrorist groups of varied political persuasions were operating clandestinely in the area. For their part, the Nazis were showing—if such were possible—ever more vicious tendencies. And the Ukrainians, who earlier in the war had thrown their allegiance to Germany, not Russia, were attempting to outdo the Nazis in deliberate acts of senseless cruelty. With each Russian advance, the Ukrainians grew more fully aware of the fate that awaited them if they fell into the hands of their former Russian comrades. It was said of them, "If it has eyes, they will shoot it." Rape, pillage, and murder were all their specialties. Their wave of terror spread in an ever-widening circle throughout the countryside.

It was a sunny day in the early summer of 1944 when a knock came on the door. A man entered the house at the invitation of

Henryk's host. Henryk had never seen the visitor before, but he immediately perceived that the two men were well acquainted. They went into the kitchen and spent some time in conversation before the stranger returned to the room where Henryk was sitting. The man's bearing and appearance impressed the boy. He was well dressed, blond, and about forty years old. When he spoke, it was apparent that he was well educated. Henryk thought the man may have been a doctor or a teacher. He spoke very precise Polish. Without introducing himself, he asked Henryk a question. "What do you think about the Germans?"

The boy was in a dilemma as to what to answer. However he chose to reply, it could mean trouble. He threw any attempt at subterfuge to the wind and answered forthrightly. "I can tell you plainly that I do not like the Germans," he said emphatically.

"Why not?" the man said.

"As you can see, I am here alone. As far as I know, all of the members of my family are dead. The Germans are responsible for it. This is reason enough for me to be against them. Maybe you are a German—I don't know. But I cannot speak otherwise."

The man smiled. "I can assure you that I am anything but a German, and I am happy to know that we share the same opinion of our enemy." The man talked on for nearly an hour, probing the boy's mind with subtle questions. Finally he got to the point: "How would you like to have a good job?"

"I will do what I can for you. But first I must ask the man I live with if it is all right for me to work for you."

"Never mind about that; it will be acceptable to him," the stranger answered confidently.

Henryk was not convinced until he had gone to the kitchen and asked his benefactor. "It is fine," he was told. "This man is a member of my family. Do what he asks you." Thus assured, the boy returned for his instructions.

"About four miles up the road is a town. Just on the other side, on the right, a unit of Hermann Göring's air command is stationed. All the telephone wires running to the headquarters are strung on poles along the road. I want you to go there and cut them. There are many of them. Be sure you cut them all. When you have finished, leave the place as fast as you can. Be very careful. If you are caught, do not tell them where you have come from. Just forget that you came from here. Do not tell them anything."

The next afternoon Henryk set out, as he was told. It was late in the day when he reached his destination. The wires were strung on low poles located close to the road. He selected a spot clustered with trees and quickly scaled the pole. The wires made a curious singing noise as he clipped them, and they snapped away and fell to the ground. When he finished the job and started to descend, he looked down to find himself staring into the menacing gaze of a German soldier whose rifle was leveled directly at him. In a cold, acidic tone, the soldier issued his order: "Come down from there, you Polish pig. You are committing sabotage. Don't try anything or I will finish you on the spot."

Henryk hung from the side of the pole for a moment. He did not want to come down, but there was no alternative. His career as a partisan, he thought, had come to a disastrous conclusion. The boy was certain he would be shot on the spot. The only small comfort that crossed his mind was in being shot instead of stabbed—a method of being dispatched he had always feared. At least death would be quick, he reckoned. The soldier, however, had another plan. "Put your hands on your head and walk toward the building beyond the wall." Henryk did as he was commanded and was marched, at bayonet point, to the interrogation officer. There he was shoved rudely into a room where two officers and a sergeant were seated.

"What have we here?" one of the officers inquired.

"He is a small partisan," said the soldier. "I found him cutting telephone wires outside the camp."

An impeccably dressed officer wearing a monocle took over the questioning.

"Do you speak German?" he asked.

Henryk did not respond to the question. They concluded that he did not understand German and sent for a Polish interpreter. When they found he could speak Polish, they began.

"Please, sit down," the officer said in a voice greasy with kindness. "Would you like to have a piece of chocolate?" The boy accepted it and nibbled some half-heartedly.

"Tell me first who it was that sent you here."

"No one."

"How did you come?"

"By myself."

"Who gave you the wire cutters?"

"I found them."

The officer turned to his comrade and spoke in German. "Here is a smart one. We will have to soften him up a bit." He addressed the interpreter next. "Tell him if he tells us the truth, we will allow him to go."

Henryk was not impressed. He knew if he told them what they wanted to know, it would be the last stop on the road for him. They waited a few moments for the offer to sink in, then started at the beginning again. "Now, tell us the truth," the man said softly, "who sent you here?"

"This was sport for me," the boy answered. "I like adventure. There was nothing to do, and I saw the wires, so I cut them. That's all there was to it."

The German began to tap a pencil on the desk impatiently. Turning slightly, he nodded to the sergeant. The man left the room and came back carrying a short, heavy club. Without a word he raised it quickly and struck the youth a brutal blow across the back. A searing shaft of pain tore through Henryk's body as white blotches danced before his eyes. "Now tell us!" shouted the officer. Henryk did not respond.

Immediately the sergeant was upon him, bludgeoning him about the head, shoulders, and back. Henryk began to feel his consciousness slip away as he sank to the floor. A strange wave of serenity passed over him. He felt as though he did not have a care in the world—nothing hurt anymore. Then buckets of cold water brought the pain coursing back into his brain. When he had regained consciousness, he was questioned again.

His head had been split open to the bone. Large knots were beginning to come up on his body. In spite of the agony, the boy was determined to hold his tongue. He felt he was going to be killed whether he gave them the information or not—he knew he could not survive much more of this. Convinced that the Germans would soon finish matters for him, he doggedly shook his head and refused to reveal any information. The beating began all over again. Suddenly it stopped. Through the fog, he could hear the officer ordering the sergeant in German to throw more water on him.

"We will let him go and have him followed. He will probably lead us to where he came from. If he does not, have the man assigned to follow him kill him. Don't bother to have him brought back here." He then addressed Henryk through the interpreter: "We have nothing further to say to you. You are free to go."

Bloodied and severely battered, Henryk managed to drag himself slowly out the door and onto the road. He knew he was being followed, but he made no movement that would betray this knowledge to his pursuer. He was just entering the village near the headquarters when he was met by an aged woman who dropped the basket she was carrying and ran forward at the sight of him. Although she appeared in her seventies, she moved like someone much younger. "What has happened to you, child?" she cried, and began wiping the blood from his head with a handkerchief. As she bent over him, the soldier who was following came along, grabbed her roughly by the shoulder and began to push her away. The enraged woman screamed at him: "You filthy beast! Leave this boy alone. I am old. You can kill me if you want someone to murder. But you will not hurt him anymore."

As they struggled with each other, Henryk saw his opportunity to escape. Suddenly, as though charged with some superhuman burst of strength, the boy dashed between several houses and took off toward the woods behind the town. Before the German could disengage himself from the woman, Henryk had sprinted into the forest and was gone. He ran in large circles until he was on the verge of exhaustion. Then he fell down to rest and await the darkness that could provide cover for his trip back home.

When he reached the house, he found it unlocked—the man and woman were not there. He crept inside and went straight to his bed. Now waves of pain wracked his body. If he died now, at least it would be in a bed like a human being, not like a dog in a field. About three hours after Henryk returned to the house, the door to the bedroom was slowly pushed open. Henryk waited apprehensively to see whose hand had moved it. A sense of relief came over him as he saw a middle-aged woman enter the room and approach his bedside. The partisans had been outside watching for him to return. When they were sure he had not been followed, she was sent in to tend his wounds. The woman examined him and told him to rest until she returned. A short time later she brought a doctor to the house to apply dressing and give him injections for pain.

The next day a man came to him to talk about the mission. He marveled that the Germans had released him, and he believed the boy's story because of Henryk's physical condition. He was well aware of the tactics the Nazis used and knew that had the boy given them information, he would not have been there in any condition.

After several days, the blond gentleman who had sent him to cut the wires paid a call. The partisan leader extended his hand along with his congratulations. "You are a very courageous young

man," he said. "You did an important job for us and we are grateful. You rest here until you are well. All of your needs will be
properly looked after. We will not forget what you have done."

The man's word was good. Henryk spent the next two weeks
in bed recovering from the beating. Each day the doctor and
nurse came by to care for him. In addition to the medical attention, they also brought special foods that supplied better nour-
ishment for him. He was overwhelmed by their kindness and
genuine concern for his welfare. It was something he had not
seen much of over the past five years.

CHAPTER SIX

IN THE PRESENCE OF MY ENEMIES

Henryk's pleasant respite was to be short-lived. Within weeks a new contingent of Ukrainians moved into the village and began at once to vent their sadistic malevolence on the villagers. Young men were commandeered for slave labor or shot at the slightest provocation. Henryk decided it was time, once more, to seek refuge in a more favorable place. He bid a fond farewell to the couple who had befriended him for so many months and headed for the bridge across the Vistula. Great changes were about to take place in Warsaw. The Polish were preparing a military uprising against the Germans. Conditions in the capital were abysmally difficult.

The boy found food more difficult to obtain than ever before. Everywhere he went he was roughly turned aside. His former troubles seemed insignificant compared to those assailing him now. Anyone who had a few morsels of food guarded it with his life. Regardless of how much sentiment one felt toward the needy, no one wanted to jeopardize his own survival by giving anything away. "Every man for himself" was the watchword of life. Henryk was mired in these bleak circumstances when an opportunity sauntered across his path from a totally unexpected source. As he idled along a Warsaw street one morning, a mounted German soldier rode past him toward a corner of the street. Henryk reached the intersection as the man dismounted his horse. "You there," he called in the youth's direction, "come over here." Although wary, Henryk felt he had better obey the order. "Watch my horse while I go into that shop for a few minutes." Without waiting for an answer, the soldier placed the reins in the boy's hands and stepped into the shop. Inspiration is often born by the convergence of necessity and opportunity. In this case, temptation and surrender struck in the same bolt of inspiration. In a flash, the youth leaped astride the surprised animal's back and, with a sharp clatter of hoof beats, made off down the street. Pistol shots rang out from somewhere behind him, but at the rate he was putting distance between himself and the policeman, there was little chance of his being hit. Henryk pressed the winded steed beyond the city limits, then slowed him to a trot when they were safely in the country. The boy was keenly aware of the bargaining power that now rested beneath his saddle.

Soon a farmer was slowly circling the horse. He had no doubt it had been commandeered, but he had little interest in the finer points of law. Possession was what counted at the moment. He and his countrymen were sure that the German occupation was coming to a close, and they regarded anything pilfered from the invaders as a legitimate prize of war.

"What will you take for him?" the farmer asked.

"One pig—not too big," answered the young businessman.

The buyer gasped. "Is that all?"

"That's all," replied the hungry youth.

The man turned toward the barn. "Come along and pick one out."

Henryk selected a plump young pig and hoisted the struggling animal to his shoulders. As the farmer led the horse to his barn, Henryk and his merchandise took the road back to Warsaw.

Offers for the prize pig came thick and fast from the hungry citizenry. When the price reached 10,000 zlotys, Henryk succumbed and he and the pig parted company. Henryk had already formulated a well-thought-out plan. On many occasions he had passed a hotel where he had often paused to watch people eat full-course meals over immaculate white tablecloths. Now that he was a man of some means, he would, at least for one night, join the company of the well-to-do. He went into the establishment and carefully selected a table by a window. After he had eaten his fill, he rented a room for the night, took a hot bath, and tumbled into a clean bed for long hours of unbroken sleep. The next morning, after enjoying a good breakfast with what remained of his funds, he left the hotel to begin the cycle all over again.

The Polish uprising against the Germans began on August 1, 1944. Orders for the action came from the Polish government in exile in London. Polish leaders were aware that the Russian vanguard was rapidly approaching the city, and they were determined to take Warsaw before the Russians could arrive and claim the victory. Even as the battle raged between Pole and Hun, tanks from the Russian advance units were being positioned along the opposite banks of the Vistula to watch the slaughter. Joseph Stalin, the Russian dictator, had everything to gain by biding his time—both combatants were his enemies. The more thoroughly they decimated one another, the easier it would be for his forces a few months hence, when they entered the capital city.

The battle raged through the months of August and September. Initially, the Polish seized half the city. Their successes were soon negated, however, as the weight of superior German firepower forced them to relinquish their gains. In the course of these conflicts, nine-tenths of Warsaw was destroyed. Civilians by the thousands were made refugees as the city became little more than an armed garrison for German troops.

Conditions for Henryk now sunk to their lowest ebb. People flooded the villages; and the Germans, who had been forced back across the river by the Russians, were seizing every edible commodity within their grasp. Even the most seasoned foragers were hard-pressed to find enough to keep them alive. Henryk sized up the situation and settled on a daring approach to the problem. A detachment of the German Wehrmacht was stationed just outside Warsaw. He would move into the camp of the enemy in quest of a small portion to stave off the persistent hand of hunger.

His opinion of the German oppressors had not changed. His body still bore vivid reminders of Nazi brutality. But the struggle for survival had now been reduced to its lowest conceivable denominator. Henryk needed food, and he needed it from any source available. Pride, ideology, and humanitarian allegiances were all immaterial—it was a matter of food and life or starvation and death.

He positioned himself outside the camp and began offering his services to the officers in exchange for a place at the table. After a number of degrading rebukes, the boy confronted a colonel who had alighted from the sidecar of a motorcycle. As the mud-spattered officer strode toward the gate, Henryk ran alongside delivering a verbal litany of his credentials. He had run through sweeping, kitchen duty, and bed-making without peaking the German's interest much. Then he struck pay dirt. "And I can make those boots shine like they were new." The officer stopped short.

"Let me see your papers," he said. Glancing at them for a moment, he made a sweeping gesture with his head. "You have convinced me, little one. Follow me and I'll give you a chance to show what you can do." Henryk, now the gentleman's gentleman, followed close behind his new master as they passed by the guard post and through the gate. A gruff word from the officer sent the private, who had charged out to challenge Henryk, scurrying back to his position.

The boy was soon occupied with a full round of duties around the camp. Bed-making, sweeping barracks, and shining officers' boots all became routine responsibilities for him. Kitchen duty was the most productive task in his small sphere of activity. It not only provided for his own needs but gave him the opportunity to put aside boxes of scraps from the mess tables to give to Polish civilians who served the Germans in another capacity.

This detachment of troops had, as a part of its duties, the oversight of the looting of the city of Warsaw. Many Polish civilians were forced to comb the ruins and ferret out gold, silver, and other valuables that people had concealed before their hastily forced departures. All finds were brought to the camp each evening for classification and transport to Germany. If a civilian retained even the smallest of these items, he was shot on the spot.

Henryk was an instant celebrity among the Polish workers. After his duties for the day were completed, he would bring his boxful of leftovers to the hungry Poles, who congregated to pull and shove for a handful of the precious cargo. He even took pains, often at great risk, to bring them things he picked up around the barracks. The most sought-after commodity was the cigarettes he supplied. All of the stubs he swept from the floor were kept for redistribution among the workers who were bound by the habit.

His horizons broadened considerably when the Germans asked him to go to a neighboring village to buy bottles of vodka for them. He explained to the soldiers that he hesitated to attempt to pass the checkpoints for fear he would be taken into custody. The commanding officer remedied the situation by issuing a pass that gave him the run of the area. This freedom afforded a valuable opportunity to do personal reconnaissance, allowing him to keep abreast of troop movements and Russian preparations to move against them. The appreciative Germans gave him money at what amounted to a 30 percent markup on what they had given him to make the purchases. He was soon operating as a young capitalist and doing a brisk business. Henryk used the money to purchase small items for his personal needs from the post commissary, as well as supplies for his civilian Polish friends.

One day, as he was making his trip, he stopped to pass the time with a work detail that was busy sifting the debris from ruined shops in a business area. Henryk began idly rummaging through some wreckage in the corner of a shop when his eye fell on a dirty jar that was half filled with small stones. "Worthless glass," called one of the Poles to him. "Throw it away and get out of here before you injure yourself." The boy did as he was told, only to see the man come over and retrieve the container himself. He later learned that he had cast aside a small fortune in unset diamonds.

This arrangement endured for about four months. Gradually Henryk sensed, through his own observation and the air of apprehension obvious among the Germans, that the Russians were beginning to make their move across the river to attack Warsaw. The youth knew that the time was ripe for him to make another flight for self-preservation. He was delicately balanced between the jaws of a great steel trap that could slam shut on him at any moment. Death could come swiftly from the Germans or Russians, depending on whose guns fired at him first. He intended to make the job difficult for both of them. His path of flight led him to a town southwest of Warsaw, Grodzish Mazowieki. It was a sizable community where Henryk found people who would trade small rations of bread for many hours of labor.

Air strikes by Russian planes had destroyed some of the buildings in the town. Henryk found one in which the floor had not collapsed and took up residence in the cellar. He converted the area used to store firewood and foodstuffs into a small apartment, complete with a bed and shelving for his small cache of food. With the passing of each new day, the Russian attacks intensified. Within a matter of days the town was reduced to a gutted graveyard of burned-out buildings. The boy roamed the streets between attacks, snatching what he could salvage from burning buildings to add to his hoard of food.

In mid-January retreating remnants of the broken German army that had opposed the Russians in Warsaw swept through Grodzish. Not far behind were the Russians, in hot pursuit. Shortly afterwards a Russian occupation unit arrived in the town to secure it and maintain order. As the thunder of the guns and the drone of planes passing overhead subsided, Henryk's tired mind slowly assimilated the fact that for him, the long war in Europe had ended. The tyrant had been banished from the land—liberation from Germany had become a reality.

That night, as he sat in his shelter and looked back over the last five years of his life, Henryk felt he had just cause to congratulate himself. Under the most adverse conditions anyone could possibly endure, he had survived. It was a triumph of determination, toughness, skill, and a lightening-quick mind over the evil instruments of intimidation, deprivation, and death. Thousands had died, but he had prevailed. In his mind, the garland of victory rested firmly on his head when he laid down to sleep that night.

It was sometime the following day when he began to realize it was no longer a capital crime to be a Jew. Slowly a bone-weary remnant of Jewish survivors began to surface. Some had concealed their identities or had hidden in the woods or had occupied lines that had not yet filed into the gas chambers. Their identifying armbands and patches bearing the yellow star of David could at last be cast aside—forever, they fervently hoped. Now, perhaps, they could begin their efforts to fit the shattered pieces of their lives back together.

What Henryk and his fellow Jews found when they emerged from the Holocaust defied comprehension. Poland's Jewish community had been reduced to an emaciated fragment. Here and there, perhaps one or two members of an entire family were still alive. The vast majority of Jewish people were not so fortunate—they had passed off the scene, never to be heard from again.

When conditions permitted, Henryk returned to Warsaw and picked his way through the ruins until he found himself on the street that had once been home to him. Some familiar faces, aged almost beyond recognition, were silently moving away the rubble in preparation for a new beginning.

The boy, now 15, sat down on some stones that had been a part of his home. No longer solely preoccupied with survival, Henryk found there was an immense void within him—he was completely and utterly alone. Had, by some miracle, any of his family survived? He would spend months trying to find the answer to that question. But until he could begin his search in earnest, he would spend the days that lay immediately before him engulfed in a consuming agony of loneliness.

CHAPTER SEVEN

THE SEARCH

Peeople were crowding into the international office of the Red Cross that had been opened in Warsaw. World War II was now history, and Jews were free to press their search for friends and family across the entire face of Europe. When Henryk arrived at the office, he was greeted by two surprises: First, he did not expect to find so many Jewish people there. Living as he had, in almost total isolation, had instilled in him a subconscious feeling that he alone had survived. It was difficult to shake off that sensation. The second revelation was equally pleasant. Here and there in the crowd, he recognized faces he had known during the days of his childhood. They had changed substantially, but still the tie with the past was revived, and this gave him a sense of being back among the living once more.

He was excited to find an old friend and classmate, Vwadik Jalonka, among those who waited at the center. The young men shared a warm reunion, complete with updates on events that had touched their lives during the long and horrifying years of war. They parted with the promise to maintain contact with each other.

For a time he was distracted from his central purpose. The meeting with Vwadik and the fascination of observing the emotional reunions taking place between old friends had captivated his attention. He was absorbed by the expressions on the faces of people who were greeting one another for the first time in years and learning who, from among them, were still left alive. The way they clung to each other, physically and emotionally, was a sight that nearly overwhelmed the teenager. These people had little else to which they could cling in those early postwar days. Dispossessed from homes and businesses, they had come from behind the barbed wire, carrying with them the indelible memories of their individual nightmares. Many bore bright blue identification numbers tattooed on their forearms. Others had left the ranks of the partisans and had lived the wild animal-like existence of the perpetually hunted. Some came to the office after years of living with forged documents and false identities. These people had somehow managed to vanish into the Gentile community, where they were seized with constant fear at every knock on the door or footstep on the street. Often they were forced to submit to extortion by people who knew their true identities but found it more profitable to bleed them dry rather than turn them in.

In one way or another, they all found that life for them was still a grim question mark. Most had been refused access to the properties they had owned before the war—those who presently occupied them simply refused to relinquish possession to Jewish people. So the Jews who had been disenfranchised by the coming of the Nazis now found themselves displaced people even after the Nazis left. A somber fact confronted the ravaged survivors—aggressive anti-Semitism was far from dead in Eastern Europe. Hundreds who filed into the Red Cross office had already felt the cruel lash of hatred for Jews that persisted in Poland after the war. Some of these same people would perhaps be among the victims who were later slain in an incomprehensible pogrom that occurred in 1946 in the town of Kielce. Polish citizens formed a mob and brutally murdered forty Jewish people, all of whom were Holocaust survivors.

In spite of it all, they still had one another. And understandably, they held on fervently to fellow Jews. They were not a people bound together by lands, social status, or monetary expediencies. They were, every last one of them, dispossessed Jews who had only other Jews with whom to identify. Thus, in a consuming sense, Henryk and all European Jewry would, for the foreseeable future, be obsessed with the search for survivors.

The woman behind the desk had a kind face that radiated a desire to help. Henryk had waited the day out to speak to her. "What can I do for you, child ?" the Red Cross representative asked.

"They told me that you might have information about my family."

"If you will give me their names, I will check the list and see if they have been registered at this office."

She wrote as Henryk spoke. "Weichert is the family name. My parents are Mendel and Ruth. They were sent to the ghetto with my sister, Tema. I have three brothers, Arthur, Hersh, and Jacob. They were taken to Germany to work."

The woman turned to consult the long list of names that had been turned in. She looked at Henryk and reluctantly informed him, "There are none by this name listed here. But do not be discouraged. We receive hundreds of names every day. Perhaps soon the names of the members of your family will be among them. Come back here tomorrow and listen to the names that are read over the loudspeaker. All new names that come in are read over it during the day."

The boy left the office determined to be back before it opened in the morning so he would not miss hearing the names of those who had joined the list of persons located by the Red Cross.

All through the following day he listened intently to the announcements. The crackle of the loudspeaker had a strange effect on the people who were seated in the office and outside on the street. An immediate hush would fall over them, and they would quickly turn to find the best vantage point for hearing the names. Occasionally people burst into tears or shouts of joy as the name of a family member or close friend came over the speaker. The response had a contagious effect as the others in the room spontaneously joined in the jubilation. It seemed, at times, as though they were sharing in a subdued tribute to a monumental triumph—another of their kinsmen had emerged from the sea of suffering and death.

For Henryk, however, there would be no tears or shouts of joy. He listened eagerly to each new listing of names. A few were names he recognized. But none belonged to members of his family.

He haunted the central office in Warsaw for many days. Finally he approached the desk of the woman to whom he had first spoken. "May I see for myself the list of names you have?" he asked politely.

"Certainly you may," she replied with understanding. She watched as Henryk ran his finger down the list—lips silently forming the names he saw on the paper. Hesitantly, he looked up and slowly slid the worn sheaf of papers across the desk.

"Are there other places where I can look for them?" he questioned.

"Yes. A large center has been opened in the city of Lodz. If you go there, perhaps they can be of some assistance." She looked at him earnestly until she had fully caught his eyes. "And young man, I do hope you locate them."

Before he left the office, he handed her the address of a Polish family he was acquainted with in Warsaw with instructions to inform them if news of his family's whereabouts came in.

Early the next morning he began his journey to the city of Lodz. The residual effects of exposure, bad diet, and the beating he had received at the hands of the Nazis caught up with him there. Henryk found that the center in Lodz had extensive listings of names of people who had been released from the death camps. He and the desk worker were poring over one of the lists when he began to feel an unsteady sensation in his legs. "Do you feel all right?" the young man assisting him asked solicitously.

"No, I feel very weak in my legs, like I am going to fall."

"Sit here. I'll call a doctor."

"We had better move you over to the hospital and have a good look at you," the doctor concluded. Henryk made no effort to protest. It was apparent to him that he needed medical attention.

A Polish physician was in the middle of examining the youth when he called a Russian doctor to the bedside. "Come over here. I want you to have a look at this." Then he asked Henryk, "Where did you get all of these scars and marks on your body?" Henryk told them they were souvenirs he had received from the Germans. "Well," the doctor replied, "they are souvenirs you will have with you for the remainder of your life." The men were astonished that he had not sustained any broken bones from such a severe beating. When they concluded their examination, they prescribed a month's stay in the hospital for rest and recuperation. Henryk would again have an opportunity to taste some of the sweet fruits of compassion he had been denied under the Nazis. As he settled into the hospital bed, he reflected on the fact that in this place, the people knew he was a Jew, but it didn't seem to make any difference. He was treated as well as any other patient.

He left the hospital with a feeling of fresh mental and physical vitality. The search, he determined, would continue until he found some trace of his family or became fully convinced they had perished.

Hundreds of new names had been placed on the roll by the time he returned to the Red Cross in Lodz. But none of the names were the ones he was longing to see. He decided to wait there a few more days and then move on to other centers. After three days of impatiently listening to the names that were coming into the office, Henryk began talking casually to a young man in his early twenties. "The largest information center in Europe is located in Geneva, Switzerland. Why don't you come along with me?" It sounded like a good idea. So two days later they boarded a train bound for Geneva. Traveling for these young men was not in the accepted fashion. They rode on the roof of the train and arrived at their destination grimy with smoke from the engine.

In Switzerland the news was the same—bad. No word of his parents. What he did find was information about other offices that might have some clue regarding their fate. For the next several months the teenager made his home on train roofs, in boxcars, and in chairs at Red Cross offices, where he sat with fellow Jews who were seeking word of their families.

Henryk looped Europe on his odyssey. From Switzerland he swung down into Italy, where a large concentration of Jews was located. Many Jews from Poland had gone there during the latter stages of the war via escape routes through Hungary and Yugoslavia. These refugees hoped to arrange passage to Palestine by way of Italy. Some fifteen thousand Jews had been smuggled into the country before the British moved against the effort and refused to allow further transit toward the Holy Land. By closing the border, they had stranded another twelve thousand Jewish people in Graz, Austria. Consequently, Italy and Austria had become fertile areas in which to seek displaced Jews. Henryk sought information in Rome, Florence, Milan, and Naples—all to no avail.

France was the next stop along the way. Results there were the same as they had been in Italy and Switzerland. His rail travel then took him to Germany and stops at Frankfurt-am-Main, Hamburg, and Munich. At each center he left an address in Warsaw where he could be contacted. By the time he departed Prague, Czechoslovakia, for the return trip to Poland, Henryk was a deeply disheartened young man. The faint hope of finding his parents was the only ray of light on his horizon. When he arrived in Warsaw, he hurried to the home of his friends. "I'm sorry Henryk, we have no word of your family." The statement seemed to hang frozen in the air like an epitaph.

For the first time in all of the years since he had last looked into the face of his mother, the question began to take on the form of a conviction—his family had perished. The conviction would not be confirmed in his mind until he had revisited the Red Cross center in Warsaw and waited several more weeks for word from the countries he had been in. In the end, he could only conclude that their names must be placed in the column alongside the three million others who had died at the hands of the Nazis in Poland. He no longer expected to hear that they were alive.

For Henryk now, his entire life seemed to have been cast against a backdrop of sheer futility. He felt as though he were enmeshed in a recurring nightmare that cycled through one horrible tragedy after another. He wondered if there would ever be an avenue of escape. Surpassing every consideration at this point in his life was the fact that Henryk Weichert had been left without hope. For years his adversity had been tempered by the hope of an eventual reunion with his family. With that gone, something died within him. He had heard people talk about God—some had even called on Him during the dark days of the occupation. But how could he place any credence in the claim of the existence of a God who had left him with no hope? If He existed at all, God only mocked him with one destructive disappointment after another. For weeks to come he wandered the streets of a war-ravaged city, without hope, without faith, without a shred of assurance that the future held anything better for him.

1945 ✡ 1948

CHAPTER EIGHT

THE PROMISED LAND

Vwadik Jalonka warmed to the subject with unbridled enthusiasm. A major decision had been made in his life since he and Henryk had last been together. "I have decided to leave Poland and make a new start," he informed his friend. "Arrangements are being make for me to go to England—I shall be leaving soon. Most of the people who are getting out of the country are going to Palestine, but I have relatives in England, so I am going there."

Henryk thought about it for a moment. "What does a person have to do to leave the country?"

"It is very simple," Vwadik replied. "A Jewish agency has a new office here that works in cooperation with UNRRA.* It is located in Warsaw. If you will go there, they will make arrangements for you. Just a minute. I will write the address down so you will have it."

Henryk's mind was working while his friend wrote the address. There was no longer any reason for him to remain in Poland. The possibility that he could leave the country came as

---

*United Nations Relief and Rehabilitation Administration.

welcome news. Although he could not explain why, his mind was immediately settled on where he wanted to go. Palestine, he had heard, was the land of promise. He would go there in search of what he had lost in the country of his birth. He would make his new home in a new land.

Thousands of European Jews were making the same decision as Henryk. The war was over, but persecution of Jews had not subsided. Jewish people were ready now to turn their backs, once and for all, on their tormentors. Between 1946 and 1948 a quarter of a million Jews would leave Eastern Europe. Immigration to the land given them by God was still an almost exclusively illegal enterprise. The British mandatory government had slowed the rate of sanctioned immigration to a trickle. Where the British occupation forces were active in Europe, they did everything they could to prevent Jews from going to Palestine; closing the Italian frontier illustrated this policy.

In spite of this obstacle, however, many escape routes were surreptitiously kept open and eventually deposited refugees on the beaches of Italy, France, Romania, Yugoslavia, and Greece. There they boarded leaky, rundown tubs that passed for transport vessels and embarked on a journey to take them to the Promised Land. Between 1945 and 1948, sixty-five of these immigrant boats sailed for Palestine. For the vast majority of those who made the trip, it was a journey into more troubled waters. The British relentlessly hunted them down, captured them, and shuttled them off to internment centers either in Europe or on the island of Cyprus.

Official sources in governments and various independent agencies defied the British dictum and cooperated with the clandestine efforts to find a national haven for embattled Jewry. The Polish government, particularly after the pogrom at Kielce, feared that it could not restrain further violence against Jews. Consequently, it considered emigration a desirable solution and assisted in the flight of Jews from their country. Czechoslovakia agreed not to hinder the mass movements and went so far as to pay train fares for Jewish people fleeing Poland. Other governments and the occupation forces of the major powers actively or tacitly approved the operation.

UNRRA, under its first director general, Herbert Lehman, was instrumental in assisting with financing the Jewish exodus. Among Jews themselves, groups such as the Jewish Agency and the American Jewish Joint Distribution Committee provided funding to help the refugees.

Operationally, a movement called Berihah (flight) was the first to move people illegally across borders and toward Palestine. Other Zionist groups joined the effort as time went by. The Jewish Brigade soldiers, Haganah and Mossad, moved fellow Jews along escape routes and onto the "illegal" ships.

As the struggle for recognition of statehood for Israel escalated, political groups began to recruit personnel for their movements. David Ben-Gurion's Haganah, Menachem Begin's Irgun, and Lohamei Herut Israel (Lehi) actively recruited, transported, and trained European Jews for their respective organizations.

"So you wish to go to Palestine." A bald, bespectacled man was seated behind a battered desk interviewing the prospective young traveler.

"Yes, I want to leave Poland. A friend of mine told me that it could be arranged if I would come here to your office."

"Does your family live here in Warsaw?" the man questioned.

"My parents, brothers, and sisters are all dead. They died during the war. I am the only one in my family who is left."

"Unfortunately, yours is a story I hear many times each day. I deeply regret that I can do nothing about the past, but I can help you with your future. If you wish to go to Palestine, it can be arranged. Take a seat over there, and wait until you are called."

Henryk waited with the other applicants until a young woman who held some papers in her hand called his name. She issued him an UNRRA refugee card and gave him instructions about the date and time he could expect to leave Warsaw. On the appointed day, he assembled with a number of Jewish people who were making the first leg of the trip with him. Their journey would take them to Lampertheim, a German town located near Mannheim.

Pleasant surroundings awaited the new arrivals from Poland. Their group was broken into small units that were moved into houses formerly occupied by German families. Meals were served in a central kitchen, where a festive communal air prevailed. A large segment of those making this trip with Henryk were young people. They all expected Lampertheim to be but a brief waylay on the road to Palestine. It would be the better part of a year, however, before they moved to the next stop on their journey to a new life.

Physically and psychologically, it was a constructive time for all six hundred Jewish transients. An optimistic mood was the prevalent theme of life during their stay in Germany. They were constantly admonished to look ahead. For the first time in years, these people had a future. Whatever had befallen them in bygone days, there was assuredly something to anticipate now. Most of them had come out of the war heavily scarred by their experiences, and it took a while for them to progress from abject despair to any form of expectation. But gradually the transformation began to take place. One saw smiles on faces more often. Some who had been secretive and reclusive began to communicate openly with other members of the group.

Perhaps the most obvious manifestation of change was the perceptible transference that took place. These refugees had come from families that had been ravished by untimely and horrible deaths. When they had fled Poland, the emptiness left by their losses was almost intolerable. But now, with the passage of time, they began to make friends. These relationships began to fill the awful void left in their lives. Although they could no longer turn to their families, they could at least turn to the familiar face of a good friend—someone who also needed understanding and companionship.

Henryk Weichert was, by the nature of his basic constitution, an outgoing individual. He was a young man who needed friends, and very soon the friends he made found that they needed him. In a real sense, during this year of waiting, Henryk began to piece things back together again. It was the infancy of a progression—one that would see his life change irrevocably and, as an ultimate result, one that would exercise an incredible influence on hundreds of his beloved countrymen.

As their stay in Germany drew to a close, impatience began to set in. A cheer went up from the group when the announcement was made instructing them to prepare to leave their quarters for the trip to Grenoble, France.

The stay in Grenoble lasted only a few days. As the time of their departure for the coast approached, a general meeting was called to brief them about the journey. The man who stood to address them was articulate and exuded optimism. He was a representative of the Irgun and would accompany the refugees to Palestine, along with several other Irgun members who had joined the travelers in Grenoble.

"Tomorrow we will leave to begin our journey to the Promised Land—Israel. It is the land of our fathers, given by God long ago to Abraham and his children.

"Many of our Jewish brothers and sisters have already gone on before us and are waiting to receive us. When we arrive in a few days, you will be welcomed by them with open arms. You will be housed and taken care of by our friends who await us in our homeland.

"Very soon, we believe, Israel will be the national home for Jews from around the world. You have the privilege of being among those who will make the dream of a Jewish state in Palestine come true.

"We have a good, sound ship waiting to take us to Israel. It will be a pleasant voyage on the Mediterranean for all of you. In a few days we will arrive on the coast of the land of milk and honey. In the meantime, enjoy yourselves—have a good trip!"

Applause followed the speaker as he turned to take his seat. It was, to their eager ears, a fine speech. Spirits were running high as the "illegals" turned in their UNRRA identification cards. If, perchance, they ran afoul of the British, there would be no sure way to trace their origin or organizational attachment. Henryk and his companions slept fitfully that night. They were taking a long step, one that would separate them from the scene of their desperate struggle for survival—they were leaving many memories, good and bad, behind them.

When the trucks rolled into camp the next day, all of the voyagers had long since been packed and assembled for their ride to the coast. Most of them had never taken an ocean voyage before. The fever of adventure was on them all. That fever would subside somewhat when they had their first glimpse of the "good, sound ship waiting to take us to Israel." It was anchored off a secluded beach in the south of France. And they discovered, with considerable consternation, that it was not a ship at all, but a fair-sized fishing boat. This instrument of their passage to the Promised Land appeared able to accommodate approximately one hundred people comfortably. Yet six hundred bodies waited on the beach to board.

They were taken on a few at a time. Their personal belongings were stowed below deck. Sitting pressed together in cramped space on the deck of the boat, the immigrants waited for the crew to raise anchor and set the small craft in motion. Before this was done, the captain issued a stern warning that because of the number of people aboard, it was essential that the weight remain evenly distributed at all times. Any sudden shift of an appreciable number of persons from one side of the ship to the other could place them in danger of capsizing. All hands must resolve to hold firmly to the places they occupied on the deck.

As the boat, loaded to the hilt, moved out into the harbor, expectant young Jewish eyes looked anxiously at the faces surrounding them—their journey to the Promised Land had begun.

CHAPTER NINE

S.O.S.

Henryk estimated that the journey to the shores of Israel would take four or five days. The early hours of the trip were spent adjusting to the new environment. Sea air washed the deck and rigging with an invigorating freshness that bore the aroma of a new beginning. Some who were seated aft watched silently as the boat's wake sent a lazy trail of wavelets fanning out behind them. The Mediterranean was, they agreed, the most beautiful azure expanse of water on the face of the planet. As if it were taking pains to return their compliment, the sea rested beneath the ship's keel with a stillness befitting a placid inland lake.

Mastering the art of moving about an overburdened vessel was a study in choreographic precision. Some were up, while others were down. People shifting to the port side would be deftly counterbalanced by movements to the starboard. For the most part, the passengers had only three positions available to them: standing, sitting, or attempting to stretch out in a relatively prone position. Each passenger exercised these postures, for the most part, within the limited confines of an area of the deck that he had claimed as his own.

Even the temperature seemed eager to please. It was early summer, but the sun seemed to fall with a muted softness upon the ship. Young faces, with eyes closed, turned toward the sky to catch the warmth sent to them by the Master of the heavens. Late that evening, they watched a brilliant orange sun dip slowly beneath the sea line spanning the western horizon. Many of them were so captivated by the magnificent pink canopy tinting a few gliding clouds that they momentarily forgot the food that was before them. As darkness enveloped the boat, someone lifted the soft strains of a familiar song. One by one, other passengers joined in until the melody lilted across the surface of the quiet Mediterranean.

Henryk and some of his shipmates talked far into the night about the future. Most, it seemed, wanted to move into a kibbutz and make their way by working the soil of their new land. Somehow, the farming life did not strike Henryk's fancy. He had been forced to do a great deal of night harvesting during his days on the run. Memories of frigid barns, rodent-infested straw stacks, and lice-laden summers had dampened the romance of the pastoral life for him. No, he was basically a man who was cut out for the city. He would learn a skill when he arrived in Palestine and settle into a quiet life near one of the centers of trade and activity.

The pleasant routine established during the first day of the journey prevailed through the early stages of the voyage. On the fourth day out, a radical change was in the wind. The elements suddenly revoked their sufferance as blue skies transformed into a sullen lead gray. Scudding clouds began to move at a low altitude toward the ship. The passengers became aware of a freshening gale that caused the gentle role of the waves to mount into unsettling, choppy swells. As the hours wore on, torrential rains began sweeping over the exposed refugees. The captain offered words of assurance: "This frequently occurs when one is traveling on the sea. Our ship is sturdy; it was built for this sort of thing. Be calm—there is nothing to worry about. Just stay in your places. The storm will soon pass."

But his listeners could not help observing that although he spoke confidently, he kept turning a wary eye toward the incoming waves.

Unfortunately, their captain's confidence rested on faulty intuitive optimism. Wind and sea ignored the pleas of the worried passengers and struck the boat with awesome fury. A storm, which had been predicted to last no more than a few hours, dragged on for days. Occasionally the deafening assaults diminished in velocity, momentarily buoying up the hopes of the beleaguered voyagers. But each fickle interlude eventually dissolved and unleashed yet another violent episode that threatened to drag them all to the bottom.

At the height of the storm, towering walls of water swelled above the railings of their small haven, then crashed across the frightened souls huddling together on the deck. The ship shuddered under the impact of the waves and began settling lower in the water. It was as though the drama of the prophet Jonah's ill-fated voyage on this same body of water was being reenacted. Unrestrained terror broke with the waves over the immigrants. It was clear to them that they were in the grip of a desperately perilous situation. Cries and prayers were flung against the deafening wail of the tempest. People protested bitterly that they had been saved from the Nazis, only to perish here in the sea. To aggravate matters, scores of passengers were reeling from the devastating nausea of seasickness. Quivering from cold and illness, they frantically clutched the railings while vomiting repeatedly.

The captain had joined his charges in forming a pessimistic appraisal of their plight. He was now convinced that the ship's pumping apparatus could not empty water from the lower parts of the vessel as rapidly as the sea was forcing it in. The boat was settling measurably, and if there was not a change in conditions soon, she would be swamped. He issued an order to the radio operator to begin pumping an S.O.S. into the wireless transmitter. The man was well apprised of the potential consequences of his action. In all probability, the S.O.S. would bring the British, who would haul them off the ship and force them into an internment camp for who knew how long. Nevertheless, this was, he concluded, a better alternative than death by drowning.

Henryk, however, sensed a strange calm amid all the hysteria surrounding him. Along with his fellows, he pondered carefully the ramifications of being snatched from the fires of the Holocaust, only to be inundated by the angry waters of the sea. He was not worried about it; nor did he feel sorry for himself, as some around him so obviously did. He acknowledged frankly that he had no control over the circumstances he now found himself in, and he was resigned to whatever happened. The phrase that had become so familiar to him in other days now crossed his mind again—what will be, will be. After all, there was no way for him to assess the future with any guaranteed degree of accuracy. Perhaps, when all was said and done, it was better this way. Having moved from one trouble to another in the past may well mean there was only more of the same for him in the future. At least this way he would die without protracted suffering.

For hours the radio flashed the plea for rescue across the face of the troubled Mediterranean—S.O.S.—S.O.S.—S.O.S. If any vessels heard their message, none responded. The six hundred were left to the thrashing dictates of the storm.

At first, the lessening of the wind held no more promise than the other mocking respites, all of which had appeared to offer hope, only to snatch it away again. But when the wind continued to diminish and the waves slackened, the seasick refugees began to lift up their heads. Tired bilge pumps finally started to take the play away from the waters that had invaded the struggling fishing boat. As the clouds started to break up over their heads, things were looking much better for the bedraggled band of émigrés. They had never seen stars appear as bright or warm as those that laid a glistening carpet across the heavens that night.

Days stretched into a week as the relieved captain followed a zigzag course in his attempt to stay beyond the reach of the British patrol ships. They passed within sight of Messina on the northern tip of Sicily, at the head of the straits separating Italy and the island just off the southern extremity of the boot. As they swung around the Italian peninsula, their course took them east past the island of Crete, then to a slightly southerly bearing that would bring them past Cyprus, well to the south of the island. They were now prepared to make their dash for the coast of Palestine.

The low drone of the aircraft engine was audible before anyone could see the plane. Anxious fingers pointed to the east; everyone seemed to spot the airborne intruder at the same time. As the plane made a slow turn to assume a heading that brought it over the vessel, the captain was yelling to his passengers. "It is a British coastal patrol plane. Get out of sight if possible. The rest of you, lay close to the deck. If we're lucky, they may think we are fishing."

The patrol plane made two passes over the ship, then flew a tight circle around her. As the craft disappeared from view, the captain quickly changed the ship's direction and strained the aging motors to the limits of their capacity. He suspected, though, that it was a vain exercise. The game was over.

Two patrol boats responded to the report from the pilot of the British plane. As they neared the ship, they separated to facilitate an approach from both sides simultaneously. After all they had been through, they were in no mood for the British. The passengers instantly transformed into an enraged mob. A smattering of sticks, the only pretense of offensive weapons on board, were quickly distributed among the incensed passengers who were prepared to defend their rights as heirs of Abraham. Their rickety fishing boat bounced on the water like a little dinghy between two battleships. The Jews were sandwiched helplessly several feet below the deck levels of the two British patrol boats. As the soldiers jumped onto the deck, guns in hand, the refugees began to vent their displeasure on them.

Henryk was in the middle of the melée, lustily swinging his firmly held stick at the helmeted heads of the British invaders. There was something about finally being on the swinging end of the club for a change that gave him a temporary sensation of satisfaction. It would not last long.

A high-pitched voice, decidedly British, shouted in their direction. It came from an officer perched imperially above them. "Drop those weapons and raise your hands above your heads. Continued resistance will force us to shoot."

The captain's voice was the next one heard above the scuffle. "Do as he says," he shouted. "It is useless to offer any further resistance."

Moans of disappointment swept through the Jewish ranks. No one knew exactly what was in store for them, but they shared a universal belief that whatever it was, it would not be good. Their suspicion proved accurate to the letter. After ten days of hoping, enduring, and hazarding their lives, the weakened band was in tow on the way to months in confinement.

Immigrants craned their necks to get a good view of the Promised Land. Haifa harbor provided the first visual exposure to Palestine. It appeared, from their vantage point, to be a very busy place. Ships were moving in and out, and the docks were alive with people.

The captain was ordered to berth the ship at dockside and await the arrival of a boarding party. As the people waited and watched, they shared their mutual frustration at being denied entrance into the land they had traveled so far to make a home in. Soon a quick-stepping contingent of British port authorities strode down the pier where the ship was moored. A uniformed man with a large, drooping mustache barked out orders. "You will leave the ship and line up along the dock as you are instructed. Any attempt to offer resistance will be dealt with swiftly and severely. Do as you are told, and you will be well treated."

Henryk and his shipmates stepped from the deck of the ship onto the first solid ground they had felt beneath them in days. They were ashore in Palestine. Their arrival was, most assuredly, not what any of them had in mind when they embarked from France more than two weeks ago. As they were being carefully searched, each of them wondered what the next move would be.

They were marched off the dock in a double column and away from the immediate area where dockside activities were conducted. A barbed wire enclosure was ready to receive them. They would spend the night confined behind the tall fence, then be put on a prison ship the next day bound for the internment camp on Cyprus.

Henryk and a number of his companions sat in a circle and talked together that night. The subject of their conversation ran heavily toward the injustices that continually befell the Jewish people. Britain's refusal to give displaced refugees access to the shores of their ancient homeland received an extended verbal examination. It was generally agreed that whatever measures were taken to bring an end to the British Mandate over Palestine were undoubtedly well justified. When conditions permitted, each promised himself he would be in the center of the conflict to establish the rights of Jewish people to live in the land in peace. The conversation wound down around some bold talk that set forth the possibilities of an immediate attempt to escape.

One of the men from the Irgun was in the circle. He spoke to them in quiet, reassuring tones. "You will all get your chance to fight for our land eventually. No purpose can be served by taking foolish chances now. There is much work for us all to do before we are ready for such a struggle. When we go to Cyprus, you will learn how to make the best use of yourself for your country. We will not be there forever. When we leave to come back here, we will be prepared to do our jobs."

He was aware, of course, that the talk by the young men was more rhetoric than resolution. Their talk had been only a small act of defiance that would serve until more realistic alternatives were available to them. This exchange would demonstrate audibly that they were not cowering under a captor's hand. Thus self-assured, they could rest the night out.

It was afternoon the next day before the ship was ready to take them on board. In due time, the authorities arrived to escort them to the vessel slated to transport them to detention on Cyprus. The combination of armed guards, close confinement on a prison ship, and thoughts of spending an undetermined amount of time behind barbed wire brought back recent specters to many of these refugees, who had suffered so much. Their faces began to betray their frayed nerves as they walked up the gangplank.

As the ship set sail, Henryk watched the shoreline slip beyond his view. If only briefly, it had been good to have his feet touch the soil of the place he was certain would become his new home. In many respects, it was a land of mystery to him. He was not conversant in biblical history and his knowledge was sketchy at best. But there was something about the place that struck a note of homecoming in his heart. They could load him on a ship and take him away, but he would return. And when he came back, it would be to stay—Israel was his home.

Chapter Ten

A HOME AWAY FROM HOME

Cyprus is an island "whose name excites the ideas of elegance and pleasure." So wrote the English historian Edward Gibbon. To the six hundred Jewish refugees who had been forcibly extracted from their little vessel, the *Ben Hecht*, Cyprus was a place that held no promise of pleasure. As for elegance, that luxury had been relegated to a period in the dim, distant past, far beyond their current powers of recall. For Henryk and his companions, the 138- by 50-mile span of sun-splashed island was to become a sea-bordered prison.

British Royal Marines had planted the Union Jack in Cyprian soil in 1878. Since that time, it had been a colonial possession of the far-flung empire upon which "the sun never set." By the time Britain issued its White Papers, which strictly limited Jewish immigration into Palestine, a complex of wire-fenced detention camps had already been readied to receive illegals attempting to enter the Holy Land. In August of 1946 the British began deporting the refugees to these camps. Fifty-one thousand, five hundred future Israelis would pass through the gates on their journey to the land they had chosen. In addition, two thousand infants would be born to women interned on "the rosy realm of Venus," increasing the numbers of Jews who were homeward bound.

Henryk and his fellow "prisoners" left the ship under the watchful eyes of armed guards. They were taken into reception quarters where they were thoroughly searched from top to bottom all over again. In the course of the search, they were relieved of many of the personal items they had managed to carry with them all the way from Europe. This was a great source of distress to those who now had precious little to show for their lives. The scene seemed all too familiar to survivors who had previously spent time behind the wire.

Henryk offered words of encouragement to a frail young woman who was apparently nearing the limits of her endurance. Her body trembled as her frightened eyes moved from one armed soldier to another.

"This is Poland all over again," she said. Her lips lifted a quick petition toward the ceiling of the room: "Oh, God," she begged, "don't let them kill us."

"No one is going to kill anyone," Henryk said soothingly. "They are just searching to see if we have weapons."

"That is what the Germans told us at Treblinka too. They just sent people to take showers, and they never came back. You don't know what they might do to us."

"But these are not Germans, and you are no longer at Treblinka," Henryk continued. "You have nothing to worry about. We are all safe."

"All of that seemed to have happened so long ago," she said as she began to weep softy. "This brings it all back again—I can see the expressions on their faces."

Her brief exchange with Henryk appeared to have provided an outlet for the inner tension—she began to relax somewhat. This girl's emotional tremor was not an isolated manifestation. Scored of internees held similar reservations about the plans the British had for them. In the end, residual phobias would stalk many of them, even to their graves.

Thankfully, their treatment on Cyprus did not begin to approximate their trials at the hands of the Nazis. When the preliminary processing was completed, all six hundred were hustled off to their home away from home—a number of squat, unattractive, tin-covered barracks inside a rambling, fenced-in area. It was a large enclosure, which relieved the anxiety of the refugees somewhat. Quarters were apportioned by lots of twenty-five people to a building.

Henryk ran an inspection of his temporary home. It was not the fine hotel where he had spent the night back in Warsaw; but it was far superior to some of the barns he had lived in. Filthy floors could be remedied by a thorough sweeping and scrubbing. Outside the weather was ideal. Sea breezes provided enough natural air-conditioning to maintain a comfortable climate. Within sight of the building were some tree-shaded woods. All in all, he thought, he had seen worse.

Detainees from the *Ben Hecht* would remain on the island for more than eight months before they came up for rotation to Palestine. A system had been initiated that allowed the Jewish people to establish selection committees charged with the responsibility of choosing seven hundred fifty persons each month for sanctioned immigration. When the time came for Henryk and his fellow seafarers to become eligible for transfer, the committee allowed the entire party to proceed to Israel together.

Since the refugees had no choice but to spend the next several months in confinement, they saw to it that their time did not pass idly. Organizational activities abounded among the internees. Youth organizations already existed to help prepare the immigrants for settlement when they reached Israel. One could study Hebrew, attend various meetings, and even participate in military training. Henryk particularly enjoyed the speeches made by Jewish leaders in the camp. He could keep abreast of the news coming in from Palestine and their political overtones. Speakers placed a heavy emphasis on preparing the immigrants mentally for the rigors that lay ahead of them. On one occasion the listeners were enthralled by an excellent speaker who challenged and motivated them dramatically.

"Every day there are developments around us that point a finger toward irrefutable evidences that our long-cherished dream will soon become a reality. Word has reached us that the matter of statehood for Israel will soon be placed before the United Nations for a vote." The impact was obvious, and an excited murmur ran through the attentive group.

"As you know, the Arabs are saying they will see to it that our nation dies at birth. They have declared that they will drive us from the land of our fathers before we can make our home there. Even as I speak, enemy forces are moving against our people who are now in Israel.

"We must give ourselves without reservation to becoming prepared to fight for our homeland. Our strength will be one that is united in spirit, will, and the ability to fight. Let each decide what his part in the struggle shall be, then move forward together to win a new life in our ancient land or death in defense of our right to live there in peace.

"May God strengthen our hands for the great task that lies before us."

An aura of expectancy shimmered over the detainees as they applied themselves to prepare for the conflict that was their collective future. The immigrants needed a secluded place where they could receive military instruction away from the prying gaze of the British. The barracks could not be used because the guards made routine visits that could prove disruptive for the trainees. So a plan was devised to build an underground chamber where a few men at a time could be taken for instruction. A site was selected in a grove of trees, where a sharp depression offered a splendid location for the digging. It was obscured from the view of soldiers who patrolled the perimeter fence.

Each evening a large group of young people gathered around the area to create a picnic atmosphere, complete with loud singing and folk dancing. As the merrymakers provided cover, select crews worked to excavate the cave. When the work was finished, the immigrants had a candlelit training center for future Jewish soldiers.

Trainees were divided into shifts for their instruction sessions. The underground classroom was small, about nine feet square, but adequate to accommodate the small units. Items covered in the curriculum included mines, grenades, artillery and military strategy. At the close of each teaching day, the entrance was carefully camouflaged with foliage.

Of course, no actual weapons were available for classroom use. To fill the need for rifles, the immigrants carved crude wooden substitutes from rough blocks of wood. Henryk and his contemporaries eagerly drank in the information and paid close attention to the instruction they were given. When the time came, they wanted to be fully prepared to fight.

News of the United Nation's historic vote to partition Palestine swept through the camp like a wave of high-voltage electricity. Many internees clustered together to listen to the particulars.

"The vote was taken on November 29. The tally was thirty-three in favor, thirteen against, and ten abstentions. On May 14, 1948, the Mandate will end and British forces will leave Palestine. The Jewish nation will be reborn." Six months later, David Ben-Gurion would stand inside the Tel Aviv Museum and declare: "We hereby proclaim the establishment of the Jewish State in Palestine—to be called Israel."

Near delirium gripped the people who had waited so long for something constructive to happen to Jewry. There was a fresh look on the faces of Jewish men and women and boys and girls who spontaneously joined hands to dance together in high-stepping circles and lift exuberant voices in song. After two thousand traumatic years of wandering, suffering, and waiting, a star had risen on the horizon of Jewish national expectation. Coming as it did, at the end of the bloodiest chapter in the pages of the human documentary, it shone brighter still. There was no gauge to measure the momentous impact this joyous news had upon the intellects and emotions of these people, who were nearest the center of potential benefit from the UN decision. The UN vote assured that their period of waiting would come to a satisfactory conclusion. At the moment, it meant little that they soon would be called on to enter a fierce confrontation that almost no one in the world expected them to win. The Star of David, soon to be emblazoned on their national flag, would be placed beside the national standards of the members of the international community. A Jewish homeland was no longer the ardent fantasy of visionaries and dreamers; it was soil and cities and mountains and rivers. But above all else, it was a culmination, an end and a beginning. It was an end to hoping and a beginning of the opportunity to turn those hopes into concrete dimensions.

Henryk joined in the communal celebration with all the fervent enthusiasm that radiated from his fellow Israelis. There was something in this news that ran very deep in the young man who had known so much rejection. In a few months at most, he would disembark from a ship in Haifa. When he stepped onto the soil of that land, he would begin his life as a citizen of the State of Israel—he would belong! There he would stand on equal footing with every Jew who called Israel his home. The humiliation of having been scorned and vilified just for being a Jew would be buried forever. In Israel he would be among his own in a truly Jewish state. It was a heady experience.

The results of the news of Israel's impending statehood were immediately evident. Jewish men applied themselves with a renewed verve to their military classes. Now they had hope, and they allowed their thoughts to wander purposefully among the dreams and aspirations they had fondly constructed in the quiet of the night. People throughout the camp seemed to walk faster and laugh louder. And always there was high-spirited talk of plans and what they would do with their lives in the future.

With the arrival of the new year, Henryk and his friends eagerly numbered the days until they would leave the island for the trip to Israel. March was hard upon them when their turn for departure came. They had made many new friends during their months on Cyprus. This time, however, parting did not have a ring of finality about it. They were happily aware that within a matter of weeks, all the people who had been interned would be making the same journey. Therefore, saying their good-byes was a joyful experience for both well-wisher and traveler.

Henryk went to his barracks to pack his belongings for the trip to his new home. That evening his mind reflected on the number of times in his brief life on earth this scene had been reenacted. He had been on the move, it seemed, for his entire life. Perhaps this would be his last journey. This time he wanted to settle down and put all of his troubles behind him. How wonderful it would be, he thought, if his family could be here with him now. He sat thinking about them for a long time that night. Ruth Weichert's face repeatedly took shape in his mind. Henryk look into her anguished features and heard her parting words all over again. Suddenly an impassioned surge of anger came over him. How monstrously unfair and cruel it all was. She, his father, brothers, and little Tema had never harmed anyone or anything. But they had been reckoned unworthy of life and were erased from existence forever. For a moment he felt almost guilty for having survived. Again, as he had almost every day of his life since their parting, he drew upon his mother's words: "Now you are a man. Be strong—be strong—be strong. . ." Henryk resolved to be strong enough for all of them.

The next day he passed through the gates and walked briskly up the gangplank to the ship that was waiting to take him and his companions to Eretz Yisrael. He was quite willing to bid a final farewell to his home away from home.

It was springtime in Israel. A touch of the season invaded his being.

CHAPTER ELEVEN

A NEW NAME FOR A NEW LAND

When Henryk Weichert stepped off the ship in Haifa, Israel, he entered a new world. The eighteen-year-old survivor of the Holocaust was experiencing a deep cleansing. No longer was he a Polish Jew. Now he was an Israeli. With the approaching establishment of the state and the subsequent implementation of the Law of the Return, he would be immediately recognized as a full citizen of the modern nation of Israel.

Not only did he have a new land, but he would receive a new name as well. "In Hebrew," he was told, "*Henryk* becomes *Zvi* [pronounced tsvee]. From now on, this is the name by which you will be known."

So Henryk became Zvi. He liked the sound of it. It graphically represented the change that was taking place in his life. He had made the transition to a new land; why not have a new name to go with it?

A new land, a new name—and now a new life. From the first hours ashore in Israel, he also officially entered a new profession, one that would become an integral part of his life for the next four decades. Zvi became a soldier. To him and the young men who disembarked at his side, it was a matter of great pride. After years of being trodden down by the heel of military tyrants, they happily shared the honor of serving a cause whose only design was to insure them and their descendants a right to live unmolested in their own land. The noble enterprise in itself brought about an immediate transformation among these young Jews. The refugee complex was falling away like the dead of winter retreating before the green breath of a clean new April. They were now Israelis, and in a very real sense, they each felt they had firmly gripped the handle of the nation's destiny.

The new arrivals were transported south to a camp located just outside Hadera, about halfway down the coast between Haifa and Tel Aviv. Hadera had been founded as a Jewish settlement in 1890. At that time it was a swampy, malaria-ridden bog, written off as worthless by its former owners. Jewish immigrant-pioneers had drained the land and planted seven hundred fifty acres of eucalyptus trees to dry the soil. Zvi and the East Europeans who accompanied him found it to be a fertile area dotted with lush citrus groves.

The newcomers were quartered in tents. This was a new experience for the majority of these young people, who took good-naturedly to their surroundings.

A tense situation prevailed in these days immediately preceding Israel's statehood, as Jews and Arabs geared for the war to come. Already, pitched battles were being fought for control of areas considered vital to one party or the other. Only the restraining presence of the British prevented a full-scale war from breaking out. In view of the situation, the raw recruits were pressed into immediate service to defend Jewish settlements in the vicinity. Marauding Arab bands were harassing residents who, in turn, called for armed relief to drive off the attackers.

Zvi's group had entered the country under the sponsorship of Menachem Begin's Irgun organization. At this time the Irgun was one of three groups vying for the dominant role in the coming government. David Ben-Gurion and the Haganah were clearly the superior faction from the standpoint of personnel, influence, and numbers of arms possessed. Both dissidents, Irgun and Lehi, disagreed with Ben-Gurion and were particularly incensed over the boundaries laid out by the UN Partition Plan, which had been agreed to in principle by Ben-Gurion and Haganah. Because of their fundamental differences, each of these entities functioned through separate operations that were often in direct conflict. Of course, Zvi and his young associates knew little about the implications of anyone's political persuasion. They were finally in Israel and quite willing to fight for her survival under any banner that provided the opportunity. To them, politics was inconsequential.

Early on the morning after their arrival, the young volunteers left their tents for an orientation session in an orange grove. All training was held inside the veil of the shielding citrus trees. Here the recruits were introduced to their first real firearms. Irgun issue during this phase was of ancient Italian vintage. These carbines were holdovers from World War I. Zvi was presented with a model that stood considerably taller than he did.

The entire operation that day seemed like a comic opera. These young men had come together from many European countries, and most of them had considerable difficulty communicating with one another, let alone with their instructor. None of them spoke Hebrew, and this was the only language the instructor addressed them in. The young soldiers did not have the faintest idea what the instructor was trying to say. Therefore, all training had to be conducted using a crude system of signs that made minimal impressions on the men. When it was time to actually practice firing the weapons, the recruits quickly learned that real rifles are capable of dealing out punishment from both ends.

The first eager volunteer stepped forward to demonstrate his prowess to the other envious trainees. His first mistake was in misinterpreting the teacher's gestures about holding the clumsy blunderbuss tightly against his shoulder—he failed to do so. The gun went off with a thunderous explosion, sending the projectile roaring away in one direction and the soldier tumbling in another. When the smoke and dust lifted, the recruit dragged himself to his feet wondering if his arm and shoulder were still connected to his body. Though the remainder of the group howled with delight at his misfortune, they developed a healthy respect for the need to properly interpret the grunts and signs of their mentors. By the time the instructors felt confident the new soldiers had mastered the basics, Zvi and his companions had suffered bloodied noses, ringing ears, various and sundry aches and pains, and many sported deep hues of black and blue. "I can understand now," said a bruised rifleman, "why the Italians sold those guns to us. They must want the Arabs to win the war."

Food for Israel's newest residents was not readily available in great abundance. Because of the friction between Irgun and Haganah, Haganah refused to make portions of their more plentiful supplies available to Irgun. This meant the men also had to spend a portion of each day foraging for food for the camp. Raiding English supply depots at night was usually a productive venture. Zvi found that his old skills were still with him. He was among the most proficient procurers in the entire encampment.

It was little more than a week after the young men had landed in Haifa when the call came for their first military adventure. Arab League countries had commissioned the Liberation Army, a volunteer force made up of units from several Arab states, to enter Israel in preparation for the war the Arabs intended to declare as soon as Israel gained statehood. Syrian and Iraqi troops were the most numerous in the country in the early days of 1948. The British looked the other way while they infiltrated from Transjordan and Lebanon. Liberation Army forces were scattered throughout an area known as "the Triangle." Points of this triangle were Jenin in the north, Nablus in the south, and Tulkarm to the west. Arab volunteers marked time as they awaited the arrival of the full complement of troops and their leader, Fawzi El Kawkji.

Arab plans called for all troops to be assembled and in position by May 14, when the British were scheduled to pull out of Palestine. The minute the English evacuated, they would begin their grand push to sweep the sons of Jacob into the sea. Advance contingents proposed to live off the spoils taken from Jewish settlements in the area—thus the crisis that brought distress to the settlers in the vicinity of the camp at Hadera.

Leaders of the Irgun conferred and decided to attack the Arabs at Tulkarm, the western point of the triangle located roughly fifteen miles from the tent homes of the immigrants.

The march to their first battle began with high-spirited enthusiasm. Immigrant boys went to face their enemies as young men always do in the early days of war, convinced that their foe was no match for them. As they moved along the road, one of Zvi's companions speculated about the encounter.

"The Arabs will not like what we have for them," he boasted. "They will probably turn and run when they see us coming."

"If they don't, it will be their funeral," predicted another.

"I have heard that Arabs will not stand and fight," said a third. "They will throw a few shots in your direction, then get away."

The first soldier offered a second observation. "I'll tell you what they are good at: stealing from women and shooting old men in the back. They won't be so brave when they are up against men who know how to fight."

A wave of agreement swept through the ranks of the untested combatants.

Their bravado cooled, however, as they approached Tulkarm. By the time they reached the scene of the attack, they had become stone quiet and visibly shaken at the prospect of being shot. They were, after all, just boys participating in a cruel and frightening enterprise.

The Arabs were caught off guard by the opening volley, and for a time it looked as though the Jewish attackers would enjoy a measure of success in their initial test under fire. This illusion was soon shattered in a hail of bullets that streamed from the superior Arab weaponry. The refugees' rifles were old, cumbersome, and inaccurate. Soon the screams of the wounded joined the whine of bullets over the battlefield. It was immediately apparent that the attackers were no match for the defenders—the call to retreat was issued.

Zvi helped drag a wounded youth out of the range of Arab guns. The boy was bleeding profusely from a bullet in the upper chest. As he was returning to aid another comrade, Zvi came upon someone else in his group who had been hit in a vital organ and died within seconds. The expression on the dead boy's face struck Zvi—it was one of complete astonishment. It was as though he could not believe he had come so far only to die so soon.

Zvi was no stranger to the pale face of death. But there was something about the quality of death in this place that was particularly hideous. Those who were taken off the field for burial were not emaciated hulks with drawn faces. These had been healthy young men who only moments before had been looking ahead expectantly to the rest of their lives. Yes, he thought, death had a different face here in Israel.

It was a solemn band of soldiers who filed back into the camp to face the barrage of questions flung at them by the women who had stayed behind. They made their glum reports and accepted the words of condolence and encouragement. Their first taste of battle had served to season them. They had faced their enemy and had found him to be a determined fighter. Now they understood that the price of independence for Israel would come high in terms of personal sacrifice. Each of them fervently hoped the price he paid would not be his life.

Over the next few weeks, some of their friends did indeed pay the highest toll exacted from men in war. Skirmishes were fought over the area in an effort to relieve the pressure on the beleaguered Jewish settlements. In each instance, the enemy repulsed their assaults and sent them away without letting them taste victory.

These were rather curious confrontations because the Jews had two hostile forces to contend with. While they were exchanging shots with the Arabs, there was always the necessity to keep a wary eye out for the British. When the emissaries of the crown were within earshot of a battle and hastened to the scene, the Jewish fighters would be forced to turn on their heels and flee. They were trying desperately to avoid both death from the Arab guns and capture by the British.

As the date set for the British withdrawal neared, the men in Zvi's group took up positions in a mountainous region where they occupied fire positions and did observation duty. A primary objective was to stay out of the reach of the English while preparing for the impending struggle.

During these last decisive days of waiting, an important climax was in the making that would change the makeup of the armed forces of Israel. On April 25, Irgun troops launched a frontal assault on Manshiya, a section of Jaffa near the center of Tel Aviv. This move was interpreted as an effort by Irgun to make a big push to gain recognition as a military force before the Jewish population. An Irgun success would reflect negatively on Haganah and damage its prestige as Israel's premier fighting unit. In preparation for the attack, hundreds of Irgun's best personnel were brought in from other parts of the country to join the operation.

The attack was launched early in the morning and met with little success that day or early the next. Consequently, the Irgun High Command felt it was time to make renewed overtures to the leadership of Haganah. Menachem Begin's proposal for a unified command was accepted. The agreement went into effect the same evening, April 26. Haganah area commanders were instructed, "This is to inform you that wherever there are Irgun positions, they will from now on come under the command of Haganah. . ."

Zvi was now a member of the group that eventually would become the Israel Defense Forces—the army of Israel.

Already, strategy was being developed for one of the first major confrontations after the British withdrawal from the country. The Arabs had succeeded in closing the Tel Aviv-Jerusalem Road—a move that placed the Jewish population in the City of David in great peril. Food supplies for the residents were being depleted. Without the Tel Aviv-Jerusalem Road, there was no way to get food into the city. And without food, the Jews in Jerusalem would either have to surrender or starve to death. This condition necessitated immediate action to relieve and resupply the city. The Jews would attack the Arabs at Latrun, the strongpoint dominating the road to Jerusalem.

Zvi and his unit swung into position to join the battle.

CHAPTER TWELVE

NO PLACE TO HIDE

"Take Latrun!" David Ben-Gurion's orders to Yigal Yadin could not have been more direct. Yadin was in charge of all Haganah military operations in Israel. He had argued vehemently against an attack at Latrun just now. Yadin felt that if there were to be any realistic hope of success, he must have more time to prepare for the fight.

In fact, Yigal Yadin had good cause to be apprehensive. Israel had been a state less than ten days when he received the order to capture Latrun. Already invading Arab forces were flooding into Israel to complement others that had previously infiltrated the borders established by the UN Partition Plan. There was not sufficient firepower available to Yadin's men; nor did he have enough trained troops to staff the operation. Besides these formidable difficulties, the paper-thin line of Jewish soldiers under his command was under attack in many other parts of the country, which he considered more strategic at the moment than Latrun.

Ben-Gurion would not be swayed. If any portion of Jerusalem was to remain under Jewish control, supplies had to be brought in immediately. In his view, a Jewish presence in Jerusalem meant life or death for the infant nation. If Jerusalem fell, he argued, it would demoralize the Jewish people so much they might lose heart for the struggle for independence. Failure to move the convoys up the Tel Aviv-Jerusalem Road to save the city would probably mean the death of the nation—there was no other choice.

Now that the final decision had been made, the problem became strictly a military one. Latrun sat astride what was, at this time, the most important crossroads in the Middle East. It was located at a point where the Tel Aviv-Jerusalem Road intersected with a road running north to Ramallah and south to the ancient port city of Ashkelon. Commanding the dominant rise on the northern side of the Jerusalem Road stood a large police station that had been abandoned by the British. Only days before the scheduled attack, the police station had been occupied by a small Jewish force. But it had been driven off by Arabs who were now in firm control of the fortress-like brown building. While Zvi and his comrades prepared for the job ahead of them, contingents of the Fourth Battalion of the Jordanian Arab Legion were digging in at Latrun to repel the attack. These legionnaires were crack troops, trained, equipped, and sometimes even led by British officers. Yet under the British Mandate, it was illegal for the Jews to even have guns.

On the slopes descending toward the road, Arab soldiers were busy implanting a network of machine gun emplacements. Any attacking army would have to cross the wide expanse of open fields and march squarely into the teeth of these guns. While some Arabs were placing the machine guns, others were reopening old trenches that had been used by Turkish troops to defend the position against General Edmund Allenby's British force in 1917. High-caliber machine guns were placed on the roof of the police headquarters, a position that provided a commanding view of the entire area. Barbed wire was uncoiled along the slope to further impede the progress of charging Jewish soldiers, and antitank guns were deployed at strategic points.

Five miles away, at Hulda, Jewish troops were being brought to a staging area in buses. Hulda was the last Jewish settlement between Tel Aviv and Latrun. This force was made up of two Israeli contingents charged with capturing the crossroads and liberating Jerusalem. The Alexandroni Battalion was a veteran unit made up of seasoned Palmach troops. This was a capable, battle-hardened group of men who knew how to conduct themselves on the field of battle. Zvi was a member of the companion battalion, the "New Brigade." Although Zvi had only been in the country a matter of weeks, he was considered a veteran in this battalion made up of immigrants. They came from many European countries and shared, as had Zvi's orange-grove companions, the problem of the language barrier. A large number of these men had been brought to the Hulda staging area fresh off the docks in Haifa—they had been in Israel only a matter of hours. Most had little or no training in firing the rifles they had been issued; some did not even know how to release the safety mechanisms. In addition to these obvious handicaps, they left the buses without helmets, water containers, or field packs. For the most part, their training had consisted of a cram course in a few Hebrew commands and some quick words about the use of the guns.

In view of the desperate urgency that dictated priorities at this stage of the war for independence, Jewish leaders had few other options open to them. They were forced to thrust untested men into the heart of the battles in the hope that military miracles might somehow be wrought.

As it neared midnight, the hour scheduled for the attack, the men were moved from Hulda to the jumping-off point two and one-half miles below Latrun. As they came into position for the march toward the crossroads, the men stood viewing a spectacular panorama. Stretching out before them lay the fertile Ayalon Valley. The moon brilliantly illuminated the vale, casting a gauzy, silver glow over the valley. Ripened wheat stood knee-deep in the rich soil. There was not a quiver of air moving that night. The entire valley seemed to be holding its breath in anticipation of what lay ahead.

As the nervous immigrants awaited the order to move out, Zvi was engrossed in conversation with a religious Jew from Poland.

"Did you know you are standing now before a very famous place?" said the student of the Bible.

"Famous in what way?" asked Zvi.

"How well do you know the Bible?" his friend queried.

"I don't read the Bible," Zvi replied.

"Well then, I will tell you. At this place, God brought about a miracle and gave our fathers a great victory.

"It was in the days of Joshua, after our people had come out of Egypt. The kings of the Amorites had formed an alliance against Israel and brought their army to this place. Joshua and his men fought hard against them until the battle started to go in his favor. Then Joshua commanded the sun to stand still in the heavens until the battle could be fully won. God heard him, and the sun did not move across the sky for a day. This is spoken of in the Bible. It says there was no day like it before, because the Lord fought for Israel that day.

"I believe God will fight here for Israel tonight. I am sure He will give us a great victory over our enemies too."

"I hope you are right," Zvi said with a skeptical edge in his tone, "but I don't think God has much interest in what goes on here now."

Their talk was cut short by the order to move into the valley and proceed toward Latrun. They walked as quietly as possible. The slim chance open to them for victory hung precariously on the element of surprise. By four in the morning they were drawing abreast of their destination. Soon it would be time to attack.

The miracle that had come to the aid of Joshua and his host was not extended to Israel's modern men of war. An Arab lieutenant would become the source of their undoing. Quite by chance, he was out on the road that night returning to his station. Through the moonlight, he caught sight of the Jewish troops as they moved cautiously through the wheat fields. He snatched up his radio transmitter to inform his superiors of the imminent attack.

Suddenly the entire hillside erupted before the faces of the unsuspecting Jewish soldiers. Before they had fired a single shot, their ranks were ripped by a whirlwind of metal-cased destruction. As the sounds of gunfire echoed across the valley, Arab villagers living nearby ran from their homes to join the legionnaries who were destroying the Jewish force.

Zvi saw several immigrants around him fall before the first withering volley. He and his overwhelmed fellows hit the ground and began looking for cover. To their dismay, there was no place to hide. The terrain on the slope before them offered few possibilities for protection. The best they could do was hug the ground and hope for help to come from some other quarter.

As the sun came up over Ayalon, a new enemy arrived. A wave of unbearable heat enveloped the valley and soon turned it into an oven of torment. Compounding the misery was an invasion of thousands of tiny mosquitoes that relentlessly assailed every exposed area of the men's bodies.

Before ordering a general retreat, the commanders attempted a flanking action that they hoped would relieve the pressure on the trapped soldiers. This attack was repelled by a shower of heavy machine gun fire from the roof of the police station. When the retreat was called, the men encountered the agony of trying to outrun the bullets and the whizzing pieces of shrapnel that flew lethally through the air. Each time the young Jews began to rise in an attempt to retreat, the Arab guns tore them apart. Shouts and groans from the wounded hung in the still, torrid air above the wheat fields, which were now ablaze around them.

As the day wore on, many fell prey to the effects of the sun. They were maddened by both thirst and swarming insects. Zvi was among those who kept trying to drag wounded comrades to whatever scant cover could be found in the fields. The sun scorched his head as heat waves danced off the valley floor to mingle with the smoke and noise. Men fell everywhere, spewing blood from gaping holes that had been torn in their bodies.

Suddenly, Zvi saw a sight that momentarily froze his senses. Arab villagers were running among the fallen Jews, pausing just long enough to bend over the wounded and repeatedly plunge daggers into their helpless bodies.

Finally, numb with exhaustion, crazed by thirst, and engulfed in the deafening sounds of war crashing about him, Zvi didn't care anymore. He got to his feet, stood erect, and started walking away from the sound of the guns. He could hear the high-pitched whine of the bullets as they passed within inches of his body. But try as they might, none of the Arab riflemen could hit him.

His course carried him toward the village of Beit Jiz, where the men had been told they would find water and a ride back to their camp. But all he found when he arrived were more Arab guns spewing death on the approaching Jewish soldiers. He paused for a moment to survey the incredible scene around him. Men were staggering around not knowing where to turn to find safety. Some were on the ground, begging to be shot by their own people in hopes of ending their suffering. Officers were pushing, cajoling, and physically beating the men to get them to their feet and out of the range of enemy guns.

If an artist had conceived a picture of hell, Zvi thought, this would be it. He could imagine nothing closer than what was happening before his burning eyes. Horrible beyond imagination, it seemed like a smaller version of the Holocaust all over again—a cauldron of devastation.

Zvi's assessment was not exaggerated. The losses incurred by these raw troops at Latrun would be the heaviest concentration of casualties suffered by the Israel Defense Forces over the span of three wars. An Arab officer would enunciate a striking oral epitaph during the victory celebration following the battle: "I have before me the identity cards of Jews from many nationalities who have come to this country from the ends of the earth." Some, who had been in the land of promise less than seventy-two hours, came from the ends of the earth to die in the smoldering wheat fields of Latrun.

It was mid-afternoon before a few battered remnants of the Jewish strike force came reeling back to the original assembly point. Slowly, the stunned fragments of the broken unit wandered to the buses for the trip away from the scene of their defeat. Zvi left the bus but did not tumble into his bunk as the others did. Instead, he walked to a secluded place and dropped down under the covering branches of a low-hanging tree. He was covered with the grime of battle. His face had been seared by the acrid smoke he had fought during the morning hours. Here and there his uniform was smeared with the blood of the wounded comrades he had tried to drag out of the line of fire. Clearly, this was not the young man who had entered the war with fresh garments and high hopes for victory. And what was perceptibly true on the outside was becoming reality on the inside. Young Zvi was in the grip of a dynamic inward transformation.

The sun may not have hung motionless at his command in some breathtaking display of divine affirmation, as it had in Joshua's day. But there in Ayalon's vale, a revelation of another kind had become crystal clear in his mind. There in the stillness of the evening, Zvi's thoughts carefully traced back over the years. The painful scenes of his childhood were vividly framed before him. The orphanage days—the German decision to send him back to Poland—the bullets that whizzed so closely past him as he fled from the ghetto—his escape from the German who was determined to kill him—his survival after the Nazis had beaten him almost lifeless—the daily groveling for enough food to stay alive—the treacherous voyage in a sea that had death written across every whitecap—and then today.

Until today, he had viewed his tenacious hold on life as a product of his own ingenuity. He was always just a little too smart for them, or a bit too quick. While others died pathetically all around him, Zvi could live by his wits. He would prevail, he had thought, while others would not. He would make it no matter what the odds were against him.

Today he knew that he had been a fool all along—an over-confident, arrogant fool. Today he should have died. Today he knew many times that he was sure to meet death. Today he had stood right next to those who had been cut down by its sickle. Today he had stood up and treated death with disdain—exposed his body to enemy fire. Yet today he was still alive.

Zvi could delude himself no longer. It was not his strength, his quickness, or his wits that had delivered him at nearly every turn in the road. How foolish he had been not to see it. There could be one answer and one answer alone—it was God! It could only be God.

How strange it seemed to him even to utter the name of God. He had not been brought up in a religious home; he had had no attachment to the synagogue, nor had he acknowledged God or sought Him during the days of his distress in Europe. He had always been too busy saving his life or congratulating himself for doing so. But now he was as convinced as he was of his presence beneath the tree, that God alone had been his constant protector and deliverer.

There was another realization of which he was now quite positive: God had spared him for a purpose. He had not survived because he was more intelligent, gifted, or worthy than the millions who had died around him. He was sure of this. But he was also sure that somewhere, wrapped in the mystery that engulfed God, was a purpose for his continuing existence. God had something for him to do.

Now the question was how to find the Lord and how to know what He expected of him. The vast void that had occupied Zvi's soul since the day he had become convinced his family had perished was replaced by a consuming hunger—a hunger to know God.

Amid the clatter and confusion that was Latrun, Jehovah had arrested the attention of one frail son of Abraham—one to whom He purposed to reveal Himself and in whom He wished to take up residence. In a sense, it was as much a miracle as had been granted to Zvi's forebear, Joshua. This time, however, it was not the sun that stood immobile in the heavens, but one young man who stood mute before his God. In the silence of that singular act, he had acknowledged the existence of God and his dependence upon Him. From that day forward, Zvi would follow an unfolding progression, one that would ultimately—inexorably—bring him to the place where his hunger could be satisfied.

Zvi's religious friend had his miracle. Not in the way he had expected—he was not even personally aware that it had transpired—but he had it nonetheless. The Jews had lost one battle; but God had won the initial engagement in the campaign for a man's soul. It was a victory of miraculous magnitude.

Before he slept that night, Zvi arrived at one more conclusion. In the valley of Ayalon that day, before the death-dealing guns of Latrun, he had searched but had found no place to hide. Likewise, he affirmed, there was no place on earth for a man to hide from his God.

CHAPTER THIRTEEN

YOU GET ONE MISTAKE

"He is a man who appears to have what it takes for the job," the officer said.

"Yes," agreed his superior. "I saw him in the field while the battle was going on. He is very quick and appears to be totally fearless."

"You talk to him and see if you can persuade him to do it."

Within a few hours, Zvi had been beckoned to the young Haganah officer's quarters for a personal tete-a-tete. As he walked to the meeting, he wondered what he had done to be called in for a personal conference.

"We've been watching you and feel you are qualified to do something for us," the officer began.

"Thank you," said the blond soldier. "I'm glad I am doing my job well."

The officer came to the point. "How would you like to take special training for a good job?" he asked.

Those words had a familiar ring to Zvi. He remembered another occasion when a handsome partisan had used the same terminology. This time he would ask a question or two before he took the bait.

"May I ask what kind of job you have for me?" he inquired.

"It is a very important one, which few men can do. One who can do this properly will save many lives and serve his country with great honor.

"We want you to work with mines. Do you know about them?"

"Not much," the prospect replied. "They told us about them while I was on Cyprus and in the orange groves, but I cannot say that I learned a great deal."

"Would you like to train for the job?" the officer concluded.

"Yes, I will do it."

"Good. There is a training camp near Netanyah. You will be taken there tomorrow."

So Zvi was enlisted in one of the most dangerous occupations in the army. During the next forty years he would remove and defuse thousands of mines, booby traps, and other lethal devices planted by Arab armies and terrorists.

The opening statement of his instructor at Netanyah made a lasting impression on him.

"You are going into an interesting business—one you will have just cause to be proud in doing well. This is the only department in the army of Israel where you must do a perfect job every time. When you are working with the mines, you get only one mistake. You will not get the chance to make the same error twice."

Zvi listened and wondered if he had chosen the right vocation. Latrun had brought about a profound change in his attitude toward life. His courage and devotion to duty remained unshaken; but he was no longer foolhardy. He took necessary risks in the line of proper service, yet he no longer dared death to take him. In a sense, his life was still barren and empty—he had not found fulfillment—but he now realized that God had brought him this far. He would not risk God's property unnecessarily.

When he returned to his unit after a few days in Netanyah, he found it had moved to the Jerusalem sector. He followed it to join his command there and help keep David Ben-Gurion's dream of a Jewish Jerusalem alive.

The Holy City was divided in two when he arrived. The Arabs held the eastern portion, which included the Old City, and the Jews had a precarious hold on the western side and a small enclave on Mount Scopus, where the Hebrew University and Hadassah Hospital were located.

The Arabs were executing a two-pronged offensive designed to crush military resistance in the general area surrounding Jerusalem while starving the residents of the city into submission. The latter tactic made it imperative that they keep the Jerusalem-Tel Aviv Road closed to Israeli supply convoys. As had been repeated with such devastating regularity throughout history, the City of Peace was under siege by a hostile aggressor.

While army and civilian volunteers labored frantically to construct an alternate supply route to Jerusalem, Zvi and his comrades had their hands full with the representatives of the Arab Legion—the unit they had been so rudely introduced to at Latrun. Fierce fighting was going on around Mount Zion as Jewish forces attempted to secure a strong position there. Zvi was thrown into the fray immediately.

Every night he and fellow demolition experts were out removing mines and planting explosives in an attempt to dislodge their stubborn enemies. Crossing from the Jewish sector to Mount Zion was an impossible enterprise in daylight. The Arab Legion troops that manned the wall of the Old City held a commanding view of the approaches to Zion's summit. Any movement drew an extended fusillade from the legionnaires.

Zvi's group managed to string a wire across the Hinnom, over which the men could ferry supplies to areas that were sheltered from the riflemen on the walls. When it was time for operations to begin, they would slip across the Hinnom and retrieve the explosives for their night's work.

Zvi was thankful to have a close friend helping him during his early days as a mine extractor. He had met David at the training center in Netanyah. The two struck up an instant association that turned into a warm relationship. David was a native Jerusalemite, a sabra, whose parents had come to Israel as young immigrants from Iraq. Since their arrival in the beloved city, they had been blessed with ten children. David was the oldest.

Having been reared in Jerusalem, Zvi's young friend had a tremendous advantage over the new immigrant from Poland. He knew every nook and cranny of the city and could lead expeditions through the darkness with unerring accuracy. On many occasions, David prevented Zvi from taking routes that would have led him into certain disaster.

After several days of extremely hard and exhausting fighting, a truce was called. Although there was still much for Zvi's group to do, he now had the opportunity to pause and take a good look at Jerusalem—and he liked what he saw. Never in all of his travels in Europe had he seen anything comparable to this city of his ancestor David. The massive wall and its stately ramparts left him amazed at the size and ancient grandeur with which it enveloped the Old City. Domed buildings, sharp-towered minarets, and ornate churches intrigued his youthful mind further. Just the ancient look about the city and its environs stirred his inquisitiveness and caused him to yearn for the day when the war would be over and he could pry open the mysteries of the city of his fathers.

Zvi had the same feeling about Jerusalem that he had when he first stepped onto the soil of Israel as a prisoner of the British. He knew at once that Jerusalem would be his home. From the moment he first saw her, Jerusalem began to spin a web tightly around the young vagabond. He was falling to the wiles of the one city in all the world that held such mystical power over the hearts of her sons and daughters. From this time on, one more Jew would say with the ancients: "If I forget thee, O Jerusalem, let my right hand forget her cunning."

Somehow he felt assured he would find the answers to his questions here. He had heard it called the City of Peace. Personal peace, he hoped, awaited him there.

His friend David was cheerful, intelligent, and patient. Zvi frequently tested his patience to the limit with a barrage of questions about his new home. He wanted to know about those walls—who built them and when? "What," he wondered aloud, "were those curious little crescents on the tops of the towers with the strange names? What was a Moslem? What did they do inside their mosques?" He wanted to have an explanation for there being so many religious people in odd dress about Jerusalem. "What made this a Holy City?" he wanted to know. "Explain, please, how Jews worship God in their synagogues?" he questioned.

On he would go, ad infinitum, until his belabored friend would throw up his hands and beg for mercy. "Oh, Zvi! That is enough questioning for now. You have my brain spinning like a top. Tomorrow I will take up the lesson again; tonight let's get a little sleep."

At this, the eager student would condescendingly extend mercy and beat a temporary retreat to ponder what he had absorbed that day.

Those critical days in Jerusalem in the summer of 1948 exhibited all the dark dimensions of war. But as it is in any protracted human experience, there were situations that produced distracting interludes.

Zvi awoke one morning in the grip of an illness that caused him to feel nauseous and feverish. About the middle of the morning his commanding officer came to him. "Zvi, I don't want you to go out anywhere this afternoon. You have an important assignment tonight, and I want you well rested for what you have to do."

"I am sorry," Zvi said, "I will not be able to go out tonight."

"Why not?" his superior wanted to know.

"Because I feel very sick. I am afraid I will endanger myself and the others if I go."

"I can't take that for an excuse. Sick or not, you will have to go."

Zvi tried to explain further, but his young commander was adamant. Soon the discussion turned into a full-blown argument. The officer had found in Zvi a man who, under the compound influences of fever and injustice, could be as belligerent and tough-minded as a leader of troops. Their heated exchange continued until the exasperated private decided to make his point more forcefully. Zvi stooped down, picked up a fair-sized rock, held it in both hands over his head, and sent it crashing to the ground squarely upon the ankle of his commanding officer. The young debater had only intended to make a firm impression in the ground and in his commander's mind. Instead, he made quite an impression on his ankle—a bone was broken.

While the officer was carried away grimacing, Zvi, protesting loudly, was ushered to the stockade. After a few hours of confinement, it became obvious that the soldier was indeed a sick man. A doctor examined him and recommended he be admitted to the hospital for treatment. When he arrived, who should be located in the bed next to him but the officer he had injured. His superior was in a deep sleep, recovering from the ordeal of having had the leg set and placed in a cast.

Zvi slept for a short time and awoke feeling somewhat better—well enough, in fact, to want something to eat. It was not near mealtime, so he began rummaging through the drawers of the table between his and the officer's beds. The hungry private found that solicitous friends of his leader had left some candy for him to enjoy during his recovery. Zvi thought he would sample some. In fact, it was good enough to keep on sampling until it was gone. Quite satisfied, he rolled over and went back to sleep.

Zvi was awakened later by the sound of visitors' voices at the bed next to his. Reluctant to face the man he had offended, he pulled the blanket up a little higher on his head and kept his face turned away. After the friends had chatted for a time, the gentleman wished to extend some hospitality to his guests. "Get some candy out of the drawer and pass it around," he directed one of the callers.

"What drawer?" the man questioned.

"The one you just opened," he said.

"You must have been dreaming there was candy in here," his friend replied. "This drawer is empty."

"I am not dreaming. I saw it put there with my own eyes."

The dawn broke. He looked around the ward and demanded a prompt confession from the culprit. Wide grins broke out on the faces of the sick soldiers, but no one betrayed Zvi. When the officer saw that only one face was not turned in his direction, he issued a stern command: "You! Turn this way and let me get a look at you." Zvi knew the game was up and turned, grinning sheepishly, toward his commander. The man slapped his forehead and fell back on the bed. "Oh no!" he lamented. "It is not bad enough for you to break my leg; you have eaten my candy too."

Pandemonium swept the room. It was the funniest thing these soldiers had ever seen happen to an officer in the army of Israel. It was a rare moment of comic relief—one they would long remember. The young officer tried in vain to contain himself. In the end, he, too, was overcome by a fit of laughter. When he had regained control of himself, he turned on his side and thrust an outstretched hand toward Zvi—all was forgiven. The two who routinely faced death together became lifelong friends as well.

The same officer, who was destined to rise to a high position in the Israeli government, later proved his friendship by coming to Zvi's rescue on another occasion. Zvi and some friends from his unit had taken the initiative to extend a pass a few hours beyond the allotted time. When they returned to their post, they found an officer who was rather perturbed by their having taken liberties with his instructions. He administered a swift brand of justice: "Three days in the stockade for the lot of you."

There was a saying in the army at the time that no soldier was worth his salt as a fighting man until he had spent some time in the stockade. As things were viewed from the perspective of those on the lower echelons, it was the test of a genuine soldier. Upon arriving at his place of confinement, however, Zvi found the stockade not to his liking. He and his companions were put to work in a small garden, raking and doing yard duty. That evening some sympathetic members of their unit came to pay them a call.

"We came to see the convicts," his friend David said. "How do you like being locked up?"

"I can tell you, I don't like this place very much," Zvi said glumly. "I may decide not to stay the whole three days."

This drew a big laugh from the visitors. "And tell me, please," said a bright-faced young fellow, "where will you go when you leave this fine hotel?"

"I haven't made up my mind yet," Zvi informed him. "My friends and I may choose to take another day or two to see the sights."

"Ha, Zvi," David retorted, "you are like a skinny sparrow in a cage. Look at you—guards, guns, a wall. All of you will stay put until they come to you and say, 'Okay boys, if you promise to be good, we will let you go.'"

The implied challenge was more than Zvi could bear. "Bring me a finger of dynamite and a detonator, and I will show you how well a skinny sparrow can fly."

"You've got it," said his cooperative friend. "Now let's see if you have the nerve to use it."

The next day his friend returned with the dynamite. Stockade security in these days was a rather loose affair, so there was little difficulty making the delivery. When their fellows departed, the escape artists huddled to lay plans. "The only thing I'm worried about," said one of the more cautious types in their company, "is that the guards have rifles. What if they should shoot us?"

"We will take care of that," Zvi assured him. "If they do what they did last night, it will be no trouble."

He was right. The guards had established a pattern of leaning their rifles against a tree while they sat around a nearby table to play cards. Since this was a place where men were brought for only minor infractions, the keepers of the keys were not afraid of being accosted. Consequently, it was a relatively simple matter, under the cover of darkness, to slip up to the tree and carry the weapons away. With the guns safely hidden, the sparrows went about the business of setting the charge in the wall.

The explosion went off with a dull "wump." Guards jumped straight up in alarm, and playing cards scattered in every direction. The guards ran for their guns but came up empty-handed. Next stop was the wall, which now hosted a gaping hole and a billowing cloud of dust. In the distant darkness, the astonished jailers could hear the escapees laughing as they said good-bye to the stockade.

A short time later the young celebrities swaggered into the camp, obviously pleased with their newly acquired notoriety. They were in the midst of a grand explanatory conference when the puffing guards came steaming in. They went straight to the commander with a request for the return of the prisoners.

"What has happened here?" demanded the officer.

"These men blew a hole in the wall of the stockade," they complained. "They have made real trouble for themselves now."

The officer addressed the man in charge curtly. "Why didn't you stop them?"

"We couldn't," he answered.

"What do you mean you couldn't?" he countered.

"Because they took our guns and hid them," the embarrassed soldier confessed.

"Well," said the commander, "if you allowed them to take your guns, there will be someone in the stockade tonight, but it won't be these men—it will be you!"

The man whose leg Zvi had broken looked at his subordinate with mock severity. "Get to your beds. And no more mischief, or you will understand what it means to be in trouble."

Zvi and his companions knew all too well that this sort of frivolity was but a temporary emollient that diverted attention from the sound and fury of combat. Within a matter of days the battle was on again, and their nights were occupied with plying their delicate skills.

"Zvi, I want you to come to my home today and meet my family," David told his friend. The young man from Europe, who had no family of his own, counted this invitation a great honor and made preparations for the social engagement.

The two went together into the Jewish residential section of Jerusalem. They walked onto a narrow street lined with crowded living quarters. When they arrived, the father welcomed them into a room that was alive with inquisitive children. At first they looked Zvi over from a distance with coy glances. Before long, though, the strange visitor had become the special object of their attention. Zvi drank in his newfound popularity with undisguised relish. He had not had much time to spend in happy circumstances with children, or to be a child himself, and he was enjoying the attention immensely.

After a simple meal, the father shooed the children out of the room, and the three of them sat talking over cups of tea. "We have heard much of Zvi in this house," the father said. "I am happy, at last, to have the opportunity to meet the man who has been such a good friend to David."

"It has been my good fortune to know him," Zvi answered. "He has been a friend who has kept me out of trouble many times."

"Yes," offered his young companion, "and we have seen much of Jerusalem together during these past months."

The conversation went on late into the afternoon and ended with warm *shaloms* and a promise to do this again before too long.

Zvi and David hurried through the streets and back to their posts. Soon they were moving out on a night mission on Mount Zion. Everything was going according to plan as the line of men bore their explosives quietly through the darkness. They were aware of the need to pass close to an Arab position, but miscalculated its exact location. Suddenly, the men found themselves almost upon the Arabs they were trying to avoid. A brisk firefight broke out. Zvi dove behind a pile of rocks in an attempt to find some protection. Nearby, David pulled the pin from a grenade and was about to lob it into the Arab emplacement when the device malfunctioned and exploded in his hand. He was killed instantly. A distraught Zvi groped through the shadows to where David's body lay motionless, and he began to drag his friend's mangled corpse down the mount amid a storm of bullets that were pelting the ground around him.

The next morning David's body was readied for burial. Because Zvi was a close friend, he was assigned as honor bearer to the funeral party. When the bereaved father met the procession, he wilted under the burden of his grief. The man threw himself across the front of the car in which Zvi was riding and wept uncontrollably. Zvi went to him and laid a comforting hand on the man's arm. David's father turned questioning eyes toward Zvi.

"Yesterday we sat together in my home and you promised to come there with him again. Now you are taking him to put him in the ground. No! Please bring him to his home again."

Zvi knew it could not be, and the procession moved along with the hysterical father protesting the death of his firstborn. This was a situation Zvi was totally unprepared to cope with. He wished with all his heart he could bring his dead friend back to life and return him to his anguished father. This, of course, was beyond human abilities, so he wanted only to get away from the sorrowful scene—to find some quiet place in which to retreat.

On the way back from the burial, a reflective young man was feeling his spiritual emptiness. Dying was an inevitable part of war, and Zvi was no stranger to it. But today he had witnessed the personal ramifications of death in an unsettling confrontation. He had nothing to contribute that could comfort David's distressed father in his trauma of sorrow. All he could do was feel his own helplessness as a human being. He had known for many months now that God wanted him alive for some purpose—but what would there be for him when it came time to die?

1948 — 1967

CHAPTER FOURTEEN

A LITTLE BLACK BOOK

The fighting had stopped, and Zvi was eager to take a look at his new homeland. He had a three-day pass in his hand and the country waiting before him. His active tour of army service would soon be over. It was high time he surveyed his surroundings. On this leave, he decided, he would visit the port city of Haifa. This time he would go neither as a prisoner nor a military conscript—he was strictly a tourist.

Zvi spent three happy days as a contented citizen, walking and gawking his way through Haifa. The spectacular view of the harbor from the side of Mount Carmel awed him.

The soldier-traveler didn't have a monetary pittance, but he had little need for much money. A nation grateful to her sons who had fought to save her now extended hospitality to those in the military. Hotels offered free rooms and meals to Joshua's modern counterparts. All Zvi had to do was walk in with his request for a night's lodging. Israel was coming alive, and the mood was sensational.

The air of optimism and self-assurance was everywhere. Exhilarating waves of confidence were breaking over the nation that had so recently fought under a question mark. This country was going somewhere—and it was good to be aboard for the journey.

Zvi left Haifa with a treasure tucked under his arm. He had picked up a copy of the Bible, written in Hebrew. It would, he figured, meet two primary needs: First, he could learn the answers to some of his questions about God. Second, it would be a great tool to help him master Hebrew.

Back in Jerusalem he spent many hours with his new source of instruction. Whenever he could persuade one of his companions to share some tent time assisting him in his reading program, he was a happy man. Soldiers had an abundance of time on their hands now, and consequently, it wasn't too difficult to find a temporary tutor.

One afternoon he was puzzling his way through the Psalms when he came across a statement that brought him to attention: "When my father and my mother forsake me, then the LORD will take me up. Teach me thy way, O LORD, and lead me in a plain path."

"Who said this?" he asked the sabra who had been chosen teacher for the day.

"King David," said his young comrade. "He was the second king of our nation. It was he who came here and made Jerusalem the royal city of Israel."

"If he was a king, living in a palace, why would he say a thing like this?" Zvi wondered.

"Very simple," said his instructor. "He was a king, yes, but a man with many troubles. He had great enemies from whom he was forced to flee. At one time even his son turned against him. Many of the things he wrote in the Psalms were about his times of troubles."

This David, Zvi concluded, was a man after his own heart—trouble upon trouble. Maybe he could learn some things from a man who had spent time in the same boat as the maturing Jew from Poland.

Zvi's mother and father had forsaken him too. Of course, it was something over which they had no control, and he had nothing but fond memories and love for them. Nevertheless, he had known the life of a forsaken waif, alone and surrounded by a host of enemies.

When this man David had suffered, Zvi reflected, the Lord had picked him up. Then David had asked God to teach him and lead him in a plain path. It seemed astonishing to Zvi that one who lived so long ago could feel exactly as he did now. From now on, he determined, his prayer would be the same—that God would teach him and lead him in a plain path.

"What are you going to do now that you are out of the army?" an officer friend questioned.

"First," responded Zvi, "I must find a place to live. The army has given me a tent to use, but I've lived in enough tents to suit me. Soon I hope to find a permanent place to stay.

"Then I will look for work. I don't care what I do, just so I find something I can learn to do well."

"It might not be easy to find work immediately," his officer said. "Until people have time to get things going, work will be scarce."

"Never mind about that," answered Zvi. "There is plenty of time ahead. I will wait for something to come along."

Zvi's tent home was something less than palatial. Often it was difficult to keep up with it. His tent developed a bad habit of blowing away when he was gone during the day. Even at night when the wind was up, it was not uncommon for him to find himself awakened by the sound of fluttering canvas descending about him. Winds in Israel, he found, paid little heed to his threats and complaints as he grappled in the dark with ropes and tent stakes. After a short time, Zvi concluded he was not cut out for the life of a bedouin. If being born a Jew had its problems, at least one of them did not have to be chasing a tent all over the Middle East. He approached the authorities and asked to be relocated.

"If you don't mind living with three or four others in one room," he was told, "you can go to the settlement at Talpiyot."

"All I am concerned about right now," said the man who needed a good night's sleep, "is that my house doesn't run away while I'm gone."

"I don't think there is much danger of that," the official answered with a smile. "I'll arrange for you to get a place there."

Zvi sacked his belongings, folded his errant tent for the last time, and set out for new quarters at Talpiyot. The settlement was located on the Bethlehem side of Jerusalem. This area had been settled by Jews in 1924. But during the recent conflict, it had become situated squarely in no man's land. From a political standpoint, the camp was as international a situation as one could find on earth. Jews from a host of nations had come to this transit camp on their way to permanent homes in Israel.

Zvi's first observation was that he would not be lonely at Talpiyot. If anything, finding a place to be alone was virtually impossible. Fifteen thousand people were jammed into an area covering no more than a few acres of rock-strewn ground. Zvi was shown to a barracks that he was to share with three young immigrants who had recently arrived from Morocco. His home measured about 6 by 12 feet, had two windows on each side, and a door. It resembled a railroad caboose, minus the viewing bays and extension. The Moroccans, Zvi found, were not the only occupants of the small room. Red ticks ranged the walls and found the new resident a particularly tasty morsel to feast on in the night.

Life in Talpiyot was an interesting, if not altogether stimulating, venture. The camp contained one toilet facility for all fifteen thousand residents. Attitudes among some of the neighbors, particularly those from primitive cultures, were communal in the extreme. If one went outside to hang a piece of laundry, he might return to find someone walking off wearing the clothing he had left behind. Rushing back to the line, he would then discover that the freshly washed piece had also been appropriated by some friendly but anonymous neighbor.

One morning Zvi, a sound sleeper, awoke to find two of the windows of the barracks missing. Some enterprising carpenter had obviously concluded that the windows were just the right size for a project he was working on. Zvi had no idea that anyone could possess such consummate stealth as to remove windows from above the head of a sleeping man. But it had been accomplished, and with apparent ease.

Food was another challenging aspect of life in Talpiyot. His Moroccan roommates did not understand Zvi's language, but they did know what to do with the food he left unconsumed on their small table. It was immediately stored in their stomachs. They stood smiling and quite ignorant of what their offended brother was attempting to communicate. When this one with the strange tongue became red in the face and particularly violent with his gestures, they would grin agreeably and nod their heads slowly. When they felt he made an especially spectacular sound or move, they would widen the smiles and speed up their nodding. Zvi quickly learned that the only safe haven for his undigested morsels was his pockets, while he had his pants on.

After he had been in Talpiyot about two months, a woman arrived She was obviously European. Zvi judged by her looks that she was in her early sixties. The woman carried a bag full of little black books. He was seated outside his barracks when she came by. As she approached him, Zvi decided to take a guess at her nationality and spoke to her in German. She smiled broadly and returned his greeting. "You were almost correct," she told him. "You only missed it by a short distance. I am from Switzerland." The two of them shared a few minutes of pleasant conversation before she reached into her bag. "I would like to give you a book," she said.

"What kind of book is it?" Zvi asked.

"This is a New Testament, written in Hebrew," she answered cheerfully.

"And what is a New Testament?" he queried.

"It is a part of the Bible," she explained. "It will tell you about the Messiah."

He had heard references to the Messiah in his ghetto days in Europe and by religious Jews in the army. "I have heard something about the Messiah, but know little beyond the name."

"Then this book will answer your questions," the woman told him earnestly. "There is only one stipulation in my giving it to you: you must promise me that you will read it."

"Yes, I will be glad to read it," he promised. "But I must tell you that I don't read Hebrew very well yet."

"Well," said the woman, "just read slowly and ask the Lord to lead you to understand what you read."

Zvi accepted the little black book with words of gratitude.

When the woman had gone, he thought about what she had counseled him to do. "Ask the Lord to lead you to understand what you read." This is what he had read about in the psalm when David had asked the Lord to lead him. The woman's words struck a chord in Zvi's spirit.

Zvi had read magazines in the past, and from time to time novels had fallen into his hands. However, he found little to interest him there. The Swiss woman's little black book was another story. As he began to work his way slowly through its pages, he found that it breathed with a vibrancy he had never encountered in a book before. Many of the quotations and references were somewhat familiar to him from what he had read in the Hebrew Bible he had picked up in Haifa. This book spoke about many places in Israel that he knew. The stories and lessons of the Gospels began to answer some of his questions, but his snail's-pace reading gave rise to a great many more.

Before long his hunger for the content of his most precious possession began to approximate the drive he had long felt to know God. Each time he picked up his New Testament, he was faced with the difficulty of understanding Hebrew. His lack of any previous exposure to these Scriptures posed another handicap. Furthermore, he knew no one who could help by explaining what he was reading. Still, he applied himself doggedly to his quest to learn what this book had to say.

Zvi had no explanation for the way he felt. Yet he was intensely aware that this book drew him like a magnet. After a while, he began to leave the busy and distracting atmosphere of the crowded camp to seek out the quiet of the parks in Jerusalem. There he would sit for hours, glued to the book. It was not unusual for darkness to descend while he sat absorbed in his reading. It was only the lack of adequate light that caused him to realize he had read his way through an entire afternoon without food or knowledge of the swift passage of time. Frequently he would pause at some particularly knotty point and think carefully through what he had read.

He was especially struck by the knowledge that the men who surrounded Jesus were simple, working people like himself. They were not highly educated men but rather, men who had a real hunger to learn the ways of God. When he read of the times they displayed fear, jealousy, or selfishness, he saw that they were just like the people of his own day. When they rose to honorable exploits or said wonderful things, Zvi silently cheered them along.

Central in his thoughts, however, was Jesus. The woman had told him this book would speak to him about the Messiah. It did not take long for him to recognize whom his little book identified as that distinguished personage. Jesus of Nazareth intrigued him. He was thoroughly captivated as the Carpenter's life unfolded on the pages before him. Zvi lingered over passages that recorded what Jesus said and did. He was moved by the realization that simple, sick, and hungry people could always approach Him and receive a sympathetic response. When he read how Jesus had raised Lazarus from the dead and returned him to his sisters, he thought of his feelings about his friend David and David's grieving father.

Above everything else, he was impressed with the troubles Jesus encountered. This Man did nothing but good, yet some men hated and opposed Him. Later they succeeded in nailing Him to a cross. He found great difficulty comprehending why this would happen. When he considered it carefully, he thought how his own people, himself included, had suffered without cause.

One afternoon he was sitting on his bed in the barracks at Talpiyot reading his New Testament when a friend came by to see him. "What are you reading?" the visitor inquired.

"It is part of the Bible," Zvi answered.

"I did not know you were a religious Jew," his friend observed.

"I can't say that I am a religious Jew," Zvi said, "but neither can I say that I am not religious. This book says many good things to me, things I don't know how to understand yet. But I can say these things interest me very much."

"This Bible you are reading, is it the Torah?" the man wanted to know.

"No," Zvi replied, "it is the New Testament."

"That is not a book for Jews," the friend warned. "It is just fairy tales and bluffs made up by Christians."

Zvi was puzzled. "I have read this book for many days now, and I admit that there is much about it I do not understand. But I have not read anything that has done me harm or caused me to want to become a bad person. I have read only good things in this book."

"If you are smart, you will take my advice and get rid of that book," his advisor stated firmly.

"I cannot bring myself to believe it will do me any harm," Zvi answered.

His friend went away shaking his head. Zvi watched him go and wondered why the man felt as he did. He was obviously very much opposed to the book—but why? Jesus Himself had been a good Jew. As a matter of fact, Zvi thought, there had never been as great a Jew on earth as this One. Why then should he, another Jew, not read about Him. He did not know how to reply to the things he had been told; he only knew that what he had read was finding a lodging place in his soul.

Periodic opportunities for work were beginning to open to him now, and he selected the building trade as his permanent vocation. Zvi learned quickly and worked very hard. It did not matter to him what the task involved. He did anything that provided a good chance to do an honest day's work. Men in the contracting business soon learned the name of the industrious immigrant from Poland who was ready to handle the toughest jobs they had.

Wherever he went and whatever he did, his little black book went with him. He was afraid to leave it behind in his room for fear someone would take it. If he had a few minutes free or was out of work for a few days, he could be found somewhere off by himself, carefully pursuing the content of its open pages.

CHAPTER
FIFTEEN

DARE I ENTER

F ew men have brought more obvious disadvantages into a spiritual confrontation with God than Zvi Weichert. Death, privation, and a recurring cycle of cruel disappointments had buffeted him during his childhood and youth. As a boy, he had looked out on a world intent on his destruction. While he clawed and fought to stay alive, his path took him from one tragic revelation to another. Zvi had seen degenerate humanity with its teeth bared and hands reddened by the blood of innocents. He had weathered a storm of demonic brutality that defied analysis by sane minds.

Bitterness, persecutions and degrading meanness, inhuman cruelty, frustration, and fear were among the ingredients that had boiled about him in the seething cauldron into which he had been plunged. By all standards of human computation, it should have destroyed him. But it did not.

Conversely (and ironically), few men have entered a personal period of spiritual crisis with more obvious openness than did Zvi Weichert. He did not carry with him the inherited prejudices of Judaism or Christianity. From the spiritual standpoint, Zvi had been brought along in a near vacuum. Satanic manifestations had swirled around him throughout his life. While he could not provide precise theological definitions for what he was caught up in, he could certainly acknowledge the reality of the experience. When it came to God, however, he was confronted by a void. His knowledge was so limited that it was virtually nonexistent.

But there was one fact available to his mental and spiritual facilities of which he was certain: He was a Jew. The force of this knowledge had been with him throughout his years of suffering. When he surfaced in Poland after the war, it never occurred to him to hide his identity and forsake his race forever. His physical features and identification papers would have made it an easy matter. Being Jewish had certainly stigmatized him and could have produced a spirit of rebellion in him that made him reject everything Jewish. Members of his family were all dead, and the future for Jews in Europe was bleak. But Zvi was never seriously tempted to turn his back on his own people. As if drawn by some mysterious inner mechanism, he had gravitated toward Israel. When he had arrived in the land of his fathers, he knew instinctively that he was at home and among his own.

From that point on, Zvi began to progress through a succession of steps that brought him to the threshold of decision. The knowledge that he was alone in the world had left him empty—and he was acutely aware of the painful void. At Latrun he had frankly faced himself and acknowledged that God existed and cared for him. Thus he awakened to spiritual reality as a hungry young man. In Haifa he had received his first exposure to the foundational portion of the Word of God. Through reading the Scriptures, he identified with Jehovah and His ability to speak to the needs of his fathers in days gone by and to his personal needs centuries later. Then he had received his copy of the scriptural component that rested securely upon the foundation and completed the structure—the New Testament.

God had divinely constructed a type of providential pyramid—one that moved from base to point in stages, drawing Zvi upward to the pinnacle that unerringly directed him toward the One who could satisfy the hunger that throbbed within him.

Without a single hand to guide him or a human voice to counsel him, Zvi stayed close to the book that he somehow knew held the answer to his longings. Day after day he soaked up its truths until he came to the place of direct personal confrontation—he felt he had to do something about what he had learned. As he read the Bible, he came to grips with the matter of his need for righteousness, not merely religious practice. Through his reading, he began to understand that it was necessary for the Messiah to suffer for the sins of the people before he, or anyone else, could approach God. When he read the accounts of the animal sacrifices of ancient days, he had wondered what could be offered to make peace for him today. When he found that the Messiah had occupied, once for all, the place of the slain lamb, he began to see that the answer to his quest was bound up in the Messiah who had borne the sins of mankind.

Zvi did not see the Old and New Testaments as isolated entities, separate and opposed to one another, but as a complementary unit, the New being the logical extension of the Old. Each was incomplete without its counterpart.

Many questions pressed upon his mind in these days, but one began to predominate: How could he enter into union with the Messiah?

It was a sunny Wednesday evening as Zvi returned from his day's work in Jerusalem. As he often did, he spent some time sitting in the park engrossed in reading his black book and mulling over its passages. The dinner hour had already passed when he decided to go up the street to a small restaurant and eat before returning to Talpiyot. As he passed a small building, he could hear the sound of people lifting hearty voices in song. The words filtering down to him came from a hymn about the person he had been reading about, Jesus. Although it was not obvious from the outside appearance of the building, he knew that inside must be a meeting of believers in Jesus as Messiah.

He had never attended such a service, so he was not familiar with how they conducted worship. Whatever they did, they certainly sounded happy about it. When he came back from the restaurant, a few people still lingered by the front of the building with Bibles tucked under their arms. Zvi fingered the New Testament he carried in his pocket and felt an urge to stop and talk with them, but did not give in to it.

For the next few evenings, he arranged his routine so he would be in that vicinity at about the same time. He saw no life about the place until Sunday night when, once again, he saw people filing into the building. He walked by the front of the meetinghouse a couple of times during the service, but did not venture inside.

Later he sat in the park and thought it over. He wanted to go inside and see for himself what went on, but he was hesitant. "Dare I enter?" he asked himself. "What if they chase me away and tell me they don't want me there? But why should I be afraid?" he concluded. He had certainly been chased away from enough places in his lifetime. If they didn't want him, he would leave.

He left work the following Wednesday evening, anxious to get to his destination on time. After dinner at the restaurant, he walked up the street and turned in at the entrance to the church. Zvi felt very self-conscious as he stepped toward the door. He did not know quite what to expect. His fears were quickly put to rest. Instead of a stone, an outstretched hand came his way. The man was smiling and extending a warm welcome to the newcomer. Zvi entered and took a seat on one of the benches near the front of the building.

He took a few minutes to look around the small auditorium. It was a simple setting. Across the front was a table with a good-sized menorah in the center of it. On the opposite side of the room sat a worn piano. A small lectern was positioned between the two pieces of furniture. Two men and a woman were talking together and looking at a book like the one he saw in the rack attached to the seat in front of him.

One by one, people entered the building, nodding to him cordially as they found their seats. Promptly at 7:30, one of the men rose and walked to the lectern. The man announced a hymn, and everyone reached for a book. Zvi was interested to find that the book was filled with songs that were written in Hebrew. Suddenly, he became aware that everyone else was standing while he was still seated. He could feel his face flush as he scrambled to his feet. The service had barely started, and already he had made one mistake. He decided he would observe carefully from now on so he would not again be caught sitting when he should be standing. After the song, the leader called on one of the men in the congregation to pray. Zvi saw that everyone dropped his chin to his chest and closed his eyes as the man addressed the Lord.

After more hymn singing, the man announced the services for the following Sunday and talked about people who were sick or needy, asking those present to pray for them. When he had concluded, another man came to the speaker's stand and laid his Bible upon it. The people were instructed to open their Bibles to the seventeenth chapter of the Gospel of John. Zvi looked around to see men and women eagerly thumbing through the pages of their Bibles to find the passage. It dawned on him that he, too, could participate in this part of the service. He reached into his pocket, drew out his well-worn New Testament, and began leafing through the pages to find the place the speaker had announced.

The words were familiar to Zvi, and it pleased him to be able to follow the reading. He was also impressed when he realized that this was the first time he had heard the Bible read aloud. Reading to an audible accompaniment established a feeling of kinship with the people who had come to the meeting.

The pastor spoke at length about the verse, which told of Jesus' prayer for the disciples. The man dwelt on the Lord's love and concern for His people, how He would meet their needs and answer prayer. "Any believer in the Messiah," he said, "could come at any time and talk with the Lord, and the Father would hear him and answer his prayer." Zvi listened with an intensity that was mirrored vividly on his face. When the man finished speaking, he wanted him to go on. It seemed to him that the man had just begun when he stopped. Oh well, he thought, there will be another time. He resolved to return for the next meeting.

Several people came up to introduce themselves when the meeting was over. They were friendly and invited him to come back again. At the door, Zvi had a question for the pastor: "Do you meet every week at this time?"

"Yes, and we meet on Sundays as well. I hope you will be back to meet with us again.

"By the way, I didn't introduce myself. I am Moshe Kaplan."

The man shook Zvi's hand as he responded to the introduction with his name.

On the walk home, he thought about the things the pastor had discussed during the meeting. All in all, it was an impressive experience. He was anxious for Sunday to come so he could go back for a worship service.

Sunday's message was different than the one he had heard on Wednesday night. Mr. Kaplan spoke on Jesus as the sin-bearer, the One who came as a substitute and took the sins of the people on Himself to make it possible for men and women to be saved from their sins. "Men," he said, "must turn from their sins and accept what the Messiah has done for them. We must be delivered from our sins by the sacrifice provided by the Messiah, Jesus."

The talk squared with the general conception Zvi had formed in his mind regarding the Messiah. He decided he would come again and hear more of what this man had to say about the book.

For the next several Wednesdays and Sundays, Zvi faithfully attended the services. He eagerly soaked up every word that fell from the preacher's lips. He even croaked out the songs as the people sang together.

Then one Wednesday night, Zvi left the service with a feeling of depression. He couldn't understand what was happening to him. The talk had been interesting, and he had agreed with what he had heard. Why, then, should he feel as he did? All the way home he turned it over in his mind. It was like a weight had been placed on him that must somehow be removed.

When he arrived at his barracks in Talpiyot, he was a troubled young man. He lay for a while listening to the heavy breathing of his friends sleeping. Zvi was far removed from the embrace that had so often taken him beyond the troubles of his waking work. Tonight sleep would not come to temporarily shut down his whirring mind.

Slowly it came to him. He needed to do something about what he had heard and read—Zvi needed to be saved from his sin. That was it! That was what had made him feel so miserable. For weeks he had heard about the Messiah—words that agreed perfectly with what he had read in the Bible—but he had not done anything about it himself. There in the darkness, he vowed that he would speak to the pastor about it on Wednesday night after the service.

"Can I talk with you after the meeting tonight?" Zvi asked Mr. Kaplan.

"Why certainly, Zvi. I would be happy for us to spend some time together."

When the service ended, Zvi approached the speaker.

"It's a long story," the young man began, "but what it comes down to is this: I want you to explain to me what I have to do to be saved."

"Well," said the pastor, "I would be delighted to tell you what you need to do. But I want you first to know, Zvi, that this is a very serious matter, one a person does not undertake lightly."

"Yes, I am aware of this," Zvi answered. "I have been thinking about it for a long time. Now I know this is what I have been searching for, but did not know how to find. I must find peace with God, and I know it can only be found through the Messiah."

"Here is a point that you must understand," counseled the pastor. "If you accept Jesus as your Messiah and Savior, you will be in for trouble. It is very difficult for people to live openly for Christ here in Israel these days. It may be necessary for you to endure suffering if you become His follower.

"For this reason, you must be very sure that this is your decision and not one you have been talked into by me or anyone else. In other words, you must be absolutely convinced that this is what you want to do."

Zvi answered thoughtfully, "Mr. Kaplan, the reason I came here in the first place was because I was searching for answers to questions I had in my life and ones that had come to me from the book. I am very sure that this is what I want to do. As far as the suffering goes, I have read about how much He suffered for me. It will be a privilege to be allowed to suffer for Him."

"Good. Now the next question is this: Do you believe in Jesus as the Messiah, and are you willing to accept Him as your Savior and Lord?"

"Yes—Yes! Without any question," said Zvi, "I am convinced that He is the Messiah and my Savior."

The two men prayed together, and the simple transaction was completed—simple, yet profound beyond anything that can be computed or communicated through human phraseology. Zvi Weichert, survivor of the Holocaust, had received the new birth. Since boyhood, he had longed for a new beginning—now he had found one. He was a new creation in Jesus the Messiah. Zvi knew that this was where God had been leading him all these years. Even when he had been blind and completely ignorant of spiritual realities, the Lord had patiently protected him, provided for him, and led him along the way to bring him to this place. How good God had been to suffer with him this long and now give him eternal life.

As Zvi attempted to analyze the results of his climactic encounter with the Messiah, he found that it crystallized into two identifiable categories: peace and joy. The void in his life was gone. All the emptiness within him that had come from all the tragedies that had beset him was now filled by the entrance of the Messiah-Savior. He was no longer at war with God or his past—he had made his peace with Jehovah. A joy overtook him that he could hardly contain. He did not believe it was possible for anyone to experience the kind of happiness that was now flooding his being. He had never known it in any measure before he found it that night in a simple building in Jerusalem, City of Peace. It was, he would find, a joy that would not diminish with the passing years.

On Sunday morning Zvi took a day off from work to attend the early service. It was another special day for him—he was baptized during the morning meeting. When he walked out into the street that morning, he summed up the experience. It was, he thought, as though he had found a mountain of pure gold studded with billions of shimmering diamonds. It was the best he could do by way of analogy, and he was aware how beggarly was the comparison to what he now possessed.

The next morning the new man whistled his way to work. On the job, he sang and smiled. It wasn't long before the Messiah's follower became the object of conversation around the construction site. "What has happened to Zvi?" the men wanted to know. "He must have had some great stroke of good luck to be so happy."

About mid-morning the overseer called him aside. "Zvi, what has happened to you? I've never seen you so happy."

"I've never been so happy," the laborer replied.

"I'll bet you have won money in the lottery," said his inquisitive boss.

"No, I've found something much better than a few dollars. I've been saved."

"You have been saved? What—you have died and come back again? What is this, 'I've been saved'?"

"You see, I was dead, yes, but not physically. I was dead spiritually. I was blind also. Now I can see. I have found the Messiah, who has saved me from my sins."

"You don't mean you have converted to Christianity?"

"Converted to what?" questioned Zvi. "I didn't have anything to convert from. Before I was nothing, now I have accepted the Messiah and have become something."

"You have become a traitor, that is what you have become," fumed the man. "Now you are no longer a Jew."

"No longer a Jew? How can I no longer be a Jew? I was born a Jew; I will die a Jew. The only difference in me now from last week is that I have become a whole Jew. I have come to know the Jewish Messiah who died for my sins."

"You cannot believe what you do and remain on this job," the foreman informed him. "Take your tools and leave here at once."

That day Zvi got his first lesson in the price he would pay for becoming a believer. It didn't matter to him. Nothing could diminish the joy he felt that morning. Over the years he would meet many who would vent their personal prejudices on him. But Zvi was thankful that in his land, Israel, a man was free to believe or not believe, as he chose.

Within a matter of days, he found another contractor. "I don't care what you believe," the man said. "On this job, a man can believe what he will as long as he does his job and doesn't hinder anyone else." There was no doubt about it. Zvi would do his job, and do it well.

CHAPTER
SIXTEEN

DARK EYES,
TENDER PROMISES

The victory of an infant nation, represented on the battle-field by ragtag bands of immigrant youths who didn't even understand the language of their adopted land, must stand as one of the unique feats of war in mankind's history. Five heavily armed and heavily manned Arab armies had moved against bedraggled little Israel and had lost in their determined effort to stem the tide of Jewish desire to return home. The sheer wonder of what was unfolding in the Middle East stopped the world dead in its tracks and delivered a resounding affirmation of what many prophetic scholars had been saying all along: A Jewish return to Palestine was inevitable.

Responsible conservative theologians saw Israel's miraculous resurrection as a return to the land in unbelief in preparation for the climactic events of the last days and the consummating confrontation with the Messiah.

To Jewish minds, it was an entirely different matter. Nonreligious Zionists considered it the fulfillment of their dream to forge a national Jewish homeland in the historical and cultural land of ancient Jewry—a place where Jewish will, dedication, and ingenuity made Theodor Herzl's words a reality: "If you will it, it is no dream."

Some religious Zionists had other ideas. This was the beginning of the end of the Messianic vision. For millennia, they and their forebears had prayed and wept for the day when they could ascend the hills of Zion. Passover cups—which had been raised throughout the Diaspora with the ubiquitous hope of "Next year in Jerusalem!"—could now be set down on tables in Israel. They were living the dream that would bring Messiah to His Chosen People in His Promised Land.

Yet here were those who disagreed. Elements of the Hasidic movement—ultra-Orthodox Jews—believed there could be no legitimate State of Israel before the Messiah comes. He alone, they said, can declare Israel a national, historical reality; and they would have no part in a secular government—except, of course, to accept selected benefits.

In reality, the victory in the War of Independence was but the first phase in a series of highs and lows that were to mark the strategic, transitional swings awaiting those first expectant citizens of the fledgling state.

Israel's optimism following the War of Independence covered Zvi as it did the nation. Coming to know the Messiah had changed everything—he had something better, Someone to live for. Granted, he was still in the army, and, as a sapper (an engineer who lays, detects, and disarms mines), he continued to practice the precarious occupation in which you couldn't make the same mistake *once*. But now he knew his life was in the hands of the Lord, and whatever happened to him was the Father's concern. In the will of God, "what will be, will be," and it was okay with him.

Zvi completed his service as an army regular in 1950. But, as is true with all Israel Defense Forces conscripts, he owed his country another thirty-three years of his life as a reservist. Consequently, he was called up for service whenever trouble was afoot. And Arab terrorist activity kept him extremely busy between 1950 and 1956.

Agitation and unrest were rampant during these years as the Arabs, so decisively beaten in the War of Independence, tried to save face and recoup their losses. After the armistice was signed, Israel's Foreign Minister, Moshe Sharett, uttered these prophetic words before the Knesset: "The storm which has been raging around us will not soon be stilled. Nor do we hold certainty in our hearts that it will not break out anew, with greater violence." He was right.

Between 1950 and 1956, the Arabs violated Israel's borders, infiltrated its lands, planted mines on Israeli roads and tracks, and waged armed incursions almost daily. During that period, more than four hundred Israelis were killed and nine hundred injured. There were three thousand armed clashes with Arab forces and at least six thousand acts of sabotage.

Egypt's president, Gamal Abdel Nasser, was a foremost perpetrator of this mischief, with Egyptian *fedayeen* (suicide fighters) acting as his primary agents. Zvi found himself almost constantly roving the roads and tracks, dislodging the mines the *fedayeen* and others were planting.

Things came to a head in 1956 after Egypt had closed the Suez Canal to shipping bound for Israel and pitched out the British as canal operators by nationalizing the waterway. To the British and French, this move posed an unacceptable danger to shipping, and they collaborated with Israel to bring an end to Nasser's adventurism.

Israel's objectives were to destroy *fedayeen* bases in the Gaza Strip and on the Sinai border, preempt Egypt's ability to attack Israel by destroying fortifications and airfields in the Sinai, and open the Gulf of Eilat to undisturbed Israeli shipping. All of these objectives were accomplished.

The Sinai Campaign itself lasted less that eight days—from October 29 to November 5, 1956. Israel, Britain, and France had secretly agreed to join forces in clearing the Sinai and securing the canal. The plan called for Israel to punch into the Sinai, after which France and Britain would land troops in order to "protect the canal." The speed with which Israel accomplished her objectives surprised even her allies. It also proved a point. Egypt, even though backed and heavily armed by the Soviet Union, was no match for the IDF. And while (in the peculiar way Arabs tend to interpret events) Nassar in defeat was viewed as a hero, Israel bought herself a few years of relative calm on her borders.

This lull gave Zvi his first real opportunity to concentrate on settling into a state of permanency in his chosen land. Over the next few years, the Lord did marvelous things to mend the holes in Zvi's life.

Among believers at the assembly, Zvi felt that he was in a family again. There was warmth, concern, and companionship. Often he looked around at his brothers and sisters in the Lord and felt that spiritually, he was the wealthiest of them all, even though he had no family and no real place to call home. While he was with the believers, he was at home with those who had received, as he had, the greatest gift in life.

These were especially difficult days for believers in Israel. Many at Talpiyot who had been close friends with Zvi became instant enemies when they learned he had accepted the Messiah. Some very close friends in the army felt the same way. In their minds, Christ was not the Savior-Messiah of Jews, but rather a "Christian" invention that had been used as a repeated instrument of persecution against the Jewish people throughout their tormented history. Jewry had just emerged from the agonies of the Holocaust—Talpiyot was filled with people who bore vivid reminders of what they had experienced among the "Christians" of Europe. For Zvi, it was not a matter of having changed camps—he knew nothing about either. His search for peace had culminated in receiving Jesus as Messiah because it was Jesus who bore all the evidencing credentials Zvi had seen set forth in the Scriptures. His decision to become a follower of the Messiah had brought the inner peace he had sought all his life. If many of his beloved countrymen did not understand what he had done, he was prepared to bear the consequences attendant to faith in Christ.

Nevertheless, it particularly distressed him when men like Karl Stern refused to associate with him any longer. Zvi and

Karl had served side by side during the War of Independence. In a hot exchange of gunfire on Mount Zion, Karl was hit in the shoulder by a dumdum bullet—a slug that flattened on impact and produced the effect of an explosion when it entered the body. The young man bled profusely from the gaping wound and would have bled to death had Zvi not thrown him onto his back and carried him to safety. Zvi's heroism had bonded them in an even closer-knit friendship than they had had before. Yet Karl would have nothing to do with Zvi now that he had confessed faith in Jesus.

Only after months of faithfully demonstrating the love and loyalty to friend and country that following Christ genuinely produces, did his friends begin to understand. While they did not agree with him, they had to admit that this son of Abraham was not a threat but an asset to them and the nation.

Zvi had not seen Karl for several weeks when they ran into each other on the street in Jerusalem. Zvi stopped his friend, and after they had passed a few moments of strained conversation, Karl broached the subject of Zvi's faith. "I cannot understand," Karl said bitterly, "how after all you have suffered at the hands of Christians, you could do this thing."

"You see," Zvi replied, "I have not joined the ones who hate and persecute us, no matter what name they choose to call themselves. I have read the New Testament through many times, and I find nothing there that tells anyone to do what they have done to us Jews. Jesus only speaks of loving and helping, never hating and killing. He sat right across that valley, on the Mount of Olives, and wept for our people.

"I can tell you this, Karl. I am a Jew. Before, I was a Jew with an empty life. Today I am a Jew who has found peace. And who did this for me—Hitler, Caesar, Pharaoh, the Crusaders, some pope? No! It was One who came to this earth as a Jew—a Jew who was put to death on a Roman cross; a Jew who, for many years, was followed by believers who were almost altogether Jewish people. Of course, Gentiles began to believe too. But this did not change how He felt toward Jews or what He, himself, was. What men have done against us and against His own Word cannot be laid at His feet—He would not have it so.

"My friend, Karl, I cannot help how you feel toward me—I only wish that I could cause you to feel differently. I will only say this. When we were in the army together, I was reading the Tenach; and I found some words that meant a great deal to me then, as they do now. David said, 'When my father and my mother forsake me, then the LORD will take me up.' I believe this also applies if a friend forsakes you. If I no longer have your friendship, I believe God will do this for me. But I will tell you this, Karl, no matter how you feel about me, or what you believe, I will never cease being a friend to you."

Karl stood for a moment and looked at Zvi. He started to speak but found he could not—tears were flowing from his eyes. "Zvi," he managed to say finally, "I ask you to forgive me. I have misunderstood. Our friendship should not be affected by what you believe. I will be a friend to you, too, for as long as I live."

Over the years that have passed since that meeting on that street in Jerusalem, these two have kept their pledge.

Days passed quickly for Zvi now. Between the periodic stints in the army, required of all Israeli men, he worked on various construction sites. Eventually he decided it was time to find more suitable living quarters. He had developed many warm friendships among the people at Talpiyot, but he felt it was high time he looked for another home. He had his eye on a place that appeared available and decided to inquire about it.

"Yes, the place is vacant," said the man who owned the house. "But nobody in his right mind would live there. It is located in no man's land. Arabs live in the house below it. As a matter of fact, they often come up to pick the grapes from the garden by the house."

"Would there by any objections to my moving in?" asked the young man, who by now was tired of life in crowded Talpiyot.

"No, if you can stay alive, move right in."

Zvi's new home commanded a stunning view of the city of Jerusalem. He could stand at a window and look across the Hinnom to Mount Zion and the Old City. Beyond the tip of Zion, on the right, the Mount of Olives and the Kidron lay quietly beneath the rich blue skyline. The room with a view was attached to the rear of a house that fronted on a street cut from the hillside.

Zvi was a happy man. At last he had a place of his own. If he wanted to be alone, this was an ideal situation. Above the room he occupied, a Jewish pillbox faced Mount Zion. Few of his callers ventured down the hill past the installation. When the postman delivered mail, he would call down for Zvi to come up the hill and claim it. If an army messenger came with some word from his superiors, he would whistle down to get Zvi's attention. It was noisy occasionally, depending on the prevailing mood of the Arabs on the other side. If they were riled up about something, they would take potshots at whatever moved on the Jewish side of the border. Zvi was thankful that his windows were covered by heavy metal shutters, which served well at such times.

His neighbors on the downhill side were Arabs. Their home was no more than fifteen or twenty yards from Zvi's quarters. Their relationship with their Jewish neighbor ran between two extremes. Sometimes it was cordial, and they would exchange pleasantries with him. Then again, when a hostile current was running, they would fling rocks up the hill to pelt the shutters and disrupt Zvi's peace and quiet.

This mattered little to the follower of the Messiah. He had a room in which to study, pray, and meditate on his newfound faith. It was a good location for growing in the Lord.

During these days, Zvi cemented a friendship with a man who was to become a second father to him. Victor Buksbazen was a Polish Jew who had immigrated to the United States. They first met at the believers' meeting in Jerusalem and struck up an instant friendship. Similar backgrounds, faith, and mutual interests drew them together. They spoke the same language, so Victor could help Zvi to better understand some things that had been a puzzle to him. On Victor's visits to Jerusalem, the two spent many hours together discussing the faith and matters of practical concern. When Victor was in the States, they communicated extensively through letters.

On one visit to Jerusalem, Victor decided to pay a call at his friend's home. Zvi had mixed emotions. On the one hand, he was honored to have his friend come to the room. On the other, he was concerned for Victor's safety. Not wanting to manifest undue alarm before his visitor, Zvi positioned himself between Victor and the Arabs on the walk down the hill.

"What a magnificent view," Victor said enthusiastically. "There is not a better vantage point in the city. I must get some photographs."

"Good," Zvi replied. "It is a wonderful place to take pictures. You can get good ones from the window inside the room."

Victor walked about snapping the shutter of his camera. Zvi hoped the Arabs were not in a testy frame of mind and was relieved when he and Victor were safely inside.

After the men had talked for a time, Victor walked to the window. "Look at those beautiful grapes," he exclaimed. "Would anyone mind if I went out and picked a few to eat?" His friend was alarmed. The Arabs had become somewhat accustomed to seeing his blond head bobbing about the hillside, but Victor was a stranger. Zvi was afraid that the sight of a newcomer plucking the grapes they enjoyed so much themselves might provoke them to take a shot at him.

Zvi was out the door before his friend could leave the room. "Don't bother to come out," Zvi called over his shoulder. "I know where the best ones are. I'll be right back." In a few minutes he returned bearing the fruit of the vine.

Zvi breathed easier once Victor was safely up the hill and on his way back to his hotel in Jerusalem.

His next home did not have the view or excitement of a no man's land. It was well within the limits of Jewish Jerusalem. If Zvi was disappointed over the lack of attractive landscape, he would find scenery of another kind. A Jewish family from Persia with three lovely girls lived in a room adjacent to Zvi's. Everyone entered the building through a picturesque stone gate that opened into a small courtyard. A series of steps ran up to a higher level, where elderly Jewish women sat to catch the sun and share the news. The activity between the rooms off the courtyard below soon gave them ample material for conversation.

Zvi and his neighbors used a common kitchen, so it did not take long for them to size each other up. The two boys, Zvi found, had brought their three sisters to Israel. Two more girls had been left with their parents until the family could get established and send for them.

The ladies who watched from their perch aloft soon understood that the young Jewish man from Poland had his eye on one of the girls next door. Her name was Esther, and she was a dark-eyed beauty. Now and then Zvi caught her looking at him, although her eyes dropped discreetly to the floor whenever she knew he had discovered her interest. Esther liked the cheerful, helpful young man. He was a handsome son of Jacob, she thought, and she began to feel her heart beat faster when they chanced to engage each other in conversation.

Zvi wanted to ask Esther to date him, but he also wanted to be perfectly honest about his faith. Her parents, he knew, were religious oriental Jews. He did not wish to do anything that would cause them or Esther to feel he had misrepresented himself.

"I would like to take Esther with me to a meeting tonight," Zvi said to the oldest brother.

"Ask her," replied the young man. "If she wants to go with you, it's all right with me."

Zvi approached Esther. His voice sounded rather stiff and formal as he registered his request. "I would like you to go with me to the believers' meeting tonight. Will you do it?"

She looked down and appeared nonplussed for a moment. Then Esther flashed a demure oriental smile. "Why yes, Zvi, I would like to go."

Activity buzzed on both sides of the wall as preparations progressed for the big occasion. Zvi sang softly as he plastered his unruly blond hair into just the right position. Esther dressed between a pair of giggling sisters who were almost as excited as she was.

Zvi's young lady listened intently as the speaker opened the Bible and brought the message of the evening. Her background had provided scant knowledge of anything to do with Christianity. Muslims were the dominant group in the part of the world she had come from. Before returning home, the two had a frank conversation.

"What does it mean to be a believer?" she questioned.

"You see, Esther," Zvi replied, "I am a Jew who believes in the Messiah, Jesus, as my Lord and Savior."

Esther was perplexed. "But how can this be?" she wanted to know.

"It would take a long time to tell you the whole story," Zvi explained. "I'll tell you what. If you want to know more, you can come with me to the meeting on Wednesday night."

"Yes, I would like to go back and hear more," she replied.

Word of the budding romance was sent to Esther's parents. Her father wrote back: "Follow him. Don't let him out of your sight. Find out everything you can about him, and let me know what you learn." A cautious father wanted to be assured that the suitor was worthy of the girl he had set his heart on making his wife.

Over the next four or five months, Zvi and Esther sat together at the believers' meeting and listened to the messages of the pastor and other speakers. Slowly, Esther began to grasp what becoming a believer in Jesus as Messiah involved. Zvi never pushed anything at her. He knew that her decision must be genuine, made of her own free will. He made no effort to force her to profess belief.

It slipped out almost casually. Before he was fully aware of just how he was going to say it, he had dropped the question squarely at Esther's feet. "Will you become my wife?"

Esther took no more than a few seconds to roll the request over in her mind. To the anxious young petitioner, however, it seemed like an eternity . . . or two. "Yes, Zvi," she replied firmly, "I would be honored to be your wife."

He rose one rung above ecstatic at the news. There was just one more matter that had to be clarified. "You know, Esther, that I am a believer. Although your family has never done anything to interfere with our being together, I know they are hostile to my faith. I don't want you to marry me without knowing that you will have problems because of what I believe. Life may be very hard for us at times. Even your family may turn against us. Also, I don't want you to say you accept Jesus as your Messiah just because you are married to me. If you believe on Him, it must be your own choice."

"I am not a child," Esther replied. "I know very well what I am doing. I know you are a firm believer in the Messiah, and I am learning to love Him too. I am prepared for whatever will come to both of us."

So the date was set. The next step was a visit to the rabbi. All marriages in Israel must be performed by a rabbi.

The rabbi was a cheerful man who appeared to be pushing fifty. He welcomed Zvi, gestured towards a chair, and sat down. "So you want to be married?" he began. "There are a few questions I need to ask you before we talk about the date.

"First, I would like to know what tribe you are a member of."

"What do you mean, 'what tribe?'" Zvi asked.

"Are you Kohayn, Levite, or Israel?"

"I have no idea," the young man replied.

"Were your parents religious Jews?"

"I don't remember either of them being religious."

"Then we will place you with Israel," the rabbi decided.

"And what about you, are you a religious Jew?"

"I have been changed," Zvi said emphatically.

"What do you mean, *changed*?"

"Once I did not believe anything. Now I have come to believe in the Messiah, the Son of God. He has come and will come again."

"Oh, yes—good, good. I believe in Messiah too," the rabbi agreed, "but you are mistaken. Messiah will come—not return."

"No," Zvi affirmed, "He was already here and will come back."

"Where did you learn such a thing as this, and who told you the Messiah will be the Son of God?"

"No one taught me this," Zvi explained. "I read it in the Bible. Proverbs 30:4 says, 'What is his name, and what is his son's name.' This is spoken of God. Look in the Bible and you can see for yourself."

"I don't have a Bible here, but I can tell you what the *Gemara* says about what you think," the rabbi said.

"You see," Zvi observed, "there is little difference between what you are saying and what a Catholic would tell me."

"Catholic!" the rabbi thundered. "God forbid you should say that I am a Catholic. How can you say this?"

"But you are," replied Zvi. "They are forever quoting traditions, interpretations, and popes—what the church teaches is more important than what the Bible says. So you have more to tell me about what the books and the rabbis say than what I can find in the Bible. I believe in going to the best source first and finding the answer there—the Bible."

"All right," the rabbi said, "let us leave the subject now. When do you want to get married?"

Esther was radiant and Zvi nervous as they stood before the rabbi to exchange their marriage vows. As they exchanged a ring, they made tender promises to become one flesh, to be faithful to each other forever, and to bear mutually all the responsibilities that marriage entails. In sickness and health, good times and bad, they would stand by one another. The immigrant from Poland and his dark-eyed bride from Persia would experience a measure of both extremes in the years to come.

CHAPTER SEVENTEEN

RUTH

It was quite a step up for the Weicherts. Esther was excited. "So much more room than we have now. At last we will be able to have friends in to visit us."

The new apartment was not large, but it was much more suitable than where they had been living. Following their marriage, Zvi and Esther had brought her sisters to live with them. Zvi became a second father to the girls. Of course, it meant sharing the small, one-room villa that Zvi had called home before the wedding. With a blanket serving as a makeshift partition, life for the newlyweds had become a crowded but happy affair.

At their new place, they had two good-sized rooms and shared a kitchen with the couple in the adjacent apartment. Another family with children lived above them, and an elderly man occupied a small room just outside the kitchen door. It did not take long for the Weicherts to get settled into their new home. Zvi worked some distance away, so it was an early-to-bed, early-to-rise life for the happy young couple.

Friends from the assembly were the first on the guest list at the new location. Zvi issued the invitation and a date was set for dinner the following weekend. Esther shopped, cooked, and scrubbed the apartment to prepare for the event.

When the day came, hungry guests were seated around steaming dishes of delicious food. After a while, they were holding up their hands and shaking off Zvi's and Esther's pressing suggestion that they eat a little more. Every visitor was filled to capacity. They all spent the remainder of the evening in warm fellowship. As his guests were leaving, Zvi thought how good it was to have close friends to spend pleasant hours with.

Esther was busy cleaning up when an insistent knock was heard on the back door. Zvi opened it to find the old man who lived behind them quivering with excitement. "Do you know who those people are?" he cried.

"Certainly I know who they are. They are friends of ours," Zvi replied.

"Friends of yours! Do you not know that those people are Christians? They are known to me; you must not bring them here again."

"My friend," Zvi said calmly, "I do not tell you who can come to visit with you. You may have anyone in your home you wish to invite—that is your business. But I must ask you to respect my right to have the people I like in my home."

"If you have them in your home, and know who they are, then you must be one of them."

"Am I not free to be a believer in the Messiah if I choose to do so?" Zvi questioned.

By now the man was shaking with rage. "I will not stand for one who has given up being a Jew to live next to me. Get away from here."

Zvi attempted to calm his neighbor. "Please, you will have no trouble from us. This is our home, and we just want to live here in peace."

"You have not heard the last of this," the man shouted.

Zvi and Esther talked the incident over after the man had gone back to his room. "Isn't it strange," Zvi said, "all of us have come so far to escape persecution for who we are and what we believe. But even here, there are a few who would do to other Jews what Gentiles have done to them for centuries.

"Did you hear him say I was no longer a Jew? It is funny, in a way, that he is quite willing to call me a Jew if there is a war and I have to fight, or if an Arab plants a bomb here in the neighborhood and I am asked to go and disarm it. But when he disagrees with my religion, I am no longer a Jew."

"He sounded as though he meant to make trouble for us," Esther said apprehensively.

"Never mind," Zvi said cheerfully, "he will get to know us, and it will be all right."

But it would not be all right, at least not for a time. When Zvi returned home from work the next afternoon, he found Esther in tears and the floor of the front room covered with glass. "What has happened here?" Zvi asked.

"Children from the neighborhood came and threw rocks through the windows," she said, crying.

Zvi knew who had incited them, but rather than say anything and stir up more trouble, he repaired the glass and told Esther they would forget it and go about life as though nothing had happened.

Ignoring the problem, however, did not seem to help matters. Things grew progressively worse. Often in the night, someone would bang loudly on the doors. More windows were broken. Taunts and catcalls from children became routine whenever they left the apartment.

Zvi decided it was time to talk to his neighbor about the problem. He tried to reason with the man. It did no good. He might reach him, he thought, by pointing out the harm he was doing to the children by encouraging them to do such things. "What are you saying to me?" the man blustered. "Are you accusing me of doing these things to you, or having the children do them? Don't come to me again with this kind of talk. You deserve whatever you get and more."

Circumstances came to a crisis when Zvi came home one day to find Esther badly shaken. She was near hysteria as she explained what had taken place. On the way to do her shopping that afternoon, she had been surrounded by a group of children who began taunting her and blocking her path. Esther did not respond, so one of them picked up some stones and began to throw them in her direction. Others soon followed the cue. As they became bolder, one ran up to snatch at her hair and give it a hard yank.

"Oh Zvi," she wept, "I don't know how much longer I can stand this. Can we look for a new place to live?"

Zvi was a burdened man. It was one thing for unreasoning fanatics to set upon him; he could cope with that perfectly well. But to see Esther upset day after day—and now for her to be physically abused—it was too much. But what could he do? He wanted to maintain his witness for the Messiah. These were only children who were doing what they thought would please the man who told them to do it. The man himself was old and embittered. Nothing would be accomplished by arguing with him. It was a grave problem.

Zvi decided he would place the matter in the hands of the Lord and ask Him to provide a solution. That evening and the next day, Zvi prayed earnestly for an answer to his dilemma. It was difficult for him to keep his mind on his work for thinking about Esther and wondering if everything was all right at home. He was relieved when he returned to find she had had no trouble of consequence.

The dejected couple sat at the table in the kitchen eating their evening meal when they heard a pronounced thump from the room where their antagonistic neighbor lived. Zvi knew immediately something was wrong and ran out the back door to see what the trouble was. The elderly man had fallen heavily to the floor and was unconscious when Zvi reached his side. In a few minutes the old man began to roll his head from side to side. Finally he opened his eyes. Zvi's face was the first thing he saw.

"I'm dying," the man gasped. "Get me help! Please get some-one who can help me. In the drawer of the table there is money—six hundred pounds. Take all of it and do what you like with it. Just help me get to the hospital."

Zvi hurried to get help, and soon he was riding beside the man in an ambulance on the way to the hospital. Doctors found that the man had suffered a heart seizure and would be confined for some weeks. Every evening, Zvi went to the hospital to check on his neighbor and ask if there were anything he could do for him.

The old man had shown marked improvement when Zvi stepped into the room one evening. "How are you feeling today?" he asked.

"Much better. Each day I am feeling a little stronger than before. The doctors tell me I will be able to leave here soon.

"I have been meaning to ask you about the money. Did you find it?"

"Your money is safe," Zvi told him. "Don't worry about it."

"But I told you it was yours if you would help me."

"I know what you told me. I don't want your money. The help I have given you is done in the name of the Lord—that is all."

Zvi's neighbor was startled at first—then ashamed. He could have understood Zvi taking care of him for his money. But to look after him for free after he had made life so miserable for Zvi—this was hard for him to believe. "You know," he said slowly, "you are the only one who has come to see me while I have been here. Even some I thought were my friends have not come. Why have you done it?"

"Already I have told you, only in the name of the Lord. A few years ago I would not have been this way. I would probably have let you die after what you did to my wife. But the Messiah has changed all this for me. I have learned to care for those who choose to be my enemies as well."

"I want to offer you an apology," the bedridden man said. "I misunderstood what belief in your Messiah would cause you to do. I am deeply sorry that I have made so much trouble for you. You will have no difficulty with me from this moment on."

Zvi took the man by the hand. No longer was he an enemy. He had become a friend. From then on, only the *shalom* of peace would pass between them.

One piece of good news soon followed another. Esther had a smug smile on her face when her husband dropped his lunch pail onto the table after a hard day's work. "Zvi, I have some news for you." She was trying hard to sound casual.

"Good news, I hope. You know that is the kind I like to hear. What is it?"

"The doctor told me today I am pregnant. We are going to have a baby."

The news jarred Zvi. For a moment he was suspended somewhere between floor and ceiling. "We are going to have what? A baby!" When he alighted, he wanted to hear it again.

Esther was walking toward him with outstretched arms. "We are going to have a baby."

Zvi stood a little taller in his shoes that night. This was news he had hoped to hear for some time. The prospective father began setting things in order for the arrival of their first child. Esther had the concentrated attention of her husband for the next several months. She had never experienced anything quite like it in her life. Zvi was determined to see that nothing would go awry.

Before the happy event took place, Zvi was called away for his military reserve service. Ordinarily, he didn't mind soldiering. He was always willing to put in his time in the interest of his nation's defense. These stints also provided the opportunity to get together with old friends and catch up on what had been happening with them. This time around, however, it was different. He was anxious to get his reserve time behind him so he could get back to the side of the mother-to-be.

One thing Zvi had always enjoyed about camp life was listening to the discussions among the reservists. In Israel, practically everyone in the country is called up for periodic service. Thus the presence of a broad cross-section of political, literary, and religious figures often spiced up the conversations and debates during off-duty hours. Politics, global affairs, religion, relevant and irrelevant topics all got the treatment in the tents of the reservists.

Among those gathered for the current session were two professors, a journalist, and one of the country's outstanding economists. The exchange opened with some observations that promised a stimulating evening. Before things could get underway, it was customary for the combatants to spar for the foremost position in the circle. The journalist told about the important periodicals he wrote for. The professors played one-upmanship over the importance of their respective positions in the academic world.

The discussion touched a number of subjects before drifting to the topic of religion. One of the professors was at the helm when Zvi felt qualified to comment and plunged headlong into the conversation. The professor was skeptical about the upstart's credentials.

"What do you do in civilian life?"

"I am a builder. I work on construction projects."

"You are not a graduate of the university?" the professor established.

"No, I am not," Zvi answered. "I have had little opportunity for formal education."

"What makes you feel you are qualified to speak about the Bible."

"I will ask you a question," said Zvi. "Moses, the greatest of our prophets, told God when He came to him with instructions to go to the Pharaoh, 'I am a child, I cannot speak.' Did God say to him: 'Go to the university and they will teach you to talk like a man'? No. He said, 'Go to Pharaoh and tell him what I have told you to say.'

"So, we need only to know the Word of God and speak about what the Book says, not what we think because we feel we are educated."

The journalist joyfully gave Zvi the point and told the professor: "The man is right, big professor. You will do well to hear what he has to say."

"What would you like to say?" the professor said.

"I would like to say that we are blind, as Isaiah tells us, 'seeing we do not see, and hearing we do not hear.'"

"What do you mean, 'we are blind'?"

"We have become so wise in our books and studies that we have missed what the Bible says we need the most, a sacrifice for our sins."

"But we have Yom Kippur," the man protested.

"Yes, but we have no more sacrifices. Repentance, humiliation, and good deeds are not enough. We must have a sacrifice that is acceptable to God. This He has given, once for all, and we need not go back year after year. The pity is, we are too blind to see it."

"You speak about the Carpenter?" the professor asked. "How do you know about him?"

"How do I know about Him? How does all the world know about Him? If you go to many places in the world and ask people if they know about some great American president or Stalin or Nero or other famous historical characters, most people will not even know who they are. But go into the jungle, in some place far away, and ask them about Jesus, the Jewish Carpenter—they will know about Him. If they know about Him in the jungles, we should know about Him in the land where He was born and lived."

"But the Christians claim He is the Son of God. How is it possible for God to have a Son?"

"First, because the Bible tells us in Proverbs 30 and in Isaiah that the Messiah will be the Son of God. It is there; you can read it for yourself.

"I will ask you a question: Was it possible for God to make the Red Sea part and cause the people to go over on dry ground?"

"Yes, of course, it was possible."

"When Sarah was old and barren, was it possible for God to cause her to bear Isaac?"

"Yes, certainly it was possible."

"Was it possible for God to feed our fathers in the wilderness for forty years?"

"Yes, that too was possible."

"If God could do all these things, why is it thought impossible for Him to send His Son for His Chosen People Israel?"

The journalist, who had begun to take notes of the conversation, broke in with a Yiddish phrase: "Zvi is right," he said, "with God all things are possible."

"It is obvious," the professor said, "that you know some theology."

"I know," Zvi replied, "what the Bible says. The Spirit of God teaches me how to apply it."

"You should be a chaplain for Christians in the army," the professor replied.

"Not for Christians only," Zvi answered, "but for all of our people. Because if He is the Savior of men, He is the Savior of all men, you and me too."

"Yes, but you speak from the New Testament. It speaks of a Savior in the way you are talking about Him."

"Not the New Testament only," Zvi explained. "What the New Testament speaks about, the Old Testament also says. Isaiah 53 tells us of a Savior and sin-bearer. Zechariah also speaks of our looking on One who was pierced. The Psalms, too, as well as many other passages, tell us that the Messiah will suffer for our sins. And not for ours only, but for the sins of the whole world."

"How do you explain Jesus' words to 'love your enemies'? How could we love the people who are trying to destroy us? And how can you, if you believe in Jesus, fight in the army?"

"When it was time for Jesus to pay His taxes," Zvi replied, "He took a coin and showed it to the people. He said, 'Render, therefore, unto Caesar the things which are Caesar's; and unto God, the things that are God's.'

"I am a citizen of Israel. This is my country and I love it very much. I am willing to fight, and if necessary, to die for it, because I am a citizen and this is my home. But also, Jesus commands me to be faithful and loyal to my country, and so I serve.

"Jesus believed all of the Old Testament and told believers in Him to do so too. One cannot be a true believer in Him and not accept the entire Bible."

The discussion continued for several hours. When it was finished, the soldiers accorded a round of applause to Zvi and the professor. They decided to carry the talk over to another night and have a full discussion of Isaiah 53.

Before he turned in that evening, Zvi sat alone under the night skies and looked up at the star-strewn heavens. He was a grateful man. God had brought him through, brought him home, and given him more than any son of Adam had the right to expect. He had a home in the land of his fathers, he was favored to live among his own people, and soon he would be blessed with a child. He was a fortunate young man indeed.

In many respects, Zvi's life has been comparable to that of the man whom he held in such reverent personal regard, Israel's own King David. Like his illustrious forebear, circumstances forced him to become a man of war. During his extended military career, Zvi fought in the wars brought upon his country by their implacable foes. As a result of his heroism, the nation honored him by awarding him a number of decorations for acts of valor in the face of the enemy. David was a man who panted after God—so did Zvi Weichert. Both saw the hunger in their hearts satisfied by a Deliverer who consistently keeps His promise that "them who honor me I will honor." The supreme reward for any petitioner of Jehovah is realized in the fulfillment of another divine word: "When thou passest through the waters, I will be with thee; and through the rivers, they shall not overflow thee; when thou walkest through the fire, thou shalt not be burned, neither shall the flame kindle upon thee." Both David and Zvi could testify to the reality of this assuring commitment. As was true with David and Zvi, some are destined to pass through both the fire and the flood. But when such men firmly place their trust in the Messiah of Israel, they become conspicuous examples of God's faithfulness and power to deliver His children, even through life's severest struggles.

Zvi rushed home after his brief tour of duty. His arrival was timed perfectly. Esther was preparing to go to the hospital. The birth was difficult, and a surgeon was called in to perform a Caesarian section. Zvi, like fathers the world over, worried, walked the halls, and prayed for Esther and the child.

A nurse finally came to him with the news he had waited anxiously to hear. "Mister Weichert, you have a lovely baby girl. Your wife is doing fine. You will be able to see them in a short time."

Zvi stood by the bed looking into the faces of a beaming Esther and a beautiful, round-faced daughter. She would be named after his mother, Ruth. His Ruth was not just another baby. To Zvi, she represented a new beginning. During the terrible years in Europe, He thought that he had lost everything he could hope to live for in this world—his family. In one sense, he knew they could never be replaced. Yet that day, at Hadassah Hospital, he witnessed the miraculous healing provision from the hand of God. In Ruth, his family would live on. The extent of Jehovah's provision for Zvi was marvelously manifested over the coming years. The Holocaust had swept away three brothers and a sister. Zvi watched in wonder as three hardy boys later joined Ruth in the family circle.

Ruth was born in 1960. Mendel joined her in 1962. Yona was next in 1964. And just as the Six-Day War was about to break out in 1967, Eli came on the scene. With his birth, the family was complete. The Lord, in His grace and goodness, had restored to Zvi what Hitler had destroyed.

As it was with Zvi and his personal experience, so it has been with Jewry. Every child born into a Jewish family anywhere in the world is a testimony to the fact that God is always true to His Word; and His people and their Land of Promise, Israel, will live on.

As the children grew in stature, Zvi and Esther rapidly grew in grace and knowledge of the Lord. The love for the Bible, which Zvi had experienced upon receiving his first New Testament, only increased; and reading it daily became a consistent and pleasurable lifestyle. Without question, he had become a man of the Book. As the head of his home, he was always ready to discuss with Esther and the children the knotty questions about Scripture and "living the life." They were active in church, and when the doors were open, the Weicherts were there and available for whatever service they could render for the glory of God.

In fact, they took responsibility for the physical needs of the building. Zvi was certainly right for the job. As a construction worker, he was a man who knew how to work with his hands and was always willing and pleased to pitch in.

Esther enjoyed it too. She was a young woman who had an aversion to anything even remotely akin to dirt. And helping to keep things squeaky-clean was a challenge she was not capable of resisting.

It was easy to see that the Lord was preparing these two for very special service. They were vessels being shaped for the Master's use. One of their first challenges was living among people who militantly opposed what they believed and stood for as followers of Jesus, the Messiah.

Little Ruthi became the first of the children to feel the lash of ultra-Orthodox bigotry.

CHAPTER EIGHTEEN

BEAT HER!

She cried all the way home. "Mama! Mama! They hit me! They hurt me!" Esther understood very well what had happened and why. But it would take some time for Ruthi to begin to understand.

The family had moved to a western suburb of Jerusalem that had a large concentration of ultra-Orthodox Jews. These black-garbed brethren looked askance at their neighbors who bore none of the distinguishing marks the ultra-Orthodox believed essential to proper Judaism. Zvi's daughter had felt the sting of their displeasure on Shabbat, when her Orthodox playmates heard sounds of a radio news report filtering from the Weichert home—a grave breech of Sabbath tranquility. For the most part, though, the Weicherts were tolerated as *Goyim* (Gentiles) would be, and their children romped and played in the neighborhood as all the children did.

Ruthi's rude awakening came at the hands of a loved and trusted grandfather figure, an old man named Rabinowitz. The strictly observant elder was a great favorite among neighborhood children. He was fond of distributing candies and gentle pats on their heads. But more than that, old Rabinowitz was a wonderful storyteller, and this talent was what Ruthi liked best of all. The children would cluster around him for long periods and sit quietly, enthralled by his animated gestures and intriguing tales.

One pleasant afternoon, the old man was standing on his stairs passing out candies to an excited swarm of boys and girls. When laughing Ruthi reach up to her friend for her piece, she was rudely refused. "You—children—beat her," he ordered. The others, eager to please their benefactor, sent the startled little girl running home amid a barrage of slaps and catcalls.

Rabinowitz had discovered that the cute little Weichert girl was not just another nonreligious Jew. She was the daughter of believers in Jesus. His command to the children was his crude way of sending his message of disapproval to Zvi and Esther. It was the exhibition of an old animosity—a vivid demonstration that in Israel, some things hadn't changed in two thousand years. As long as Zvi was just another nonpracticing Jew, perhaps even an atheist, he was tolerated. But as Jew who believed in "that Jew, Jesus," he became an enemy whose presence was unacceptable.

Mendel suffered the same abuse during their days in Ir Ganim. One boy in particular took great delight in taunting him at every opportunity: "Hey, look at him—Mendel the Christian!" To Jews steeped in rabbinic Judaism, calling someone a Christian was worse than cursing him. And to a child anxious to be accepted by the other boys, it was a heavy indignity to bear.

To a large extent, it was only the ultra-Orthodox who tormented Zvi's family and other believers. Their lack of compassion was as obvious as their black garments. To this day, their conduct has been one of the great incongruities of the modern State of Israel. Jewish people who have been scorned, hated, and assailed by Gentiles for centuries simply because of who they are, now scorn, hate, and assail their own Jewish brothers who will not conform to sectarian strictures. That sad fact has divided the nation since her rebirth, and the scars of resentment run deep.

A nonreligious Jewess who was a secretary to a former prime minister, harbors caustic memories of Orthodox hypocrisy. "It was during the siege of Jerusalem in 1948. We, in the city, were on the verge of starvation. Our survival was very much an open question in those days. The Arabs had control of the Tel Aviv-Jerusalem Road, and supplying the city with food became virtually impossible.

"Then our boys managed to scrape out a road beyond the reach of Arab guns, through the hills to the city. They were heroes who had risked their lives to save us—some died in the effort. But when they came into the city with food, those idiots stoned the trucks carrying the food needed to save Jerusalem because it happened to be Shabbat.

"I can never forget how I felt the next day, when I saw those same men pushing people aside to get their hands on the food that was carried by the trucks they had stoned the day before."

She would gladly have hurled their stones back at them with appropriate velocity.

Many of her fellow Israelis shared her resentment. The ultra-Orthodox, or *Hasidim*, have been the single most disruptive influence in the Jewish community.

Branches of the Hasidim manifest a variety of extremes. Some actively participate in the affairs of the Jewish state, while others refuse to recognize the legitimacy of Israel altogether. Most Hasidics wear the special garb familiar to travelers in the Holy Land. Their long black coats *(kapotes)* and black or fur hats *(spodiks)* set them apart in a manner reminiscent of the ostentatious Pharisees of Jesus' day. Most of them wear beards and carefully nurtured earlocks *(pe'ot)*.

The term *Hasidim* was used in rabbinic literature to designate those Jews who maintained a higher standard in observing the religious and moral commandments. Hasidism, from its inception, promoted joy, dance, and song as vital expressions of piety in living the good Jewish life. The modern version of these "men of piety and good deeds" often shows little evidence of being worthy of the ideal.

One of the qualifying elements in the Hasidic system is a fanatical loyalty to charismatic personalities who provide leadership for the movement. These *rebbes*, also called *zaddikim* (righteous ones), provide the spiritual illumination for the individual Hasid and the Hasidic community from "his own all-pervasive radiance, attained through his mystic union with God." [1] The *zaddik* is viewed as a wonder healer and miracle worker. In the eyes of his followers, he is a combination of confessor, moral instructor, and practical adviser. He is also their theoretical teacher and exegetical preacher.

"In Hasidism the *zaddik* is conceived of as the ladder between heaven and earth, his mystic contemplation linking him with the Divinity, and his concern for the people and loving leadership tying him to earth. Hence his absolute authority, as well as the belief of most Hasidic dynasties that the *zaddik* must dwell in visible affluence."[2]

Thus each branch of ultra-Orthodox Jewry follows a small group of powerful leaders, each with his own contingent of unquestioning followers to whom he is the authoritative representative of God and His exclusive interpreter. In reality, these rebbes are revered as mini-messiahs—messiahs who are militantly at odds with *the* Messiah, Jesus.

For his part, Zvi opted to follow a course of action much different from that of the prime minister's secretary. He chose a bread-for-a-stone approach. "If these people are ever to come to the light," he reasoned, "it will be because someone has sown one seed at a time before them. I must show them kindness and give them the Word of God. It is the only way."

His perception and patience was tested with neighbors like Ruthi's tormentors. The severest tests, however, came in the yeshivas (Talmudic schools)—the hallowed ground of extreme ultra-Orthodoxy in the Mea Shearim section of Jerusalem.

The shabby quarter's entrance is marked by a warning: "Jewish daughter—The Torah obligates you to dress with modesty. We do not tolerate people passing through our streets immodestly dressed." The "Jewish daughters" who inhabit the area even today fit the prescription perfectly. Long, plain dresses hang loosely over thick-stockinged legs and heavy, styleless shoes. Kerchiefed heads bob behind ever-present baby carriages, as the wives of the pious go about their shopping and errands.

Streets are littered with trash, and the quarter's squalid buildings appear as prime candidates to be condemned. It's obvious that the residents of Mea Shearim have their minds on something other than local beautification. Usually the men are found inside the yeshivas, studying.

The approaches up staircases into the schools often appear as dingy as the rest of Mea Shearim. Narrow passages open into the austere rooms where boys attend daily classes. These young men move about in unregimented groups, wearing white shirts buttoned to the top and black pants, the tassels from their *talitot* (prayer shawls) visible under the shirts flapping about their hips. Long curled earlocks swing under *yarmulkes* (skullcaps) that cover their shaved heads.

The inner sanctum, where adult males spend innumerable hours hunched over their cherished books of Bible commentary, is another world altogether. Ornately decorated walls rise toward stately ceilings. In one yeshiva, magnificent paintings of the symbols of Israel's twelve tribes grace the ceiling. A raised, banistered platform stands in the center of the room, with candelabra placed at intervals about the table where the Torah is read. Exquisitely carved woodwork with elaborate niches that are supported by large marble pillars frame the ark that contains the Torah scrolls. Above the veiled chamber where the scrolls rest is a large gold crown placed directly above replicas of Moses' tablets of stone inscribed with the Ten Commandments. The veil itself is royal blue with rich gold fringe and golden Magen David sown into the corners. Another crown and richly embellished Torah scrolls are embroidered into the fabric.

From this impressive riser, their messiah-figure rebbe addresses his ecstatic, perpetual students who jam the room.

Zvi was a familiar face as he moved through the streets and into the yeshivas of Mea Shearim. His boldness seemed rather like that of a man walking unarmed into the lion's den—an inadvisable situation for most men. But Zvi came uniquely equipped, properly burdened, and unimpeded by a lack of courage. Watching him witness to the black-garbed denizens of the ultra-Orthodox quarter evoked but one logical conclusion: only God could prepare a man to do this.

Zvi's foremost credential was his fluency in Yiddish, the favored tongue of the Hasidim. Hebrew is regarded as the holy language, reserved for reading the Torah. His approach was always direct, but kind and tactful. And somehow, one had the inescapable feeling that the Holy Spirit was at work in keeping the peace and opening opportunities for him to share the Lord.

A few times, open hostility made it advisable to beat a hasty retreat, other times, flying saliva enlivened the exchanges. Once Zvi found himself circling to the rear of a building to elude his irate pursuers. But this was the rare exception, not the rule.

One such excursion found him bounding up the steps, armed only with his Bible, to a yeshiva with a sign out front proclaiming the Solomonic desire for "Wisdom, Understanding, Knowledge." It was afternoon, and the attitude was much more relaxed than in the morning when intensive study was going on.

Wisdom called for some casual conversation to break the ice and perhaps open the way to a witness for Christ. Within a short time, Zvi was probing the students with questions about just what their revered rebbe taught on certain subjects. "And what do you believe about Zechariah 9:9, 'Rejoice greatly, O daughter of Zion; shout, O daughter of Jerusalem; behold, thy King cometh unto thee; he is just, and having salvation; lowly, and riding upon an ass, and upon a colt, the foal of an ass'?"

"This is without explanation," a rabbi responded, as others began to join the proceedings.

"Well then," Zvi continued, "maybe you can explain a passage that has been on my mind for some time. It is Isaiah 53."

"That passage is not familiar to me," the rabbi answered.

"Perhaps I could read it for you and refresh your memory."

"If you know Hebrew, go ahead, read it."

Zvi read the verses slowly and carefully.

When he finished reading, he looked intently into the face of the man standing before him. "Could you please explain the sixth verse: 'All we like sheep have gone astray; we have turned every one to his own way, and the LORD hath laid on him the iniquity of us all.'"

The man stroked his beard thoughtfully before he gave his reply. "The answer to your question will come when the Messiah will come."

"But this is very strange to me," Zvi countered. "You have studied here since you were three years old and don't have an answer to this question?"

"Some things are hard to understand."

"If you would like, I will give you an explanation," Zvi said with a boldness that startled even him. "Who was He? I am sure you know but will not say. It must be speaking of Jesus, who was crucified."

Tension built with his statement. "You have come to the wrong place with talk like this," a man in the circle fumed.

"No, I have come to the right place and asked you questions you should be asking yourselves.

"You know as well as I that our whole system for forgiveness of sin is built on the offering of proper sacrifices. Why, then, was our Temple destroyed and the offering of all sacrifices stopped—but only after the crucifixion took place?"

"We are Jews here," called out another angry voice. "Do you want to make us Christians?"

"No. I want to make you good Jews."

"But you are not a Jew, you are a Christian."

"I am as much a Jew as you are. But I am one who believes in Jesus. And why? Because I believe in the Bible. We can be Jews and believe the whole Word of God.

"Answer for yourselves. If I don't tell you what the Bible says, do what you will to me. But you must ask yourselves, 'What does this mean?' What does Isaiah 9:6 mean when it says, 'For unto us a child is born, unto us a son is given, and the government shall be upon his shoulder; and his name shall be called Wonderful, Counselor, The Mighty God, The Everlasting Father, The Prince of Peace'? Yes, and many other Scriptures you ignore while reading the rabbis' fables."

As the conversation grew more intense, Zvi felt a quickening kinship to the apostle Paul, who had similar exchanges with the forebears of Zvi's audience.

Upon leaving the yeshiva, Zvi thanked God for His divine protection. His opponents had uncharacteristically invited him to sit with them for coffee before his departure. This and other subtle indicators led him to believe that perhaps a little light had penetrated the spiritual murk of that place. The Lord's Word had given these men food for thought and perhaps some pointed questions for their rebbe.

In any case, it had been seed sown. And Zvi prayed that some fell on good ground.

ENDNOTES

[1] "Hasidism," *The Encyclopaedia Judaica*, Vol. 17, 1971, p. 1400.

[2] Ibid., p. 1401.

1967  1973

CHAPTER
NINETEEN

SIX DAYS IN JUNE

For the Western world, World War I (1914–1918) was to have been "the war to end all wars." But history quickly dispelled such naïve, wishful thinking. Zvi and much of Israel flirted with the same delusion concerning the Six-Day War, which lasted from June 5 through 10, 1967. It proved to be the high-water mark in the short history of the modern State of Israel. Jewish emotions spiraled to dizzying heights in a euphoria that surpassed even the establishment of statehood. The joy of victory lasted only a few years, but the significance will last forever. This was the war that gave the nation her singular most spectacular achievement—the reunification of Jerusalem.

From beginning to end, this conflict was different. To begin with, it was preemptive. Israel struck first in order to employ the element of surprise against enemies who were poised to attack her once again. Shortly after 7 A.M. on June 5, 183 Israeli aircraft swarmed over 11 Egyptian air bases, making a shambles of Egyptian President Gamal Abdel Nasser's air force. From the second the first bomb struck, Israel had secured clear supremacy.

An overwhelming sense of history in the making accompanied the opening sortie. As Israeli planes began their initial bombing runs, a coded message was received: "'Nahshonim, action. Good luck.' Nahshon, leader of the tribe of Judah during the Exodus, is traditionally believed to have been the first to enter the waters of the Red Sea as they parted, setting the example to the rest of the Children of Israel, who promptly followed."

Two days later, modern-day Nahshons courageously stood atop Abraham's Mount Moriah and transmitted the heart-stopping message: "The Temple Mount is ours!" At long last, the words of the Israeli national anthem, *Ha-tikvah* (The Hope), had come true: ". . . to live in freedom in the land of Zion *and Jerusalem.*" Historians, national leaders, and men of war were captivated by Israel's military victory for decades.

For the women and children who stayed behind, however, it was quite another story. Jerusalem was a battlefield, and they were in the middle of the war zone. The last engagement of consequence with the Arabs had been the Sinai campaign in 1956. It had lasted only one hundred hours and was fought far from Israel's centers of population. So in Jerusalem and other towns and cities, it was business as usual. But this luxury did not exist in June 1967.

King Hussein of Jordan had received bad advice from his Egyptian allies. "We were," he would later lament, "the recipients of false information about what had happened in Egypt." His was one of the classic understatements of the war. Egyptian President Nasser and his generals had told the king that their forces were winning sweeping victories and crushing Israeli bases. Based on that news, Hussein decided to honor his pact with Egypt and join the effort to "drive Israel into the sea. "It was the biggest mistake of his political career.

About mid-morning on June 5, Jordanian forces began heavy artillery shelling of Israeli villages and town, including the outskirts of Tel Aviv. They also bombed a number of inhabited areas from the air. Jerusalem felt the major brunt of the shelling; and at 11 A.M., Jordanian ground forces began their assault on Jerusalem.

Five-year-old Mendel, Zvi's oldest boy, was playing in the yard with a friend when Hussein's gunners opened fire. "We were playing in the garden near the fence [it marked the border between Jewish and Arab territory] when the sirens went off. It was a new sound to us, so we didn't know exactly what we were supposed to do.

"There was a valley beyond the fence, and we couldn't see into it. Our imagination had created visions of a huge elephant living over in the valley. I called to my friend, 'Hey, maybe the siren means the elephant is coming! Let's go to the fence and see.' So there we were, sitting by the fence, looking toward the valley on the Arab side."

Their childish fantasy was shattered when Mendel looked up to see his mother running toward them carrying newborn Eli wrapped in a blue hospital blanket. With a stricken look on her face, Esther began to scream "Mendel! Mendel! Come! Hurry! We must get into the shelter."

When the boys saw other neighbors running toward the shelter too, they knew the game was over. Something serious was happening. The scene had turned ugly; it was time to run for their lives.

The shelter was small and overcrowded. Light filtered through the windows in strange, crisscrossing patterns fashioned by the masking tape that had been stuck there to discourage flying glass. The light gave an eerie look to the place as it fell on fear-twisted faces and merged with the muffled sounds and vibrations of artillery fire. The noises intruding into their small haven were not reassuring. The roar from aircraft swooping overhead, the bombs, and the pop-pop-pop of small arms fire made the hearts of the children race and their lungs strain for breath. It was all much too close for comfort.

After a while, Mendel left the family huddle and made his way toward the door of the shelter. Trembling, he began to pray for Abba to appear and tell him that everything was okay. Perhaps, he thought, God would think him more

earnest if he imitated the Hasidic Jews he had watched praying from time to time. Methodically, he began rocking back
and forth, engaging his entire body in the act of prayer to
prove to God just how serious he was. If only Father would
come, as he always did, his bad dream would be over. They
could all go home again.

Mendel's earnestness and fears were not misplaced. Even as
a five-year-old child, he knew the facts of life regarding the survival of Israel.

"I would sit listening to the guns," he would later remember, "with one thing in my mind: If we lose, I won't be alive
for ten minutes."

Women and children were not the only ones with troubles
when the men went off to fight their nation's battles. The men
had troubles of their own.

Zvi had a very real problem when the soldiers came bearing
the red notice card that ordered him to report for duty. The Six-
Day War had not actually begun, but because of the nature of his
responsibilities, Zvi was required to report early. (For Zvi, six
days of war meant eighty days of military service.)

Zvi was still in the "every time a perfect job" section of the
service—planting and removing mines. After nearly twenty
years, his commander's first words to him were as fresh in his
mind as on the day he first heard them: "This is the only
department in the army of Israel where you must do a perfect
job every time. When you are working with the mines, you
only get one mistake. You will not get the chance to make the
same error twice."

Before he had family responsibilities, Zvi didn't think a great
deal about himself or his situation. But now it was different. He
had three children at home and no mother there to look after
them. That knowledge gnawed at him relentlessly as the beginning of the war approached. He was a man distracted, doing a
job that did not allow for distractions.

When he was called to duty, Esther was in the hospital delivering Eli. She had experienced complications during the birth, necessitating an extended stay.

"You see my problem," Zvi explained to his commanding officer. "I have no one to take care of my children. If I could just have a little time to call someone in."

"I can appreciate your situation," he was told, "but there is really no alternative. You must go, and you must go immediately. Don't worry, we have capable volunteers available. I'll have someone sent right over."

The officer was true to his word. Within minutes, it seemed, the temporary mother was at the door.

"Good evening," she said with a smile, "I'm Rebecca. I'm here to take care of the children."

Zvi took a look at Rebecca the babysitter. "Oy," he murmured to himself, "this one needs a sitter herself."

He had a question for the young lady who was about to play mother to his children: "How old are you, child?"

"Fourteen," she replied cheerfully.

"Do you know about caring for children?"

"Oh yes, I do it all the time."

He wasn't convinced, but he had already taken more time than the army wanted to allow him. "Here, I'm giving you all the money I have. It should be enough to last until I return."

So Zvi was off to help get the nation ready for war while Rebecca tended the home fires for the three Weichert children he was forced to leave behind.

Under the circumstances, Zvi's mind kept leaping from the minefields to the hospital to the house and back again. These were tough days for Abba.

As soon as his unit returned to the Jerusalem sector, Zvi requested permission to make a quick visit to his home in Ir Ganim.

"I'll do better than give you permission for the visit," said the officer, who knew about Zvi's predicament. "I'll arrange for a car to take you there."

When he entered the house, he thought it looked as though a volcano had erupted in the middle of the living room. A grimy-faced Ruthi ran to him with outstretched arms. "Oh, Abba, we love Rebecca," she chirped.

"And just why do you love Rebecca?" he asked, trying hard to cover his astonishment.

"Because she gives us candy and ice cream."

Mendel, too, thought Rebecca had taken them to paradise. "In the morning, candy. At noon, ice cream. In the evening, maybe some of each."

Where, they wondered, had their mother been when such wonderful lessons in how to feed children were being taught? She certainly hadn't paid as much attention as had their new friend, Rebecca.

The only break in the sweets routine came when Uncle Nathan showed up at the door with two cartons of eggs. Nathan was a family favorite from the church and was eluding sniper fire to deliver food during the crisis. His eggs, however, seemed rather common fare compared to Rebecca's exotic menu.

Not only had the sitter exhausted all the funds Zvi had provided, but her somewhat extravagant food service had put him in debt at the neighborhood market. It took him quite a while afterward to dig himself out.

Friends from the church eventually came to the rescue. Relieved, Zvi sent Rebecca home. He was in a much better frame of mind when he returned to the front. His children, left in orderly surroundings, were scrubbed, well fed, and cared for by people who adhered to Esther's concept of meal planning.

When the episode was over and things had settled down, Zvi had a good, long laugh. First, he laughed about Rebecca. Poor child, she would have to do a lot of polishing on her prowess as a homemaker before she would be ready for matrimony. Zvi could just see her giving a chocolate party every day for a husband and children, none of whom would have a tooth in their heads because of all the sweets.

His heartiest laugh, however, was reserved for himself, because when it came to working in the kitchen, Zvi was downright pitiful. The incident with Rebecca brought him back to his days in Talpiyot when he lived with the immigrants from Morocco.

After they had surmounted the language barrier, Zvi and the Moroccans adjusted to one another's personal habits and became good friends who shared and shared alike.

The Moroccans took turns cooking, while Zvi did his part by paying a share of the cost of their food. One day they had business that kept them away most of the afternoon. "Zvi," they said, "it is about time you began taking your turn at the stove. This is a good day for you to begin. Today you will be responsible for our supper."

While Zvi had had a great deal of experience as a scrounger, he had never done any serious cooking.

"I can't guarantee the result," he called after them. "I've never done much cooking."

"It's easy," they shot back. "You can do it."

Of course he was sure he could do it. He could do just about anything he set his mind to.

The stove was a kerosene contraption with two or three burners that billowed great clouds of black smoke if you turned it up too high or the wick was bad. Zvi fired it up and rummaged through their meager supply of pots to find one to his liking. He made his selection, dumped in healthy portions of rice and beans, then poured oil over the whole concoction.

He was quite pleased with himself. His no-frills meal was also no fuss, and he found himself with time on his hands as he waited for his culinary masterpiece to cook.

"I may as well go to town for a while," he told himself. "I'll be back in plenty of time to have things ready for the fellows."

So off he went to enjoy a couple of leisurely hours amid friends on the streets of Jerusalem.

As he was returning, he could see a plume of black smoke rising in the air above the camp. "I knew it would happen someday," he said to a friend who was walking in the same direction. "Some of those old women at the camp are so feeble they can hardly get around, much less take care of themselves. I'm surprised one of them hasn't burned a barracks down before this."

Once Zvi entered the camp, however, he saw that the area smoldering was suspiciously close to his own barracks—or, more correctly, what had been his own barracks. Wisps of smoke fluttered in the air over all that remained of the place he and the Moroccans had called home. Later, when he dug around in the rubble, he discovered the charred pot and remnants of the stove. Wouldn't you know—the rice and beans were ruined.

"Well," he chuckled to himself, "at least Rebecca didn't burn the house down. Maybe if I see her again, I'll tell her that story and give her some advice about cooking. On second thought, I'll have Esther do it!"

CHAPTER
TWENTY

MOVE, MOVE, MOVE!

Fighting in Jerusalem during the Six-Day War had a profound affect on Israel, Jewry, Arabs, the superpowers, and the world at large. The religious impact alone was monumental. Within a few hours, Messianic tides began to swell that will culminate one day with the great Second Advent of Jesus Christ. Whatever can or cannot be said about hard biblical confirmation of modern Israel's place in prophecy, the reunification of Jerusalem demonstrated to the world that something was taking place among the Jewish people that could not be humanly orchestrated.

The war not only changed the geographical face of the Middle East, it altered fundamental facts of life for the region. With the cessation of hostilities, Israel was no longer as vulnerable to attack as she had been with the armistice lines of 1949. She now had ample warning time if her enemies decided to start another war. Jordanian artillery no longer dotted the Judean hills, and terrorists could not as easily reach Israeli population centers. In the north, the Syrians could no longer take potshots at Jewish kibbutzim.

Israel's political and diplomatic situation also changed dramatically. Before the war, Israel had little to bargain with.

Now it had territories that provided valuable negotiating power. And the Arab states were beginning to get the message: They were not going to bully Israel by weight of arms. Rather, it was the Arabs who were reduced to pleading with the United Nations and the superpowers, asking them to get Israel off their backs before the IDF went sightseeing in Damascus, Cairo, and Amman.

Prophetic overtones were reflected in the fact that the superpowers were now clearly involved in the conflict. The United States and parts of Western Europe were aligned with Israel, while the Soviet Union actively intruded on behalf of the Arab states.

But for Zvi and most of his Israeli brethren, Jerusalem was where the action was.

Fierce fighting raged in Jerusalem and around the Old City all day and most of the night on June 6. Zvi and his sapper comrades were hard-pressed to open lanes through the minefields for men and tanks.

Teddy Kolleck, who later became mayor of the united Jerusalem, remembers their heroism. In describing the fighting around the Rockefeller Museum, he said: "The tanks were there only because while fighting was going on in the Police School, paratroop sappers were clearing a path through the minefield alongside the school compound. It took them several pre-dawn hours, for they were under continuous and accurate shellfire, mostly from 81-mm guns, and mine clearing had to be done by hand between salvos. They would rush out from cover during the brief lulls, clear a few mines, and then race back as the rounds came over."

Caution was thrown to the winds in those desperate and decisive hours, when getting lethal mines out of the way of advancing troops was more than a convenience; it was indispensable if Jerusalem was to be taken.

Teddy Kolleck recalls that troops were "bent on speed, even at the cost of higher casualties. They had no flailer tanks to crash through the minefields—these were all in Sinai—so their sappers simply cleared the mines by hand with prod and knife. Operating in daylight and under fire from the enemy on high ground, they suffered forty casualties in less minutes from enemy fire and exploding mines."

This quick-and-dirty method of handling such deadly devices went against all Zvi's instruction and instincts. He had seen the high cost of hurry too many times over his years of service to his country, and he carried many unpleasant reminders in his mental notebook.

Working carefully and deliberately was an absolute necessity in the sapper business. "If I work quick, I will go quick," he kept telling himself. Since he had come to know the Lord, he had acquired a settled sense of patience as well. Second Timothy 2:24 taught him, "the servant of the LORD must . . . be . . . patient." No need to hurry. One step at a time; one day at a time. God is in control.

Others, however, had not yet come to his settled lifestyle in the Lord, and they didn't quite understand Zvi's operational procedures.

One day, while he and the men he commanded (Zvi was a sergeant at the time) were clearing an area where the Arabs had planted mines, a young officer gave him a dressing down.

"You are working like a grandfather," chided the youngster. "If you don't get a move on, you will never finish this job."

"The Arabs," Zvi explained, "have planted mines like potatoes in this place. There is no pattern to them, and we don't know where they are. We must move slowly, or we will lose men."

The officer, long on schooling and short on experience, didn't want to hear that kind of talk.

"You get out of here. I will do your work and show the men how it's done."

Zvi didn't want to leave, but he had no choice. An officer had issued an order. He had no alternative but to obey. He knew all too well the danger his hotheaded superior was walking into.

The Arabs did not follow the rules of war prescribed for civilized nations by the Geneva Convention. Their mines were planted indiscriminately, with no discernible patterns or retrieval maps. They had also learned the nasty German trick of planting sandwich mines—one on top of the other. Pulling up the top one detonated the one beneath it.

Within minutes, Zvi and his comrades were shaken by the dull *whump* of an exploding antipersonnel mine. The young officer lay unconscious on the ground, a foot and part of a hand missing. For him, the war was over.

"It is so sad," Zvi told his buddies. "The same thing could have happened to any one of us. But as long as we keep moving with the caution of grandfathers, we have a chance of seeing our families again."

But this was a time when there was no time, so he worked feverishly, a little phrase running repeatedly through his mind: "Trust in the Lord; what will be, will be."

With Zvi and the sappers opening the way, the Old City became encircled by Jewish forces, and the dawn of June 7 found young Israelis poised to attack the Mount of Olives and make their heart-stopping charge on the walls of the Old City.

The sense of history and destiny shone before them that morning as brightly as the brilliant Jerusalem sun cutting through the choking smoke of battle. Every soldier seemed to have been ordered in position in a precise display of planning from an unseen hand.

General Moshe Dayan, the fabled one-eyed warrior and recently appointed minister of defense, passed the High Command's attack order to IDF Central Forces commander, Major General Uzi Narkiss. Narkiss was the Palmach Brigade commander who, in 1948, briefly penetrated the Old City but failed to secure it because of too much enemy pressure and too little time before the cease-fire.

Narkiss, in turn, issued the order to Colonel Mordechai "Motta" Gur. For years the young soldier had sketched plans in his mind and rehearsed his brigade for this moment, should the opportunity ever come. Colonel Gur was one of Jerusalem's native sons. Yet because of nineteen years of Jordanian refusal to open the Old City to Jews, he had been denied access to his birthplace.

Also on hand was chief chaplain of the forces, Major General Rabbi Shlomo Goren. His presence completed the symbolic encapsulation of Israel's strength, national heart's desire, and transcending religious dream of dreams—-to possess *their* Holy City: Jerusalem.

Indeed, it would take a rabbi to say it best for all of Jewry: "To us the world is like an eye. The white is everything else. The iris is Israel, Land of the Jews. And the pupil, it is, of course, the Holy City, Jerusalem. But the gleam in the center of the pupil—that gleam is Moriah, the Temple Mount."

Young Motta Gur was so taken with the historical moment and a desire to pay it due respect that he commanded his half-track driver, a bearded farmer from Galilee, to stop in mid-charge. They had raced down the southern slope of the Mount of Olives on a road that took them out of sight of the city. "Turn around," he shouted to his somewhat confused subordinate. "Drive up to the overlook in front of the Intercontinental Hotel. I want to give the command for the conquest of the Old City from an appropriate place."

Ignoring strict regulations against giving unit designations on the radio, he began: "Paratroop Brigade 55. We stand on the heights of the Old City. In a little while we will enter it—the ancient city of Jerusalem, which for generations we have dreamed of and strived for. Our brigade has been given the privilege of being the first to enter.

"Move, move, move! Move to the gate!"

Their fervent response to his command will forever shine from the pages of Jewish history.

Soon members of the 55th were assembled before the Wailing Wall, and Gur was sending out his historic message, telling the world that the Old City was safely in Jewish hands.

When the chief rabbi arrived, the loud wail of the shofar could be heard piercing the air before the ancient stone wall in an act that heralded the reunification of the two Jerusalems, old and new. Its tones echoed throughout the far-flung world of Jewry—a symbol inviting Jacob's sons and daughters to come back home. Ecstatic paratroopers hoisted Rabbi Goren to their shoulders and ceremoniously paraded him through the street as he waved the shofar and Torah scroll wildly above his head.

To complete the fact of an Israeli presence on the Temple Mount, Gur's men hoisted the Israeli flag above the Islamic shrine, the Dome of the Rock. Their revelry over such an emblematic sight, however, was, short-lived. When General Dayan came to the Wall with General Narkiss and General Yitzhak Rabin, he spotted the flag and ordered it removed.

The memory of that day will endure forever in the hearts of those who love Israel: the Torah, cradled in a craggy niche in the giant stones; battle-blackened faces streaked with tears, gazing up at the Western Wall with unbridled awe. One young, bespectacled soldier stood with his helmet in hand, yarmulke on his head, and a shell-studded bandolier lapped around his shoulders like a prayer shawl as he leaned his forehead against a war-dirtied fist pressed hard to the stones.

"This is the greatest day of my life," said one of the state's most illustrious architects, David Ben-Gurion.

General Narkiss was speechless. He said later, "It was as though I was in another world—in a cloud of happiness . . . I felt a part of the whole Jewish people, who for two thousand years had longed for this."

But Moshe Dayan made the most compelling declaration of intent: "We have returned to our holiest of holy places . . . We earnestly stretch our hands to our Arab brethren in peace, but we have returned to Jerusalem never to part from her again."

An appropriate tribute to the epochal events of the day had been presented only a few weeks before the fighting broke out. Naomi Shermer's hauntingly beautiful song, "Jerusalem of

Gold," had been introduced to the nation at the Independence Day celebration held on May 15, 1967. Her stirring lyrics caught the mood and voiced universal Jewish commitment: "If I forget thee, O Jerusalem, may my right hand its cunning lose."

A bone-weary Zvi had done his part and witnessed his countrymen's euphoria. He, too, had gold on his mind.

CHAPTER
TWENTY-ONE

THE GOLDEN CALF

I n the final phases of the attacks prior to Israel's penetration of the Old City, Zvi was busy clearing mines with knife and probe near the Rockefeller Museum, not far from Herod's Gate. His feet and legs were badly swollen from all his running to change positions during what seemed like interminable hours of duty. He had been clearing entryways for tanks while under withering fire that often sent him diving for cover.

By the time the 55th brigade was prepared to launch its conclusive assault, Zvi's unit had been moved to a position near the Dung Gate. Gur's initial plan to enter through Herod's Gate had been scrapped in favor of an assault through the Lion's Gate (St. Stephen's) on the eastern side. So, while members of Gur's brigade were making their entry, Zvi's group was preparing to enter from the south. Moshe Dayan described activities there: "As they were entering the Old City from the east, Eliezer Amitai's Jerusalem Brigade was about to enter from the south, through the Dung Gate. His troops did so half an hour later, having captured several Arab positions and cleared the mine-fields between Mount Zion and the Church of Peter in Gallincantu. It was soon after this that I entered liberated Jerusalem and visited the Western Wall."

Like his fellow Jews who were privileged to be at the scene during such a momentous occasion, Zvi was grateful Jerusalem was no longer a divided city. David's words were in his mind as he watched the near delirium gripping the soldiers at the Wall.

> *I was glad when they said unto me, Let us go into the house of the* LORD. *Our feet shall stand within thy gates, O Jerusalem. Jerusalem is builded as a city that is compact together, . . . Pray for the peace of Jerusalem; they shall prosper who love thee. Peace be within thy walls, and prosperity within thy palaces*
> (Ps. 122:1–3, 6–7).

How deeply he longed for peace within her walls, for an end to the killing, and a good life for his family in the City of Peace. He felt all of this. But, strangely, Zvi did not feel the fervent exhilaration he saw in his brethren. He watched and listened as Rabbi Goren sounded his ram's horn and Narkiss led the troops in Israel's national hymn, *Ha-tikvah.* "But why do we conduct ourselves so before a wall of stones?" he wondered.

"We have our city. Good. This is a wonderful day in the history of Israel. But this is not a holy place. It is a wall built around our ancient Temple by an enemy, Herod. There is nothing sacred here."

Indeed, the Arabs had done their best to desecrate the spot. They had given literal meaning to the gate named *Dung.* It was piled high in the narrow street, so near the Arab houses that Zvi wondered how anyone could stand to live with the flies and stench. To the Arabs, however, dung piled before Jewry's great shrine was a symbol of superiority. So was kicking over Jewish grave markers and using them for stepping stones, demolishing synagogues, and building in the captured Jewish Quarter. It was all a matter of symbolism. Your enemies knocked down your venerated places and sacred objects, and you raised them up again when you prevailed and drove your foes from the hallowed ground. It was the Arab way.

Zvi understood symbolism very well. Hardly a Jew alive comes up short in that department. It wasn't that Zvi objected to national monuments. Rather, he was saddened for his people, who had returned to Jerusalem after so long, only to worship cold, lifeless stone. "This place," he thought dejectedly, "will become a new golden calf for Israel."

Moses' experience, Zvi thought, should serve the nation as a solemn warning and an invitation. Before Moses had even returned from Sinai with his revelation of the Law from Jehovah's lips, the Israelites were reveling before a lifeless golden calf they had molded to take the place of the living God. Moses' challenge rang in Zvi's mind: "Who is on the LORD's side? Let him come unto me" (Ex.32:26).

The Temple built by King Solomon had been Israel's first national house of worship—home for the Shekinah glory that flooded the Holy of Holies with the light of God's presence among His people. But Israel's disobedience and rebellion had so grieved the Lord that the Shekinah was replaced by *Ichabod*— "the glory has departed."

The Messiah had come to a house of worship where the holiest chamber knew only darkness. And He drove out those who traded merchandise in Jehovah's courts to fill their pockets rather than empty hearts; He told them, "make not my Father's house an house of merchandise" (Jn. 2:16). Zvi wondered what Jesus would say to them today.

"If they only realized that stones cannot save them," he cried out in his heart. "If only they would come to Him, instead of to a wall, how wonderful this day would be."

Weeks later, while doing guard duty at night, he watched as people flocked to the wall. The approaches through the streets were now clean of dung and debris. All through the night they came. Through the Dung Gate, down the gentle descent, past the path leading up to the Temple platform, through the narrow street, and on to the wall. Little groups of women and men came silently, as though entering a great cathedral. They positioned themselves there, dwarfed by the great stones, to weep and pray. Some rolled up pieces of paper containing their petitions and wedged them into the crevices between the stones.

Some of the women reminded him of Hannah, the wife of Elkanah and mother of the prophet Samuel, who had come to the Temple greatly distressed to pray to the Lord and weep bitterly. She had been so overwhelmed in her agony and lamentation that Eli the priest thought she was drunk.

These women, many of whom were deeply lamenting their own darker days, perished dreams, and shattered families, stooped before the wall like modern Hannahs.

While walking his post along the wall one night, Zvi stopped to speak to a woman who seemed particularly overwrought.

"I see you crying here before the stones. Why are you weeping?"

"I am a woman who has passed more trouble than you can ever know. I come here to find peace and an answer to my prayers."

"Dear lady, do you think your answer is here in these stones?"

"It is a sacred place," she replied.

"No, these stones are not God, who alone can answer your prayers. You must know the Lord. And when you know Him, you won't have to come through the streets of Jerusalem at night to pray before a wall. You can pray to Him there in your home, and He will give you your answer."

He would give that same advice to many such troubled people over the nights and years to follow. Most would only turn again toward the lifeless stones to seek solace.

Twenty years later, Zvi and his son Eli stood not far from the spot where he had talked with the woman. It was in the yeshiva under Wilson's Arch, where Orthodox Jewish men come to study and pray. There they encountered a man who looked like someone who might have stepped out of the pages of history—perhaps one of David's mighty men. He was big, in his early twenties, with jet-black hair and a full beard. Tefillin (phylacteries) were strapped to his forehead and right arm by leather straps. His white yarmulke was on his head, his prayer shawl hung almost to his white running shoes, and a prayer book was open on the table beside him.

While Eli leaned against the railing around the deep shaft running down the wall, Zvi began a conversation with the young Jew.

"Hello. How is everything going?"

"I'm doing okay, thank you."

"Do you live here in Jerusalem?'

"No, my home is in Tiberias. I came to Jerusalem to pray."

"And why did you come all the way to Jerusalem to make your prayers? Can't you pray in Tiberias?"

"Yes, of course, I can pray in Tiberias," the young man said, "but the Shekinah is not in Tiberias. It is here in the Old City. So I come here to pray near the Shekinah."

"Oh, I see," said Zvi. "But these are only stones. Do you mean to tell me you have come here to worship stones?"

"No, not stones. I have come here to be in the presence of God."

"Well, my friend, you have made a big mistake. The Shekinah was here many centuries ago, in the first Temple. But when our people sinned, the Shekinah was taken from the Temple. When this wall was built, the Shekinah was not in the Temple, and that building was destroyed. And in spite of all the praying that has been done here, see how our people have suffered.

"The trouble is that you are only praying from books, not from the heart. When you come to know the Lord, really know Him, you can pray from your heart. Why? Because the Shekinah will be living in your heart, that's why."

Zvi's listener was not pleased by what he was hearing, but he did not react the way the Orthodox sometimes do. He disagreed but remained respectful. Zvi and Eli had prayed before they left the house that their witness would not be human words only, but the Spirit's work in empowering His Word. Perhaps, like a small mustard seed, something was sown that would raise a question in this man's empty heart; and one day, the Shekinah would indeed reign within him.

Whatever the eventual outcome, their meeting showed that things had not changed spiritually for Israel over the centuries.

The fact is, the Six-Day War raised more spiritual problems than it solved. While there were resounding surges of emotion unparalleled in modern times and tremendous historical implications, Israel's sweeping triumph took her even farther from an attitude of reliance on God.

Zvi met the prevailing mood head-on when he talked to fellow soldiers one night in the aftermath of the war. The conversation revolved around how strong and clever Israel had been to catch Egypt by surprise and then defeat three countries with such comparative ease.

"Did you ever think that this may not have been our own strength?" Zvi asked. "It might just be that God wanted to free us from so much pressure and to put Jerusalem back into our hands. We should give some thought to what the prophet Zechariah said: 'Not by might, nor by power, but by my Spirit, saith the LORD of hosts' [Zech. 4:6].

"I think God wants to teach us that it is time to seek the Messiah. We can rejoice, as we are now, but it should be as Zechariah told the daughters of Zion to rejoice: 'Rejoice . . . thy King cometh unto thee; he is just, and having salvation'" (Zech. 9:9).

At that point, an officer broke in abruptly. "Now you are talking about Jesus. This is no place to bring up a subject of this kind. We'll have no more of such conversation."

The officer's opinion expressed the hostility and resentment Zvi and fellow believers frequently encountered after the Six-Day War. At those times, Jesus' words to disciples of a much earlier day came to mind: "I send you forth as sheep in the midst of wolves" (Mt. 10:16). Israeli self-sufficiency was not, for the time being, open to question.

In the days following the Six-Day War, Israel was a nation much like Zvi himself had been until he saw his need of the Lord. He had survived the Holocaust, he fancied, because he was smarter and quicker than his enemies. It was "Zvi, the master of his own destiny." Then he learned just how wrong he had been. Others, he confessed, were smarter and just as quick. But they perished and he did not. Why? He came to understand, in an intensely personal way, what Jeremiah had meant when he said, "It is because of the LORD's mercies that we are not consumed" (Lam. 3:22). Then, and only then, was he ready to seek God's provision in the Messiah.

So, in the postwar days, Zvi and other believers met in their little assemblies to worship together, edify and encourage one another. They witnessed faithfully without much outward evidence of success. But they lived in the assurance that the Lord was doing His own work in a quiet and faithful way. And the day would come when many in the nation would acutely feel their need for help outside themselves.

CHAPTER
TWENTY-TWO

BUT WHERE'S
THE BABY?

An unpleasant part of army life in Israel is the necessity to occasionally enter civilian homes to search for arms. One day following the Six-Day War, Zvi was on a detail working a short distance from Jerusalem on the road to Ramallah. The area was dotted with expensive villas occupied by affluent Arabs.

The usual, ritual questions were asked of the owner of the house, a tall, solemn-looking son of Ishmael.

"I must ask you if you have any weapons on the premises," Zvi began. "In the event you do, if you will turn them over to us, there will be no problems or further questions asked."

"No, I am a peaceful man. I do not keep guns in my home," the Arab replied.

"I'm afraid I must ask you to allow us to look through the house to be sure."

"If you insist. But I can assure you, you will find no weapons here."

Zvi entered and walked slowly through the house, poking into closets and would-be hiding places. When he returned to the spacious room where the man and his wife were seated, he noticed that the man of the house appeared extremely nervous. "Well," he told himself, "he looks like a man who has something to hide."

Over in one corner of the room, Zvi saw a baby carriage. It was completely covered with a light blanket. "Oh, I see you have a little one," he said, as he strode toward the carriage. When he glanced at the man, the Arab had a stricken look on his face. It appeared that the fellow, who had risen from his seat and was pursuing Zvi across the room, was about to pass out. Zvi was certain he was about to uncover a cache of weapons intended to be used on Jews.

When he lifted the blanket, he was astonished to find it filled to the top with gold, precious gems, and U.S. dollars. Zvi's reluctant host, his face now scarlet, tottered on the brink of collapse. He propped himself against a piece of furniture and, with a resigned gesture, awaited the inevitable. The soldiers, he was sure, would promptly empty the buggy and rob him of his treasure—or so he had been told.

This type of misinformation was disseminated liberally by Arab leaders in order to convince the population that the "Jewish devils" would loot their property to the last saleable item. The term *devil*, Zvi learned, was an appellation some Arabs applied literally to the Jewish people.

When Zvi had been on duty in an isolated Arab village, he and his companions had filled a large container with bread and began distributing it to Arab children. A swarm of eager, receptive children kept circling around the soldiers. When the soldiers asked the giggling youngsters what they were looking for, they ran a short distance away, frightened that their maneuver had been detected. As soon as the soldiers were again occupied with passing out bread, the children again would be craning their necks in an effort to see the soldiers' backsides.

The father of one of the children had been observing from a respectful distance. Grinning widely, he walked over and said, "You know what they're looking for? They want to see if Israeli soldiers really do have tails of devils, as they have been told. Why don't you turn around and give them a good look."

It wasn't the only thing those youngsters had been told about Jews. In some Arab families, when children were reluctant to go to sleep, they were assailed with a recurring warning. "If you don't lie down and get to sleep right now, I will go get a Jew with horns, and he will come and eat you alive!"

It was little wonder that the wealthy Arab feared the worst.

When Zvi returned from surveying the contents, covered the carriage, and was preparing to leave, the man's relief was mitigated by a look of dismay.

"I was afraid you would take everything," he explained.

Zvi, who after the Rebecca fiasco didn't have an agora in his pocket, replied with a hearty laugh, "No, yours is not the kind of treasure I'm looking for. The treasure that really concerns me is the treasure I have in Heaven."

Now the Arab was genuinely perplexed. "But we have heard that the Jews would take everything we have as spoils of war."

"Let me explain about Jews, and myself as a special Jew. No, Israeli soldiers will not take your personal belongings as spoils of war. And I will not take them for two reasons. The first you have heard already; the second is this: I was born a Jew, yes, but then I became a born-again Jew."

Now perplexity turned to curiosity. "What do you mean by this phrase, 'born-again Jew'?"

"What I mean is that I am a Jew who believes in the Lord Jesus Christ as my Savior. So I have chosen to serve only the Lord God, not mammon.

"We have a song we sing in my church that expresses how it is. 'Nor silver nor gold has obtained my redemption. Nor riches of earth could have saved my poor soul. The blood of the cross is my only foundation. The death of the Savior now makes me whole.'"

You could have knocked the Arab over with a feather. "This is amazing!" he exclaimed. "You see, I, myself, am not a Muslim. I am a Christian Arab."

So the Hebrew Christian and the Arab Christian found they were not enemies after all. They were, in fact, brothers in Christ.

Now the wealthy homeowner wanted to become a willing host. "Come back and sit with me. My wife will make coffee. You will be a welcome guest in my home."

"That's very kind, but I'm afraid I must decline your offer," Zvi told him. "We are not allowed to eat or drink in homes where we are conducting searches. Maybe some other time."

Several months later, when he was walking through the Old City, Zvi was hailed by an insistent voice. "Hello! Hello! Hello!" It was the kind of urgent invitation tourists get accustomed to hearing from Arab merchants. This time, however, there was no intent to sell. When Zvi turned around, he found himself looking into the beaming face of the owner of the treasure-filled baby carriage. The man owned an antique shop in the Old City. It was a proper occasion for accepting hospitality, so Zvi and the merchant sat down together, drank coffee, and talked of the things they shared as brothers in Christ.

On a subsequent visit, Zvi learned that his Arab brother had departed for heaven and was glad that God's providence had brought them together in the kind of relationship that money can't buy.

Zvi had been thoroughly indoctrinated regarding the spoils of war long before he met the antique dealer. Back in 1949 his unit had been transferred from the Jerusalem area to a camp near Tel Aviv. The cease-fire had been declared, and upon their departure from Jerusalem, some of the junior officers had gathered quite a number of "souvenirs" from the homes of Arabs who had fled the country. Arab leaders had urged them to do so, promising that the Arabs would win the war and would return to their homes and confiscate Jewish property. Although it was forbidden, the officers indulged themselves with a few choice items to take home with them. When the truck containing the booty arrived at the new camp, it was quietly deposited in an out-of-the-way barracks for disposition later.

Zvi and some of his friends from Europe were sitting together one day discussing the state of their finances and prospects for future employment. "If we could only get our hands on some money," lamented one young man, "we could have the celebration we deserve after so much hard fighting."

"That may not be such a hard thing to do," Zvi said with a knowing look.

"What do you mean?" his companion asked. "I mean, I know how we can come by enough money to put on any kind of celebration we want."

"How?"

"Well, you know about the truckload of things those officers brought over from Jerusalem and stored in the barracks. We have an ammunition truck to use. Tomorrow night, when we are on guard duty, we will load it on our truck, take it to Ramla, and sell it to the shopkeeper there who deals in such things."

"Count me out!" said the lad who made the inquiry. "I don't want to make that kind of trouble for myself."

"Now wait a minute," responded another, who happened to be a lawyer. "Even the Talmud says it is not wrong to take from someone who has taken something illegally. They know as well as we do that they were not supposed to take those things. I agree with Zvi. We deserve a good time—and they could use the lesson. It will be good for them. Anyway, even if they catch us, where will they go to complain?"

The next night, the conspirators quietly rolled their vehicle alongside the barracks and began loading it up. The truck soon lumbered away toward Ramla with appointed representatives of the impromptu trading company ready to deal for the lot of it.

"You've got a lot of stuff here," observed the proprietor of the no-questions-asked establishment.

"I know," replied the sales rep. "It ought to bring a pretty good price."

"Well, I don't know. There is so much of this kind of thing floating around these days, I really won't be able to get much for it."

So the dickering began. The boys didn't argue long. After all, they didn't have a great deal invested—just a little time and ingenuity.

When the man's offer slid into the appropriate range, the young entrepreneur yelled, "Sold!" and it was done. The soldiers slapped each other's backs and congratulated themselves all the way back to camp.

The air had a festive feel as they carried in the meats and other embellishments they had purchased with the profits. A brief meeting settled minor details. The guest list was the leading topic of discussion.

"Just to cover ourselves," suggested their resident intellectual, the lawyer, "let's invite the officers to join us. It isn't necessary, really, but I think it's a nice touch, and a little more insurance won't hurt anything."

It turned out to be a memorable evening. Not one officer ventured to ask about the finances for the feast. There were smiles all around when the evening ended and everyone went to his bed contented. The smiles disappeared the next morning, however, when the officers discovered what had happened. Zvi was among the first to be called on the carpet.

"You were in charge of the watch the night the barracks was emptied," a sullen officer charged.

"Yes, sir. I was," Zvi answered. "But may I say, I was not the only one on duty. Why am I called in as the chief suspect?"

Consequently, the whole detail was called in, and questions began to fly. Their resident lawyer fielded the heavy queries.

"We frankly admit, sir, that we had some little part in the events in question. I suppose that the only recourse open now is to have the matter referred to higher authorities."

He was steering a straight line, and the officer knew exactly where the track would end. "You're dismissed for now. But I want you all to know you haven't heard the last of this."

His words had a foreboding ring to them, and they didn't have to wait long to get his drift. About two days later, Zvi heard:

"Weichert, I want you to scrub the latrine today. I want it cleaned like it has never been cleaned before. When I inspect it, it had better be perfect, or you'll find out what trouble is all about."

"Yes, sir! It will be clean," Zvi promised.

Inside, Zvi was seething. It was, he knew, pay day. His officer was after a generous pound of flesh, and Zvi wasn't about to give him that satisfaction. These were the days when Zvi was new in the faith and the Lord's grace had not yet tempered him. A counter-injustice plan was almost instantly in place.

As a sapper, Zvi had access to the camp's explosives magazine. A little dynamite placed at strategic intervals would do a very nice job of cleaning the latrine "like it had never been cleaned before." It did. The explosion shook the camp and brought people running from all directions.

The officer was livid.

"But you said you wanted it cleaned as never before," Zvi reported. "As you ordered, it's clean."

"And I'm putting you up on charges," railed his superior.

"Do what you choose."

The senior officer who was selected to judge Zvi in the incident turned out to be a man he knew very well. Zvi had served under him in Jerusalem. The officer also knew the circumstances that had prompted the whole episode. The theft/sale/feast scenario was much too good a story to be kept under wraps—although the information was all quite unofficial.

"You have the right to stand before another officer if you wish," Zvi was told.

"No, sir. I will be pleased to have you as my judge."

The senior officer listened intently as particulars about the instant cleaning of the latrine were laid before him. When all the evidence was in, he sat back and announced his decision.

"First of all, let me say that I am well aware of what brought on this whole situation. And I want the entire matter dropped at once. The charges are dismissed. You are free to return to duty."

The junior officers were thus put on notice that there would be no more "spoils of war" activities or reprisals, and Zvi and his companions returned to the less colorful pursuits of soldiering.

When the Six-Day War came to a close, Israel not only possessed the Old City of Jerusalem but was also in control of the Gaza Strip, the Golan Heights, the West Bank of the Jordan, and the Sinai Desert. It would take some time for the Arabs to stop accusing one another of responsibility for the fiasco and get back to hounding Israel. Zvi welcomed the bit of breathing space this gave him and quickly got back to his first love—Esther and the children. War had deprived him of more than a glimpse of his newest arrival, Eli. He was anxious to get home and see just what kind of stuff the boy was made of.

1973 — 1982

CHAPTER
TWENTY-THREE

GROWING UP
WITH LEGENDS

T he Weichert children grew up surrounded by legends. They were really only men. But from the vantage point of the very small, who had to look up at everyone and virtually everything, these men seemed much larger than mere mortals.

Yet Father was the first and most ardently admired. To Ruthi, Mendel, Yona, and Eli, Zvi was like the proverbial man of steel. Although he was not tall, he was strong and muscular. When the children conspired to catch him by surprise and pile on top of him with war whoops and fierce fits of determination, he could raise them all to his shoulders and stride around the room like Samson, as though he hadn't noticed they were pestering him. Each of the boys took turns trying to dethrone him as the family arm wrestling champ. It was a waste of time.

Their walks through the streets of Jerusalem added to the aura. Strolls that took ordinary people five or ten minutes often stretched into an hour for them, as shouts of "Hey Zvi!" or "Hi Zvi!" or "Zvi! Wait a minute," constantly impeded their progress. Old army buddies, people he had worked with, and a seemingly endless procession of others all had something to say to Zvi and his kids. There's a saying that every Jew has a story.

You didn't have to argue that theory with Zvi's children; they thought they had listened to them all—war stories, work stories, Old Country stories, etc., etc., etc.

They became accustomed to being thumped on the back by strong men as they passed along some commentary on *Abba* ("father" in Hebrew). "Ah, you are a lucky child to have such a one as this for a father—he is a good man. You want to grow up to be strong? Then be like your daddy."

This was all well and good and left an indelible and constructive imprint on them all. But sometimes, for those intent on getting to the store for an ice cream cone, a walk down King George or Ben Yehuda Streets often proved an exercise in self-restraint.

Also adding temper to the development of personal self-discipline was the stream of visitors pouring into their home. This was particularly bothersome to Mendel. No turf was guarded more tenaciously than Shabbat afternoons, when a boy could come home, eat a sumptuous meal, take the newspaper to his room, close the door, flop down on the bed, and enjoy a serene siesta. Too often, or so it seemed to Mendel, he opened the door on a host of smiling faces offering "Shaloms" that did not add up to "peace" for his afternoon. Sometimes they were local people just in for the day. Other times, they came from far-off places and bedded down for a few days or weeks—perhaps in his bed!

As Mendel grew older, however, his resentment of these intrusions began to fade, and he grew to understand that these occasions were not designed to shatter his Shabbat siestas but were an integral part of the ministry of hospitality that his parents so warmly extended to one and all.

One shortcoming their father appeared to evidence was that of being perpetually broke. He never seemed to have two agora to rub together. Money for the pressing necessities of life to children—candy, chocolate, ice cream—was not often dispensed from Abba's pockets—unless, of course, he had something left over from his bus fare.

But there were two very good reasons for their father's financial state: indifference and design. Handling money did not rank high on Zvi's scale of priorities. He was vitally interested in providing well for his family, and the Lord enabled him to do so. What he kept for himself was an afterthought. Whatever it was, it was always enough. Esther was a much better commissar than he would ever be. She knew what to do with money. She also knew what not to do with it. Therefore, Zvi was willing and wise enough to leave household matters in the hands of a woman who could have been the model for the worthy woman in Proverbs 31.

Other legends were two elders from the church. The first, Joseph Davidson, was a sedate, patriarchal figure who looked like one of the upper-class European Jewish men one saw in old pictures. His bearing and lifestyle held true to the image. Mr. Davidson was a man of substance and dignity—solid all the way through. That appraisal went beyond the man's appearance. His spiritual depth and character were reflected in his outward demeanor. The children watched the Davidsons as they sat together at worship. If you sat close, you knew you had to be on your best behavior. Mr. D. did not countenance any monkey business in church. A look was sufficient to restore and maintain order. But what the children learned from Joseph Davidson was not cold severity; it was disciplining grace. Knowing him became a memory they would cherish.

Uncle Nathan was another story entirely. He was warm, friendly, and drew children to him like a magnet. He laughed loud and loved fun—a good man for young children to have around. Unlike Joseph Davidson, who was an infrequent visitor, Uncle Nathan often dropped in for tea and talk. The joke was: "Good old Nathan, you can buy him with a slice of bread and a cup of tea." They could all testify of his fondness for both. He would sit in the kitchen, a teacup on the table and a slice of bread (always unbuttered) in his hand. You could be sure that while he was there, the children would be close by.

That's what set him apart. Uncle Nathan noticed the kids and cared very deeply about what God was doing in their lives. He demonstrated what Christian love and caring were all about. It was Uncle Nathan who had risked his life under sniper fire to bring eggs to the family whose dad was on the battlefield. His life and lessons would stay with them. In a land where living for the Lord was sometimes pretty tough sledding, it was good to have an Uncle Nathan. His charm and smile light their memories even today.

Some time after Nathan had gone home to be with the Lord, Mendel was baptized. At the conclusion of the ceremony, Nathan's wife came up to him, joyously proclaiming: "You have made my Nathan so happy today. He is jumping up and down in heaven!"

Like churches the world over, not every member evidences the type of deportment that qualifies for *legend* status with those who need constructive Christian role models. The church the Weicherts attended was no exception. But as the children began to mature, it would be people such as Joseph Davidson and Nathan whose influence God would use to make a difference.

As Zvi's children were touched by sound, strong personalities, they were also affected by the traditions and festivals that make Israel unique. The feast of Esther (Purim) that comes each spring was an especially good time for small boys and girls.

Purim is for children, and during this happy festival, it seems everyone in Israel becomes a child again. To be on the streets in Tel Aviv then is somewhat like walking down a midway at a carnival in small-town America. People are laughing and bopping each other on the head with squeaking plastic mallets, walking around in strange costumes, and generally enjoying the merriment. For a nation stressed by living under the perpetual threat of war, Purim is therapeutic.

It is celebrated by Jews the world over to commemorate Mordecai's and Persian Queen Esther's triumph over the infamous Haman and his plot to exterminate world Jewry approximately 2,500 years ago. As is true with many Christian observances, it has been added to and altered over the centuries.

For religious Jews, the celebration is an annual reminder of God's protection for His people. In Hasidic literature, much is made of Purim as a day of friendship and joy and as a celebration of God's unseen hand at work behind the scenes.

In the synagogues, the main feature in the commemoration is the reading of the book of Esther. When what has been termed *the four verses of redemption* (2:5; 8:15-16; 10:3) are read, it is in a louder voice. And whenever the name of the hated Haman is heard from the text, the children scream wildly, stamp their feet and make loud noises with Purim rattles to demonstrate their contempt for him. The objective of the noise is to blot out the name of Haman and "the memory of Amalek"—Haman was a descendant of Amalek, a perpetual archenemy of ancient Israel.

It is customary at Purim to "send portions" to friends and give gifts to the poor. The rule is to send at least two portions of food to a friend and give a present of money to at least two poor men. A special meal of boiled beans and peas is eaten on Purim afternoon, which is said to be a reminder of the cereals the prophet Daniel ate when he was in the king's palace at Babylon. A favorite treat are special cookies called *hamantashen* ("Haman's ears"), eaten during the celebration.

For those who are less inclined toward the religious aspects of the holiday, the Mardi Gras flavor gives the season its appeal. Today the carnival atmosphere is accentuated with elaborate costuming, excessive indulgence (heavy drinking, for some people), and allowing children to do pretty much as they please.

For the Weichert children, it was Purim plays, dressing up, and having good, clean fun.

There was the year when Ruthi showed her skills as a producer and director by preparing a Purim play for the church families. She was also in charge of talent selection and coaching the participants. Her casting ability may have seemed a bit biased when Mendel appeared as Queen Esther, and Yona peered at the audience from the Mordecai costume. All the same, the play was a big hit and enhanced the spirit of joy and friendship reflected in the season.

As a child, Ruthi especially loved Purim. Her favorite role was that of Esther—beautiful and queenly—going about the business of being a heroine and deliverer of her people.

Costumes are important to little girls with such grand fantasies. She always fancied herself and her mother—the real, everyday Esther—in one of Jerusalem's finest shops, selecting the most elegant gown Purim had ever seen. But, as is so often true, reality fell a little short of fantasy. Esther was not the sort who frequented boutiques—even in her dreams. She leaned toward the clean and sensible. And spending good money on a play dress to be worn for a day or two did not fall within the parameters of *sensible.*

"This year it will be different," Esther told her daughter with the expensive taste.

"What will be different? Are we going into the city to buy me a Purim costume?"

Mother quickly dashed that prospect. "No, we are not. But I have been giving it a great deal of thought, and this year you will have the perfect costume."

"Can you please tell me—or better, show me—what it will be?"

"No, that would spoil all the fun. You'll just have to wait until Purim. Then you will see."

Ruthi was a picture of anticipation that year when she bounded out of bed on Purim morning. Suspense had disrupted her thoughts for days. At last she would find out just what her mother's idea of a "best yet" costume was.

"Stand still," Esther instructed as she began to create. She worked deliberately over her impatient daughter, like a master craftsman on some great project. First, an immaculate white shirt, open at the collar. Then she slipped her into a black suit— it turned out to be one of Zvi's. A pair of black shoes finished the creation. "Now hold still, while I put this on your face." Ruthi could feel a pointed object being moved expertly over her upper lip. The masterpiece was done when Esther wrapped Ruthi's head with a bright red kafiyah and pulled a thick black cord to forehead level.

Esther stepped back for a survey, made a few adjustments here and there, then smiled approvingly. "Go look at yourself," she instructed. By this point, Ruthi was not so sure she really wanted to look.

Zvi's eldest child studied the image in the mirror. Her voice was composed as she spoke to her mother. "Would you tell me, please, just who, or what, I am supposed to be?"

"An Arab, of course," Esther replied.

"An Arab! I don't want to be an Arab! Besides, this is not an Arab costume. They wear long robes."

"No. Old-fashioned Arabs wear long robes. You are modern Arab!"

As has happened the world over after well-meaning mothers have lent their best efforts to help their daughters, Esther watched her little girl burst into tears. It was, in fact, a terrific Purim costume. But Ruthi could not see it that way. After all, how could a queen be comfortable in a scratchy black suit?

As things would have it, Ruthi's dream came true. The source was consummately appropriate. Her grandmother, Esther's mother, sent her a special dress to wear to the wedding of an aunt from Persia—Esther's birthplace. The exotic white garment was beautifully embroidered and flowed gracefully to the floor. And it had come from the land of her queen and Mordecai. It was one of those rare instances in life when a child's dream really did come true.

The following Purim, when "Queen Esther" stepped from her door, she looked every inch a queen. All the boutiques of Jerusalem and Tel Aviv combined could not have produced one so regal, elegant, or happy as Zvi and Esther's daughter.

It was a fitting climax to Ruthi's play days. She was growing up, and the fantasies of childhood were giving way to life as it must be lived in Israel. Too soon she would trade her beautiful Persian gown for olive drab Israeli army fatigues. It was the way sabra girls came of age.

CHAPTER
TWENTY-FOUR

FADING NUMBERS

I n the years between the wars, Zvi and his family enjoyed the best of two worlds. They were living in the most exciting period in the history of their new nation. Maturing in the Lord and watching Him work His will was even more fulfilling. But with all he was involved in with family, work, and church, Zvi never forgot the people who had known the bad times in Europe. Most of his fellow survivors of the Holocaust had not yet found the peace they desperately needed. He wanted to do what he could to help them.

The dark numbers tattooed on their forearms had faded somewhat over the years—the memories had not. Many survivors were haunted daily by thoughts of barbed wire, stench-filled barracks with narrow wooden beds, and empty stomachs. They remembered when their minds had been dulled with hunger and fatigue; when their bodies had withered into skeletons with every rib showing and every joint distended. They remembered the scowling guards, the swastikas, guns, clubs, mud, moans, excrement, and the long lines of naked Jews waiting their turn in the "showers." For them, the fumes of the gas chambers and the atrocities too inhumane to describe still tortured them in their thoughts. Rape; dissection; striped suits on grotesque hulks clutching electrified fences in quivering, self-induced death spasms; and piles of human hair, shoes, gold-rimmed glasses, and clothes stacked before the "processing chambers" were all specters lurking much too close to the surface. They wanted to forget. But most never could. The Holocaust was not a dark historical pause for them; it was an eternity of anguish compressed into a lifetime.

Many of the survivors are gone today, but a remnant still keeps a vigil at the Holocaust memorial, Yad Vashem, in Jerusalem. Their representatives, most of them old, sit on benches, handkerchiefs to their faces, outside the building housing the grim artifacts of anti-Semitic insanity. Theirs is a presence that gives life and breath to the storied "weeping Jews of the Diaspora" who inspired Byron to write,

> *The white dove hath her nest,*
> *The fox his cave,*
> *Mankind their country,*
> *Israel but the grave.*

In the great memorial shrine, an eternal light flickers over the entombed ashes of victims and illuminates the names of the extermination camps, which the world—like it or not—must remember: Auschwitz, Belzec, Chelmno, Kulmhof, Majdansk, Sobibor, Treblinka.

All Holocaust victims bear lifelong scars of their ordeal. Some wounds are physical, as those inflicted by the "doctors" at Dachau and Auschwitz in the name of racial and medical research. Others are psychological and run far deeper than those inflicted by knives and guns.

Zvi moved freely among them all. His easy demeanor and obvious desire to help in any way he could soon taught survivors that this was a friend who could be trusted. Some encounters bore spiritual fruit; some did not—at least, not immediately. When he had lived with the people who wore the numbers, Zvi learned that pathos and humor sometimes ran in the same stream. Shulman was a prime example.

Following Zvi's misadventure as a cook in the transit camp, the man in charge of placement directed him toward a new barracks.

"The only place we have for you now is with a man named Shulman. He's much older than you and, I must warn you, is an odd sort of fellow. Maybe it's because he spent so much time in concentration camps. Be patient with him and try to get along the best you can.

"I'm sorry we can't place you with someone nearer your age. If something opens up, I'll let you know."

"Well, at least it is a place to lay my head at night," Zvi said, as he went looking for his new quarters.

Shulman was an odd sort. Zvi judged him to be about sixty. He was short in stature and wore glasses so thick it was hard to believe his nose could support them. His face was round and not the most appealing one Zvi had looked upon. "Oy," he thought, "if I had to choose between kissing that face and a monkey, I wouldn't think twice—it would be the monkey!"

Shulman didn't wait long before laying down the law.

"I will tell you now that I don't like the idea of having anyone living here with me. But since I have no choice in the matter, you will have to keep some rules. The first one is this: you cannot bring your friends here. I will not permit it. And I want this place kept clean. Furthermore, you are to leave my things alone. Don't touch anything that belongs to me."

"You don't have to worry," Zvi assured him, "I like things clean too. And I will respect your wishes about having my friends in while you are at home. Your belongings will be safe, and I promise to do what I can to help with what needs to be done."

It was soon obvious that Shulman had not completely shaken the lifestyle of the concentration camp. He was secretive and suspicious. Often, after they had eaten the evening meal, Zvi would see him slipping uneaten pieces of bread under his pillow. Every nook and cranny in the place seemed to be stuffed with packages. He recognized them as parcels of clothing sent into the camp by various relief agencies around the world. This clothing was supposed to have been distributed without charge to anyone who needed it. Shulman, however, had been gathering it all up and building a carefully guarded hoard. Periodically he would run checks on his goods to see that everything was still in place.

Living arrangements under these conditions were tolerable, but not exactly what one would call congenial. Absence helped, so Zvi spent much of his time away, and his housemate often ambled around the camp talking with people who were nearer his age and interests.

One day while Shulman was away on a ramble, some of Zvi's friends dropped by to invite him along on a trip into town. While they were waiting for him, a young fellow noticed all the clothing packages. "These are supposed to be given away," he said. "What are they doing here?"

"It is Shulman's hobby," Zvi laughed. "He just picks them up and stuffs them away."

"Well, let's have a look and see what's inside some of them," his inquisitive visitor said.

It turned out that Zvi's friend liked what he found much better than what he was wearing; so he helped himself, as did some of the others, and replaced the garments they had taken with their castoffs. It was, indeed, a better dressed company of youths who walked to Jerusalem that afternoon.

What had been good fun for them, however, was no laughing matter to Shulman. "You are a thief!" he shouted, trembling with anger. "I knew your being here was no good. Get out! Get out of my sight, and don't come back."

"That would be all right with me," Zvi replied, trying to remain calm. "But, you see, I have no place else to go."

"Then I will call the police and have you arrested! They will give you a place to stay."

"No," Zvi countered, "I don't think you should call the police. You know as well as I that those clothes are not to be kept as you are doing. They are to be distributed to whomever needs them. They don't belong to you or me, and the police won't like what they see if they come here."

Shulman knew he was right and said no more. The two lived with an uneasy truce from that point on. But, as things would have it, the cease-fire was not long-lived.

The old man's snoring was so bad one night it woke Zvi up. Finding himself extremely thirsty, Zvi began poking around, looking for something to drink. There was no electricity in the place, and since he did not want to disturb an already irritable Shulman, Zvi groped around in the dark for what he needed. His hand moved over a table until it bumped a glass that was partially filled with water. Just what he was looking for. Zvi flipped the contents out the open window, filled it from the pail on the table, had his drink, and went back to bed.

Around 6:00 in the morning, Zvi awoke to a verbal assault that made the clothing incident seem like a light warm-up. When Zvi sat up on his bed and looked at the old man, he was certain that Shulman had gone completely mad. He was ranting and raving with uncontrollable rage about what Zvi had done to him, screaming that Zvi was not going to get away with it this time. Further complicating the tirade was the fact that Shulman's words were spewing through severely puckered lips, which were emitting strange whistling noises. Zvi had no earthly idea what this was all about or if—and it seemed entirely possible at that moment—his accuser had become insane.

When Shulman finally paused to take a breath, Zvi injected a question. "But what have I done to you?"

"You know very well what you have done to me, you thief! My teeth! You stole my teeth during the night! What have you done with them?"

A deep wave of nausea swept over Zvi, momentarily blocking out the man's words. That partially filled glass had contained Shulman's teeth! Zvi had thrown the old man's teeth out the window. But far worse, to Zvi's mind, than Shulman's missing upper plate, was the fact that Zvi had drunk from the glass! For a few distressing moments, he felt as though he were about to lose more than Shulman had.

Shulman's accusation of thievery was, of course, preposterous. At his age, Zvi had a full set of his own teeth. And where would one find a customer for a used set of teeth—especially in the middle of the night? The irrational outburst reflected the residual effects of the Nazi concentration camps. Shulman never recovered from them. He did, however, get new teeth free of charge. *irrational responses due to previous problems*

The placement officer had been correct when he had warned Zvi about the difficulties of living with Shulman. The arrangement did not work out. And it was Shulman himself who decided to make the break.

"I'm moving out," he informed Zvi.

"But where will you go?"

"Oh, I have a place. I am moving in with a friend of mine. We are the same age, so this will be a much better arrangement for both of us."

That day Zvi got a glimpse of what his roommate probably had been like before the concentration camps ruined his life. He was a good man, but a man so deeply scarred that one had trouble finding him beneath the rubble. The summary tragedy of what Hitler did to victims of the Holocaust was not just what he took away, though that was unspeakably horrible; it was what he left them to live with for the rest of their days.

As one who had been there, Zvi was fully aware of this reality and had a deep desire to reach out to Shulman. He hadn't been a believer long himself, but he knew that Shulman needed what he had found in the Lord. But how to approach him and what to say— those were the questions. Zvi asked the Lord for the appropriate words to give the man before they parted. The Lord supplied them.

"You tell me that you have found a friend with whom to live. I am very happy for you. It will be good for you to have someone your own age with whom you can live and talk.

"I want you to know that I, too, have found a friend with whom to live. He is here with me all the time. When I came to Israel, I was alone like you. All my family was lost, and, in another way, I was lost too. I wondered what I had to live for. Then I came to know the Lord Jesus Christ as my Savior. When I did, I found the friend I needed. I hope that one day, you can find Him too."

It was a short, simple witness for the Lord Jesus—nothing detailed or profoundly theological, just one heart telling another that there is a friend who, in love and grace, sees through the scars and reaches out to us with His peace.

Shulman listened. Zvi hoped he understood. They parted company to move away to very different personal worlds. Only eternity will tell if the old man with Hitler's tattoo found a new friend in the Lord Jesus.

It was different with Leo.

His nervousness caught Zvi's eye. The man worked in quick, jerky little movements. During idle moments, he paced around the construction site puffing on one cigarette after another.

One day during their lunch break, Zvi motioned him over. "Come, sit down, let's eat together."

Leo hunkered down beside him, munched a bit of food, then lit another cigarette.

"I'm curious," Zvi began, "I don't think I've ever seen a person smoke more cigarettes in a day than you do. How many packs do you put away?"

"Four or five," he answered.

"Well, if you don't mind some friendly advice, you had better cut down or you'll wind up with emphysema, and that's a hard way to live and die."

His companion bristled. "If you only knew what I've been through in my life, you wouldn't be so smart and quick to pass out advice." With that he walked off to another corner of the job site.

Of course, Zvi didn't know what Leo had been through. But he knew enough to draw some general conclusions when he noticed the blue numbers tattooed on his arm.

Later in the day, Zvi approached the man with a grin. "I'm sorry if I offended you. I didn't mean to hurt your feelings.

"I'll tell you what. Why don't you and your family come over on Shabbat. My wife will prepare a nice meal for us, and our families can get acquainted."

Leo seemed eager to accept Zvi's invitation. The next Saturday afternoon, introductions were made all around and everyone sat down to enjoy one of Esther's culinary masterpieces.

After dinner the two men took a walk and shared some quiet conversation. Zvi's new friend began to talk freely. Clearly, he bore a burden he wanted to unload.

"You asked me on the job the other day why I chain smoke. Well, I'm going to tell you. Then I want you to answer a question yourself: If you have experienced what I have, would you be any different?"

"Good," Zvi replied, "I would like to hear your story."

"As a young man—it seems so long ago now—I had a beautiful wife and a healthy baby boy. We had a good life from my trade as a cabinetmaker. Life couldn't have been better for us.

"Then came the war, and, as you know, we Jews were in trouble. Eventually we were picked up by the Germans and sent to Auschwitz.

"I will never forget the smell of the boxcar we rode in to the concentration camp—maybe that's why I smoke so much. For days we were locked inside. People had no food, and some were suffocating for lack of air. I pushed us into a little space near the door of the car so at least we could get enough air through the cracks to survive.

"The stink from body wastes and the people, alive and dead, was unbearable. But we were, of course, in no position to alter our circumstances.

"When we finally got to the camp, the door was opened, and we were herded off like so many starving cattle.

"I was relieved. At least, I thought, we are still alive and together. But hunger was eating at our guts, and I knew we must have something to eat soon.

"After a while, I saw a cart loaded with potatoes passing nearby on the way to the kitchen. I couldn't resist. I quickly grabbed one—only one—and stuck it under my coat. Unfortunately, a guard saw me do it.

"'We don't like thieves here,' I was told. 'When we catch them, we make examples of them. Take this shovel and dig a hole over there.' I did as I was told. When I was finished, the guard shouted at me. 'Now get in!'

"I thought they were going to bury me alive. But when the dirt was up to my neck, they stopped kicking it in on me.

"We were all at Auschwitz for only one purpose: to die. But it was even more grotesque to think that these animals were going to play games with us while we did.

"I stayed there for about 24 hours with my head sticking out of the ground. Some of the guards even came over and kicked it like a soccer ball as they walked by.

"Now I was sure that I would never get out of that hole alive, and I didn't really care. I began hallucinating—I couldn't remember—I was waiting for death.

"The sight of my wife and boy snapped me out of it. At first I thought I was dreaming. But, no, there they were standing above me. Maybe, after all, I told myself, there was a small spark of humanity in this awful place.

"I was crazy to even think such a thing. A big guard came over and took our son away from my wife. He was only a year old. Another guard, who had a rifle with a long bayonet attached, was standing nearby.

"'Here, see if you can catch this,' he said. And he threw my baby into the air. The guard caught him on his bayonet.

"My wife screamed, and I struggled with all my might to free myself. She ran toward the baby—reaching out for him. They knocked her down; and as she was trying to get up, they shot her dead before my eyes.

"It was like my life ended too. I wasn't physically dead, but I wasn't alive either. The Germans, I would soon learn, had no intention of extending that favor to me. For the moment, at least, they had need of me.

"I was registered as a carpenter, and after they dug me up, I was put to work on a building detail.

"I worked like a mechanical man. Time after time I could see them again—hear the gun. My only thought was, I wish they would have shot me too."

Leo looked at Zvi intently. "Do you understand now why I can't sit still, why I smoke so much?"

Zvi had heard it all before—not the same gruesome details, perhaps, but the same story of death and despair. Unknown to his friend, he had seen it—lived it. And for years he had spent a great deal of his time going in and out among the aging people who bore the faded blue numbers.

"Now I will tell you just how much I understand what you went through. For you, all this started when you were twenty-six years old. For me, in Warsaw, the nightmare came when I was only ten. I was like a little cat surrounded by a thousand dogs—and so I lived during the war."

Now the door was open for Zvi to tell his friend how to find a new beginning. Patiently, at every opportunity, he unfolded the story of what he himself had found in the Lord.

Zvi's faithful witness and God's power ultimately brought the man, who had wished himself dead, back from his spiritual grave—he came to know Christ as his Savior. As a result, his children by a second marriage were placed in a school operated by Christians. One by one, they too became believers.

Everything changed for Leo after he came to the Lord. The blue number, of course, was still there. But it no longer told the whole story of his life. With God's help, the horror and pain it symbolized finally retreated from an everyday reality into a memory for the carpenter from Europe.

One day when they were working together, Zvi had a question for his friend. "Leo, I notice that you aren't smoking today. What has happened?"

"Believe me, Zvi, only the Lord could have taken the cigarettes away. He has. And I thank Him for doing it.

"And it's not just the cigarettes—this was only a small thing. He has brought me out from my troubles. Best of all, I know where I'm going when all this is over."

Leo's and Shulman's stories are only two of thousands that could be told by Holocaust survivors. Sadly, they are not often stories of spiritual triumph. But for Zvi and those few other Jewish believers who outlasted Hitler's Europe, the fires of suffering have created unique opportunities. While Holocaust victims will sometimes, almost grudgingly and in guarded terms, discuss their trials with a few who ask, they will reveal their stories and their hearts to those who have shared their ordeal. Thus God gives the opportunity to bring the light of the gospel—dimly at first, because for them, the night has been so dark. But for this segment of Jewry's precious remnant, the light increases until it illuminates and shows the way home.

CHAPTER TWENTY-FIVE

A MEAT-GRINDER WAR

"Howbeit on the tenth day of this seventh month is the day of atonement; there shall be a holy convocation unto you, and ye shall afflict your souls; and ye shall bring an offering made by fire unto the LORD" (Lev. 23:27, Masoretic Text).

Yom Kippur is a day for the collective "afflicting of soul" for world Jewry. As Israelis went quietly to their synagogues for early services on the Day of Atonement in October 1973, little did they realize the intensity of the offering by fire that was just hours away. Their offering would not be a lamb sacrificed unto the Lord on a great Temple altar. It would be Israel's finest and bravest young men, offered on the altar of national survival.

In the crucible of affliction that lay ahead, many a Jewish soldier would question the *haftorah* reading for Yom Kippur, which promised,

> *He will turn again; he will have compassion upon us; he will subdue our iniquities; and thou wilt cast all their sins into the depths of the sea. Thou wilt perform the truth to Jacob, and the mercy to Abraham, which thou hast sworn unto our fathers from the days of old* (Mic. 7:19–20).

To Israelis, those wonderful words of promise seemed light-years removed from anything they experienced in the Yom Kippur War.

The war was the cruelest of all confrontations between Israel and her enemies—a fact precisely in line with Egyptian planning. Egypt knew that Israeli military manpower limitations could not sustain heavy loss of life. In terms of Israeli lives lost, the previous conflicts had not been unduly expensive: Sinai Campaign (1956), 200 casualties; Six-Day War (1967), 800; War of Attrition (1968-70), 400.

The chief Arab priority, as in other wars, was the annihilation of the Jewish state. Short of that, Syria and Egypt wanted Israel to pay far more than she could afford in manpower, morale, and economic security. Egyptian war minister and commander-in-chief, General Ahmed Ismail, concluded, "Our strike should be the strongest we can deal. We must 'chop the Israelis up.'" Egypt's chief of staff, General Shazli, phrased it in forebodingly terse terms: It will be "a meat-grinder war."

The war, which disrupted the most solemn commemoration on the Jewish religious calendar, also held religious overtones for the Arabs, who reasoned that Israel would not expect an attack during the month of Ramadan (a month of Arab fasting). October 6 had further meaning to the Arabs because it corresponded, according to the Moslem calendar, with the day on which their prophet Mohammed began preparations for the battle of Badr—a battle that opened the door to the capture of Mecca and the spreading of Islam. Accordingly, the code name "Operation Badr" (lightning) was given to the operation that inexplicably caught Israel by surprise and did, indeed, put her into Shazli's "meat grinder." But, as had been the case in each of Israel's modern wars, the grinder ultimately turned to mangle the Egyptians and Syrians, and Israel turned almost certain defeat into a stunning victory.

In the process, however, Israel was badly mauled. In just 18 days, 2,522 young men lost their lives, and thousands were wounded.

Military considerations aside, the Yom Kippur War was a major turning point in the modern history of the Middle East. The decisive Six-Day War had been the high-water mark for the Jewish people, who had returned to Zion with such high hopes. The very euphoria that had emanated from their sweeping victory over the Arabs and their climactic reunification of Jerusalem actually helped set the stage for the near disaster of Yom Kippur. The Arabs saw Israeli overconfidence as a weapon in their hands. Egyptian General Ismail commented to this effect, saying, "He [Israel] is, moreover, an enemy who suffers the evils of wanton conceit." Israel learned the hard way that conceit could be lethal.

For Israelis and Arabs alike, Yom Kippur both opened and closed doors. Once again the Arabs claimed that their crushing defeat was a victory of sorts. Egyptian and Syrian achievements in the first days of war were, in their eyes, proof that Israel had lost her deterrent power. Arab leaders concluded that with larger quantities of modern weapons and more intensive preparation for the next round, they might solve the Middle East problem by military rather than diplomatic means. Their attitude opened the door for the militant Palestinian action that eventually create a quagmire in Lebanon.

Of equal or greater importance was the decision by some of Israel's allies to reassess their commitments to the Jewish state in the wake of Arab inclinations to make Arab oil a weapon of war.

For Israel, the war of 1973 squelched its grandiose feelings of military invincibility. And while Jews, out of brutal necessity, have always been realists, they began to seriously question how far their "friends" were willing to go to support Israel's right to survive. Some of her allies, such as Western Europe, Japan, and several African nations, headed for the door as soon as their oil supplies were threatened. The upshot was that Israel had to face the reality that staying alive in the Middle East meant living among enemies determined to destroy her and friends who seemed quick to sacrifice principle for petroleum and commitments for cash.

Of greater significance to the people of Israel, however, was the fact that this war took a giant bite out of the Zionist dream that Jewish ingenuity and effort could produce peace. The question that only time could answer was this: Is the Zionist dream of living in peace and security in the land of our fathers, after all, obtainable? Many were beginning to wonder.

In the final analysis, the war left a legacy of psychological and emotional residue within the population of Israel. The key question was, after all, essentially religious and Messianic. And from a completely different perspective, it brought the nation back to the fundamental elements of the Day of Atonement with which it had been involved when so rudely interrupted only days before.

Before the Arab attack, the Day of Atonement had been largely a religious ceremony—one taking place in an environment of confidence and security. Now, with its confidence shattered and its security badly shaken, some Israelis began to look beyond themselves and their nation for personal assurance of peace with God and confidence that whatever the future held for Israel, they personally could know better days. Some Israelis were finally beginning to ask the right questions; and few among them could supply the right answers. Zvi Weichert was among that few.

Zvi awakened on the morning of Yom Kippur expecting to spend a quiet day with family and friends. He was surprised to hear what sounded like a radio playing faintly in the distance. "Playing a radio on Yom Kippur?" he said to himself. "Whoever this is must be out of his mind. He could get rocks on his head in a hurry."

As he was dressing, he casually looked out into the street. More people were moving about than was normal at this hour on the Day of Atonement. Here and there, he could see cars moving slowly through the streets. That was a sure sign something was up. He reached for the radio and turned it on. Esther rushed from the bedroom when she heard sounds coming from the radio. "Zvi, Zvi," she warned. "Turn off the radio. Did you forget today is Yom Kippur? If anyone hears it, they will be over here making trouble for us."

Her voice barely penetrated. Word was out that Egypt and Syria were preparing to make war. A partial call up of reserve forces had already begun.

At 4:30 that morning, the High Command had concluded that the enemy intended to attack. The decision against a preemptive assault was made, and the limited call up of reserves began. It was much later (9:30 A.M.) when the order for total mobilization of forces was issued. (The Egyptians and Syrians launched simultaneous attacks at 2:00 in the afternoon.)

Zvi watched as neighbors were being picked up and whisked off to duty stations. A friend called to him as he was leaving his house. "Hey Zvi! You had better enjoy your holiday quick. The guys with your invitation can't be far behind." The scene was all too familiar to Zvi, Esther, and the children. Soon the men would come with the red call-up card and ask him to sign the verification that he had been officially notified. Accordingly, he would get his things together, say a quick good-by, and leave them standing in the doorway, stretching their necks to watch him until he was out of sight.

This time it turned out to be different. "You must come with us immediately," he was told. Urgency bordering on distress sounded in their voices. If war was imminent, they knew Israel was up against it, and they all had their work cut out for them. They could only hope it was not too little too late.

When Zvi and his unit reached the assembly area from which troops would be deployed, there seemed to be an air of confusion totally atypical of the IDF. The men waited for their weapons, but none were delivered. They spent the first night without arms, wondering when they would be supplied. "We're sitting ducks," one soldier complained. "As things stand now, a few Arabs could wipe out a regiment."

That fear was quieted with the arrival of supplies, and the men went to work. For Zvi and his fellow sappers, it was again wartime musical chairs. Up to the Golan to plant mines; down to the Sinai on the same urgent mission; then off to the Jordan to place a protective buffer between Israel and the Jordanians, who were mobilized as a diversion. The Arabs wanted Israel engaged on three fronts so she would be unable to concentrate totally on Syrian and Egyptian forces.

The heat was oppressive along the Jordan. Soldiers who went days without sleep were tormented by the threat of dehydration, which drained precious energy from their exhausted bodies.

Israel's plight demanded heroism and sacrifices that went far beyond those normally expected in the dreaded game men call war. Zvi came very near making the ultimate sacrifice on the Golan Heights. The Syrian onslaught there had been devastating. One hundred MIG-17 fighters led the assault across the Golan. Next, Syrian artillerymen "walked" a curtain of fire toward the squadrons of Israeli tanks assembling at their firing stations. Behind the shelling, seven hundred Syrian tanks rolled to the attack against Israel's skeleton force. If things did not change soon, the Syrians would be sipping tea in Tiberias. The Israelis worked frantically to stop them.

"We need mines here quickly," Zvi was told. The area was being swept by intense fire, but the Jewish commanders did not have the luxury of waiting for a more propitious moment. "Don't worry. We will provide cover for you."

Zvi went to work with the total concentration his occupation demanded. Only when he had managed to finish the job unscathed did he notice that he was completely alone. His unit had gone and left him to finish his work unattended. He had some words for his commanding officer when he later found his unit. "You made a promise you didn't keep," Zvi complained with obvious justification. "Exposed as I was, I could have been killed."

His officer understood his frustration. "In this fight," the man answered, "one man cannot be our first priority. Our job is to save the State of Israel." Zvi nodded his understanding of the larger situation. Every soldier had to be considered expendable;

Israel must survive. Zvi had, in fact, been well-covered, but not by Israeli soldiers. The Lord God of Israel Himself had protected His chosen vessel.

Strange events, which remain unexplained fully to this day, assured Zvi that this war had larger ramifications than man could manipulate with tanks and missiles. Both Egypt and Syria, when they appeared to have complete victory in their grasp, stopped dead in their tracks. Humanly speaking, it was a fatal blunder. With the passing of each irresolute hour, the Arabs were delivering time to their Jewish foes—time to get men to the field, time to regroup, time to formulate strategy, time to strike back, time for the Israelis to wonder why they were being granted enough time to assure their survival. "Who gave us time? And why?"

Those questions and the somber realities of war wiped the smiles from the faces of Jewish combatants. When there was time for reflection, despondent young men began to seek answers.

"Why do you think the Egyptians stopped?" a swarthy sabra asked Zvi while they were sitting together.

"I must believe two things," Zvi replied. "First, God has allowed us to be punished because we have been proud and believed that we always win because we are great fighters—so strong. Second, while God has punished us, He has also preserved us. We are, after all, a people who cannot be destroyed. And why is this? It is as it says in the Bible: 'thou shouldest be my servant; . . . I will also give thee for a light to the nations' [Isa. 49:6]. Someday it will be so. We are being preserved to do this. For too long we have believed that our success was from our own strength. I tell you that is wrong. Think seriously about all our wars. In '48, we should not have won, but we did; '67 was the same. We were so few, they were so many; but it looked so easy for us to defeat them. Now there is a good lesson for us, if we will only take it to our hearts. We almost lost—yes, we were punished—but somehow, we were saved. That 'somehow' was always God watching over us. There is no other reasonable explanation." Zvi's fellow soldier had heard some points to ponder.

Israelis who were not acquainted with the Scriptures seemed to get at least some of the message. Almost universally, the mood after the Six-Day War had been, "Look what we did in our power." In 1973 that mood was swept away. Now many of Zvi's companions were shaken to the point of asking themselves what—or who—was responsible for this miraculous victory. Now they were hard pressed to say, "We did it."

As a result, the Bible became required reading for serious inquirers. Zvi came back to his tent one day to find a sergeant on his cot reading Zvi's Bible. He made a habit of leaving it out where it could be seen, hoping someone might become curious and pick it up. Zvi had attempted to speak of the Lord with this man on several occasions before the war. Each time he had met with a stone wall. The sergeant had been very outspoken, telling Zvi he wanted nothing to do with such conversations. Now, however, provoked by what they had all been through, his sergeant friend also became an eager participant in discussions on the Bible and the sergeant was not the exception. For the first time in his experience in the Israel Defense Forces, men were asking him to get them Bibles. A supply he brought back after a brief visit home was soon gone. "When you leave the tent for work," he suggested, "leave the Bible behind so others can read while they are off duty." It was a stimulating sight for a man who had witnessed so earnestly and prayed so faithfully for God to open the eyes of his comrades to spiritual truth. Zvi took stock of the men serving with him and estimated that at least 40 percent were reading Bibles in the aftermath of the Yom Kippur War. Not all, however, were pleased by Zvi's efforts.

"Let me see one of those Bibles," demanded a bearded Orthodox soldier.

"Certainly," Zvi answered, and handed the man a copy.

As the man thumbed through the Book, a frown began to wrinkle his forehead. "It is as I thought. This Bible has the New Testament. What do you think you are doing bringing such poison here among Jews?"

Before Zvi could answer, another soldier spoke up. "This Book may bother you," he said, "but it is not a problem for me. Here, give it to me. I will read it."

In other times, the incident would have precipitated an unpleasant scene. But now, after all they had endured, there wasn't much heart for another fight.

Out of that terrible time for the country, there was blessing from the Lord. At least for a while, He had captured the attention of many in the nation. To be sure, they did not come all the way—although, thank God, some did. But it was as though Israel had taken a few halting steps toward Him. The sobering effects of Yom Kippur opened great doors of opportunity for those who really knew God to witness of His power in Messiah.

Zvi served for seventy-three days before he was finally sent home. As he started his trek toward Ir Ganim, he was, like his nation, a troubled soul—but not for the same reasons. He faced returning home to his faithful wife and four expectant children without a shekel in his pocket. How strange it seemed to experience such a sudden and dramatic change in priorities. During the war he had no time for such thoughts. Now it became his foremost consideration. Saving the nation had given way to facing the family. What would he do?

He decided to go by his place of employment and talk to them about his situation. Everyone was smiling when he walked through the door. "Zvi!" his boss called out. "We are so happy to see you. Come, sit down. Let's talk about getting back to work."

"Yes, I'm happy to see you too. It will be good to get back to our work after the job I've been doing for the past couple of months. At the moment, I have a problem. I'm going home, and I don't have any money to take to my family."

"I'm sorry to have to tell you this," his boss said in a very serious tone, "but, my friend, you do not have a problem."

Zvi answered with a bit of perplexity in his voice. "What is this, 'I don't have a problem'?"

"You see, Zvi, while you were fighting for us, we were thinking of you. Here is a check for a full two months' work. And for good measure, we have thrown in another half-month's pay as a bonus!" Before Zvi could say thanks, the man continued. "And that is not all. Over there in the corner is a big box of chocolate and presents for you to take home to the children. They have been prepared for all our men who went to the war. Take it. Go home to your family and enjoy."

Someone, a frequent traveler no doubt, once said: "Going home makes being away worth it!" Zvi may not have known the phrase, but as a man who loved his family as much as a man can, he shared a full portion of the sentiment.

"It's Abba!" Mendel shouted at the top of his lungs, and promptly fell down three steps in his effort to be the first to tackle his father. They were all on him in a flash. Ruthi and Esther covered him with kisses. Mendel and Yona hugged and wrestled, while Eli rode his shoulders like a conquering Roman. And, yes, in a way only soldiers who survive the fray can know, going home was worth it.

Zvi soaked up a full ten minutes of uninterrupted adoration. Then the children turned their focus to the mysterious package. It was time for the triumphant soldier to become Abba the Distributor and Arbitrator. He was, once again, back to being Abba, and that was how he liked it. And Esther? She didn't get much from the box. The candy went to the kids; but the check— and Zvi—went to Esther. She was quite willing to settle for that.

CHAPTER
TWENTY-SIX

THE HAPPIEST DAY

"And Moses said unto the people, Remember this day, in which ye came out from Egypt, out of the house of bondage; for by strength of hand the LORD brought you out from this place; . . . And thou shalt show thy son in that day, saying, This is done because of that which the LORD did unto me when I came forth out of Egypt" (Ex. 13:3, 8).

There is a sense of immediacy about the Passover season in Israel; and understandably so, because one hundred fifty miles to the east, beyond the sands of the Sinai, lays Egypt—the land where Israel lived out her days of debilitating slavery. Abraham's sons and daughters passed long years of suffering among the dunes and desert winds known so well to the modern descendants of those ancient pilgrims. Finally Israel had seized the dream reckoned by the promise: "And he brought us out from there, that he might bring us in, to give us the land which he swore to give unto our fathers" (Dt. 6:23). Those who live in that Promised Land lift their memorial glasses in the true spirit of Passover, feeling in their souls the ties that bind them to Israel's history and to the faithful God who performs what He promises.

Today's Israelis are an unmistakable witness to the awesome and enduring bond Jehovah has had with His people from the days of Moses and the patriarchs. For two thousand years their forefathers wandered in the desert places of a hostile world. Often enslaved by hard taskmasters, they bled out the centuries and millennia weeping to be home and crying, "Next year in Jerusalem!" As in Pharaoh's Egypt, the nations finally lost their grip; and from deep chasms of persecution, men such as Theodor Herzl raised the cry, "Let my people go!" And they came out of the nations to enter into their land. Emaciated masses from a hundred countries crossed over on their journey home. But just as it had been with Joshua, Canaan was not a place of peace and rest. "Entering in" meant struggle and war. So each year, when Israel's sons and daughters read from the Haggadah the story of their forebears' exodus from Egypt and declare "we are no more slaves, but free people," they do so reclining on Passover pillows, their weapons of war close at hand to insure that the statement remains a reality.

Hebrew Christians retain those links with biblical origins and historical actualities. But for them, there is so much more. Behind all the events depicted and remembered in Passover, there are prophecy, providence, fulfillment, and shadows of a future destiny.

Zvi's Jerusalem is where Jesus and His disciples lived out the events of the consummating Passover. Jerusalemites routinely walk over the streets and sites where it all came to pass. It is the Jerusalem where groups of believers huddled around tables in remembrance of Him, while forces dedicated to their extinction vowed to eradicate every remembrance of the Nazarene. Nearly two thousand years later, believers are still there—and in growing numbers. And while living every day amid such sacred scenes may tend to become routine, to them, they are all freshened again by the spring breezes of Passover.

The first Passover Zvi and his family spent in their new home was a rather symbolic experience. Ir Ganim was a place of crowded, narrow streets with cramped houses and the problems such situations can create. This latest move took them into an area near the section where Zvi had lived as a newcomer to the city after the War of Independence.

So many things were different from life in Ir Ganim. This place didn't have the look of just having grown up of its own accord. It was a new, planned housing area. Ample space, lots of good places for the children to play, wide streets and flower-lined walks—you could smell spring in this place.

And the view! The area offered a spectacular panorama of Jerusalem. One could look right up the convergence of the Kidron and Hinnom valleys, over Mount Zion to the stately walls of the Old City, and on to the golden Dome of the Rock. Seeing the city from that spot at night is a breathtaking experience. The children could look out a window across the shepherds fields and on down to Bethlehem. From a vantage point behind the house, the haze-covered Dead Sea rests in full view. In between, the light brown hills of the Judean wilderness run like a soft carpet down to the sea. Moab's silent mountains occupy the skyline on the other side of the Jordan River. Beyond them is Hussein's Jordan. Herod's palace-fortress, Herodium, juts up from the desert like a chopped-off, inverted ice cream cone. The man so violently opposed to the Christ who could move mountains literally built one for himself there in the desert.

As it was with Israel's initial Passover, this was a new beginning for Zvi and his family. Pesach was a fitting setting for celebrating the event.

For the kids, this was "the happiest day of the year." But it was not just one day on the Weichert calendar. Preparations began a month in advance of the festive occasion with Esther's dismantling of the premises in a relentless search for anything remotely resembling dirt. Ruthi was her first mate on the spring cleaning detail. To her childish mind, it all seemed so unnecessary, boring, and just plain wearing on a person's body. The worst thing was wondering if this was ever going to end. Although she was firm in her conviction that Passover was "the happiest day of the year," that sentiment did not cover the month that preceded it.

Pesach provided Esther with her brightest opportunity to do justice to preparing a meal. She was not particular about how many guests came through the door—the more people, the greater satisfaction in a job well done. Her children would rise up to call her blessed just remembering the aromas that floated from the kitchen. The sharp smell of horseradish (bitter herbs) was tempered by that of fresh-cut greens, fruits, cinnamon, and other pungent spices. Bubbling pots of dumplings and other sumptuous dishes combined to provide pleasantries for the nostrils. Perhaps the most appealing in tempting young appetites toward inordinate desire was the smell of *teyglekh* (honey cakes) browning in the oven.

The table itself was something to behold. The heavy, sparkling white tablecloth was graced by shining new dishes— the very best family resources could provide. Deep goblets filled with blood-red fruit of the vine cast scarlet shadows down on the linen. Platters were stacked high with food in such abundance that the children stood in wide-eyed amazement at their mother's handiwork. Passover greens—it seemed every green vegetable grown—were richly contrasted against the beautiful silver plate on which they had been carefully arranged. An ornate Passover plate held the representative shank bone, egg, bitter herbs, and charoseth. A three-tiered matzo dish held its precious ceremonial wafers with proper dignity. And, just like every year they could remember, there was the prettiest goblet of all—filled to the brim—in the exalted position of "the Cup of Elijah." Stately candles sent a flickering, soft aura to light the room and beam a sort of regal affirmation of the children's belief that this was, indeed, the happiest of days.

Zvi practiced an open-door policy at Passover. Literally anybody who wished to come was welcome—relative, friend, or stranger. Special care was taken to invite singles and people who had no family with whom they could share the celebration. Friends from the church were always present. But among the great spectacles of Pesach was to see faces at the table completely unknown to anyone in the family—they just decided to come, and so they did. It was not unusual for as many as thirty people to gather with Zvi's family. He was happy that the Lord had provided a place large enough to accommodate the crowds.

When all were seated and he began the *seder* service, Zvi always found himself looking out on a mixed multitude. Many were, of course, believers. But there were inevitably a number of unbelievers at his table as well. He was, therefore, presented with a prime opportunity to share Christ. Consequently, he had at his disposal a Passover Haggadah (a guidebook for the traditional Jewish *seder* ritual) and his Bible to expound how "Christ, our passover, is sacrificed for us" (1 Cor. 5:7).

There is probably no setting superior to Passover for bridging over to a clear and simple presentation of the gospel with Jewish people. Simply put, Christ is everywhere in the Pesach memorial. Even traditional ornaments of Judaism demonstrate this. For example, "artwork on one Jewish *seder* dish features the Messiah entering Jerusalem on a donkey, led by Elijah blowing a ram's horn, while David is playing his harp" (*Encyclopedia Judaica*). The emblems on such a dish would give a golden opportunity to present both the suffering and reigning aspects of the Messiah's ministry to us.

Zvi used tradition and truth to seize the moment for his Savior. As they moved through the ceremony, he selected statements and events consistent with biblical objectives. "Our fathers were enslaved in Egypt. On the night that the plague of the death of the firstborn came upon the Egyptians, Israel was spared because of the Passover lamb. They put the blood of the slain lamb on the doorposts and lintels of their houses, and when God saw the blood, He passed over and they were safe. Moses then led them out of Egypt, and they began life as free people."

The kids were impressed with Zvi's practical comments on slavery and freedom. "Pesach was to show how people could pass from not believing to believing—from darkness to light— from being slave to finding freedom in the Lord.

"We also learned that we should never forget who we are or where we came from. No matter where we go or what we become, we are no better than anyone else. Always treat everybody with respect, and do your best to be good to everyone."

Jewish tradition arranged the matzo (unleavened bread) in such a way as to almost, in itself, preach Christ. Three matzos are stacked in a compartmented tray. As is done by Jews the world over, Zvi selected the middle matzo, broke it, wrapped it in a napkin, and hid it. That broken matzo becomes the *afikomen* (literally: I came). At the conclusion of the *seder* meal, the wrapped half of the afikomen is unwrapped and comes forth to be broken to provide a portion for all to eat—everyone must partake. "Christ our Passover" is also "Christ our afikomen." He came to us as the second (middle) person of the triune Godhead. He was broken for us on the cross; wrapped in grave-clothes; *hidden* in a garden tomb in Jerusalem; brought forth in resurrection; and for two thousand years, He has been present-ed to Jew and Gentile alike as the One who will give eternal life to all those who will partake of Him. Many who sat at Zvi's table had never before heard that news coming out of Jewry's most revered ceremony.

His major emphasis, however, came straight from the divine Haggadah (his Bible), not Judaism's.

"We must understand that Pesach is not just a story of matzo and slavery. The lamb was the most important part of Pesach, and the lamb's blood had to be shed and applied. If it had not been so, none of them would have been saved.

"The lesson for us is this: We, everyone of us, were slaves. There is no way this kind of slave can free himself. Only God can show us the way. And he has. The Lord himself came to become the Lamb for you and for me. He shed His blood for us, so we can be free.

"Many of our Jewish people are saying at this very moment, 'We are no longer slaves, we are free.' If they are only talking about the nation, this may be true in a sense. But if they are talk-ing about the Lord, this is not true. If we receive the Lord, we are free. If we have not received the Lord, we are not free. It is as simple as that.

"My family and I, along with thousands and thousands of others, have received the Lord Jesus Christ as our Messiah and Savior. Now we can say, 'Once we were slaves, but now we are free.'

"It is possible to come together and have a wonderful time, as we are doing here tonight, to go home, and in a matter of a few hours, to forget what we have done.

"The main thing the Lord wants us to remember tonight is that we all can be free if we will receive the blood of the Lord."

Festivities continued long after the *seder* service was concluded and they had joined in singing the Hallel (Psalms 115—118). With bulging belt lines and merry hearts they sang and fellowshiped far into the night. The evening, which began around the table at 7:00, would reluctantly conclude well after midnight.

As the children settled down in their beds, they reflected on the fact that this was certainly a night unlike all others. They couldn't wait for a year to pass so they could do it all again.

CHAPTER
TWENTY-SEVEN

LET'S HEAR IT
FOR THE CARTERS

When Jimmy Carter stepped off Air Force One at Lod International Airport outside Tel Aviv on March 10, 1979, he held high hopes for making history. The American president and his top aides had already met with Egyptian President Anwar Sadat in Cairo to work on details of a peace plan that Sadat declared had placed Egypt and Israel "on the verge of an agreement."

After days of exhaustive discussions filled with soaring emotional highs and lows, the Israeli Cabinet approved the treaty by a vote of 15 to 2. On March 21 the Knesset overwhelmingly ratified the decision. On March 26 President Sadat and Israeli Prime Minister Menachem Begin signed the historic treaty at a White House ceremony in Washington, D.C., as President Carter looked on. The state of war that had existed between the two countries since Israel's birth as a modern nation was now officially over— Israel and her foremost adversary, Egypt, were at peace.

It was a fact that felt to many on both sides like a dream from which they would be rudely awakened. Sadat had, indeed, startled the world with his vow in November of 1977: "I am ready to go to the Israeli Parliament itself to discuss [peace]." Begin countered with an invitation to do just that; and on November 19

Anwar Sadat walked slowly down a line of Israeli dignitaries assembled on the tarmac at Lod, shaking hands and exchanging pleasantries. One Israeli government official later recalled: "I watched it all, but I simply could not believe it was actually happening. Anwar Sadat here in Israel, addressing the Knesset? It was incredible. I still pinch myself once in a while."

Sadat's reasons for seeking peace with Israel were both profound and pragmatic. First, he was sick of fighting wars he knew he could not win. He recognized only too well the truth of the statement: "When the Arabs go to war against Israel, Egyptians die." Since the rebirth of Israel, Egypt had been in the forefront of every significant military conflict. She had paid more, suffered more, and lost more than any other Arab nation.

Second, Sadat's nation was awash in devastating poverty that threatened the stability of his government. Sadat could no longer countenance a poverty-for-belligerence lifestyle.

Third, his relationship with the Soviet Union had so deteriorated that he expelled Russian military advisors (1972) and later renounced the Soviet-Egyptian Treaty of Friendship and Cooperation (1976). This move left Egypt with a 4-billion-dollar debt and no more credit from the U.S.S.R. Sadat's only other big-power option was the United States. A bold move to bring peace assured solid U.S. military and economic support.

And finally, the humiliation of losing the Sinai was further compounded by the futility of Arab attempts to regain it by military force. Negotiation was the only avenue that held any likelihood of regaining lost territory.

For his part, Jimmy Carter also believed that the dream of peace could come true, and he invested vast amounts of his time and energy in an all-out effort to make it a reality. Carter convened the historic Camp David negotiations on September 5, 1978, with some basic commitments, prayer, and a Bible under his arm.

"I went to Camp David with all my maps, briefing books, notes, summaries of past negotiations, and my annotated Bible, which I predicted—accurately, it turned out—would be needed in my discussions with Prime Minister Begin.

"The Judeo-Christian ethic and study of the Bible were bonds between Jews and Christians which had always been part of my life," Carter said. "I also believed very deeply that the Jews who had survived the Holocaust deserved their own nation, and that they had a right to live in peace among their neighbors. I considered this homeland for the Jews to be compatible with the teachings of the Bible, hence ordained by God. These moral and religious beliefs made my commitment to the security of Israel unshakable."

The president told U.S. Secretary of State Cyrus Vance: "We'll ask the religious leaders to set aside a week of special prayer." When it appeared the talks at Camp David would fail, "I remained alone in the little study where most of the negotiations had taken place. I moved over to the window and looked out on the Catoctin Mountains and prayed fervently for a few minutes that somehow we could find peace.

Participants and observers shared Carter's sense of history and destiny. The leaders of nations representing the world's three major religions—Judaism, Christianity, and Islam—were meeting and occasionally referencing a Bible in an attempt to secure peace for their region of the world. It was indeed a time that caught the imagination and fueled the dreams of men and women around the globe. One Egyptian official saw things in millennial terms: "I envision a day when Israeli farmers will be harvesting crops in a Negev made green by the waters of the Nile."

In the midst of all of this, the Israelis, who were at center stage during the negotiations, were buzzing with excitement and anticipation. When Carter and his entourage came to Israel, everything else in the nation became incidental to where he was, what he was doing, and what he might say.

The Weichert family was no exception. As all Israelis, they were accustomed to world leaders visiting the Promised Land. But this was different. This time their future was directly affected, and events lay in the balance that held the potential of quieting at least one major battle front. Zvi was paying close attention.

For the Carters, activities were not confined exclusively to stuffy conference rooms. Occasionally the president and his wife would leave their suite at the King David Hotel to enjoy the hospitality Israelis were eager to extend. Among the engagements on their itinerary was a performance by the Jerusalem municipal orchestra—Ruthi, Mendel, and Yona were all members.

Music had been a part of their lives almost as long as they could remember. Their association with it was born of Zvi's love for music and the fact that it was almost a social necessity.

When the children were small, Zvi and Esther had been concerned that there was no area where they could play except on neighborhood streets. This was not acceptable, and they spent a lot of time discussing their desire to be in a better place. But finances squashed any serious thoughts of moving.

Then one day, Zvi answered a knock on the door to find a pleasant young woman who turned out to be the bearer of good news. "The city," she began, "has decided to begin a program of music instruction for children in this neighborhood. Classes in flute will begin soon. If you have children you wish to enroll, I'll tell you what you need to do."

Zvi and Esther saw this as an answer to their prayers, and when enrollment opened, Zvi was among the first in line. In their turn, Ruthi, Mendel, Yona, and Eli soon livened up the household activities with sour notes and impromptu concerts.

From flute, they progressed to a variety of instruments. Ruthi demonstrated such proficiency in mandolin that she was offered an opportunity to study at the conservatory in Jerusalem. She was delighted, and Zvi could scarcely keep the buttons on his shirt when he told friends of his daughter's accomplishments. Soon Ruthi was holding classes and music clinics for her younger brothers, who were, more or less, happy to have her help them along.

When her instructor was forced to take time off for eye surgery, he asked her to teach his classes in mandolin and electric bass. At fifteen, she was accustomed to helping younger children one-on-one, but forty students at one time? That was a test, particularly since she had never played a note on the electric bass. In true Weichert fashion, Ruthi was up to the challenge. She did fine with the mandolin students, and her knowledge of theory sufficed for electric bass until a student asked for a demonstration to help him correct what he was doing wrong.

"Look at me," she said to the impressionable boy. "I will teach you a valuable lesson: Every teacher you will ever have has a method of teaching. My method for electric bass is never to touch a student's instrument. You must develop you own technique. I can tell you what to do, but you are the performer. It is up to you to learn to play to your best potential." The students were impressed with their teacher's innovative instructional style and were inspired to seek their own highest level of proficiency.

By the time the Carters came to Jerusalem, Ruthi was lead mandolinist for the municipal orchestra—a group comprised of the best students from various orchestras in the city. Her prize students, Mendel and Yona, were also part of the select aggregation.

Playing for dignitaries was nothing new to them. They had played in the Knesset and at the president's residence on special occasions. Teddy Kolleck, mayor of Jerusalem, was fond of having the orchestra perform before his guests.

The Carters were to be entertained at the president's house. The President, Prime Minister Begin, and other top dignitaries would be on hand to contribute their portion of dignity to the occasion. There could be no doubt about it: this was a big day in the life of Jerusalem's brightest young musicians.

Members of the orchestra were accorded celebrity status by friends and neighbors. It seemed everyone wanted to find out as much as they could about what was planned and what would be played. Zvi was cool and confident that his children would play up to the standard dictated by such an auspicious occasion.

Esther was not so cool. She was concerned that her children did not leave the house with a hair out of place or one button undone. It was spit and polish in the best tradition of official functions.

At the presidential residence, orchestra members sat nervously awaiting the entrance of the dignitaries. When they were assembled, the children found that they were placed very close to President Carter and the First Lady. They would have to do their very best. And so they did.

They played with skill and precision, and their notes gracefully and melodiously filled the air. The Carters and their companions obviously enjoyed the level of expertise exhibited by the young musicians. Everything was proceeding as rehearsed when, from the corner of her eye, Ruthi saw Yona's music slip from the stand and flutter to the floor. She was hit by a quick wave of light-headedness as she wondered how he would react and what this slip-up would do to the performance.

For his part, Yona was unperturbed. He was, after all, an Israeli. And faced with a fracture of the conventional, Israelis simply take matters in hand and improvise. Stooping to pick up his music was inappropriate. He had to keep on playing. So without missing a beat, he continued. There was one slight hitch, however. He was playing, yes; but Ruthi and Mendel detected an entirely different melody coming from his direction! Unfortunately, Yona had not memorized his music. But since he had an extensive repertoire of other selections to choose from, he simply switched pieces and kept playing!

If the Carters had been pleased to this point, they were now clearly delighted. When the music ended, Mrs. Carter retrieved the fallen pages and, with a smile, handed them to Yona Weichert.

Again and again, after they returned home, Ruthi and Mendel retold the story of Yona's plight and performance in the face of adversity. If Carter, Begin, and Sadat were making history for the world, Yona had made some history of his own. For as long as the Weicherts remember that day at the president's house, they will retell once more the story of Yona's ingenuity and his concert within a concert.

1982 — 1986

CHAPTER
TWENTY-EIGHT

WE KNOW
WHO YOU ARE!

Judaism's ultra-Orthodox extremists fought hard for a law they hoped would bring an end to the kind of witnessing Zvi and other believers had been doing in the land of their fathers.

They felt they had won a partial victory with passage of the "Enticement to Change of Religion" amendment in the Knesset. An outright prohibition of Christian evangelization could not be obtained under Israeli law because Jews have an inherent right to the freedom of religion.

Although Israel does not have a formal constitution, the guarantee of religious liberty was carried over from the days of the British Mandate, when the mandatory government was required "to insure complete freedom of conscience and the free exercise of all forms of worship for all."

Furthermore, in 1948 Israel signed the Universal Declaration of Human Rights adopted by the UN General Assembly. Article 18 of the Declaration states: "Everyone has the right to freedom of thought, conscience and religion: this right includes freedom to change his religion or belief, and freedom, either alone or in community with others and in public or private, to manifest his religion or belief in teaching, practice, worship or observance."

The controversial legislation, which has become popularly known as the "Anti-Missionary Law," was enacted because of the peculiar makeup of Israel's coalition government. Since the inception of statehood, no political party has been able to achieve a clear majority. Consequently, forming a government requires pulling together a coalition from diverse elements that are often at odds with one another on fundamental issues. In this delicate balance, minority religious parties, such as the militant Agudat Israel (Hasidic), exercise influence far beyond their numerical strength. These parties only occupy about 10 percent of the Knesset seats at any given time. Yet, if they withdraw their support from a coalition government, they can bring down the government and force new elections.

In this scenario, bargaining and tradeoffs are an ongoing fact of political life; and some legislation that is unpalatable to the great majority of Israelis must be swallowed in order to keep the government running. The "Anti-Missionary Law" is a case study in the strong-arm tactics of the ultra-Orthodox.

"Enticement to change of religion" is the essence of the amendment. What the law really says is, *You can't buy converts for your religion.* Giving "money, or another benefit" to a would-be convert can result in heavy fines or five years imprisonment.

This law does not specify discrimination against Christians or missionaries. Ostensibly, it covers all religious activity by all religions represented in Israel. But it was introduced by a rabbi with the stated objective of stopping missionaries who "ensnare souls" among the public at large or Israel's military personnel.

On the surface, the bill appears to carry little weight. What serious evangelical Christian would be the least bit interested in "purchasing" souls? The idea is ludicrous. But extremists see it as a valuable device in harassing, threatening, or otherwise intimidating believers who share their faith in Jesus as Savior and Messiah of the Jews. To be charged with being a "missionary," therefore, looms as a potentially serious accusation when unprincipled fanatics choose to use it against you.

Zvi saw the face of the process close up when a man and his son stopped him on the street not far from his home. "Zvi, wait a minute, I need to speak with you."

Zvi recognized the pair and stopped. "Yes. What can I do for you?"

The man hesitated before saying, "I think you know what I want to discuss with you."

"No, I'm afraid I don't know what you are getting at. You will have to explain."

The son spoke up. "Zvi, we know who you are."

"So you know who I am. I know you know who I am—my home is just up the street. What does you're knowing who I am have to do with our conversation?"

They didn't seem anxious to end the game there on the street, and Zvi didn't have time to waste. "Look," he suggested, "I don't have time to talk now. Why don't you come around to the house later. Then you can tell me what you want."

Later that evening, a knock on the door announced their readiness to reveal the purpose of their mission.

"Zvi, we know of the book that has been written about your life. We know who you are. We also know that you have connections with missionaries."

"Yes," Zvi replied, "I make no secret that a book has been written about my life. Furthermore, whom I chose to associate with is not something of which I am ashamed."

"Perhaps not. But if this information fell into the hands of certain authorities, you know you would be in for a great deal of trouble. It wouldn't be good for you or your family if they knew these things."

Now his visitors were approaching their point.

"I can do you a big favor by seeing to it that your secret stays with us and goes no further. In exchange, you can do us a little favor too. I am in some financial difficulty. If you will help me a little, we will forget what we know."

The cat was out of the bag. The men had their answer just as quickly.

"I will tell you," their host smiled, "if you want to do me a favor—not a little one, but a big one–go immediately and tell them. I can assure you that they already know who I am. Better yet, go to the newspaper and take out an advertisement. I will be glad to give you a picture to print, if you wish."

Obviously deflated, his visitors did not know quite what to say. Just then, Esther told them she had prepared the evening meal with the intention of sharing it with them. So they sat down to eat as Zvi continued the conversation.

"We don't live in fear because we are believers in Jesus. There is nothing to hide. We live openly and talk freely of our desire for other Jews to come to know their Messiah. This is my hope for both of you. Let me tell you why."

Over the next several hours, Zvi gave them a detailed witness for Christ and explained carefully why they, as Jews, had every reason to become believers too.

At one point in the conversation, the man stopped his host with a question. "But why do you take the time to tell us these things, knowing how we feel about you and what you believe?"

"My reason is very simple. First, I have already told you why, as Jews, you have every reason to become believers. But there is another reason. It is found in the book of Ezekiel in the Bible. Let me read it for you. 'When I say unto the wicked, Thou shalt surely die; and thou givest him not warning, nor speakest to warn the wicked from his wicked way, to save his life, the same wicked man shall die in his iniquity; but his blood will I require at thine hand. Yet if thou warn the wicked, and he turns not from his wickedness, nor from his wicked way, he shall die in his iniquity; but thou hast delivered thy soul' [Ezek. 3:18–19].

"If you were listening, you heard that a believer has an obligation to the Lord to try to get wicked men to turn from their sinful ways and come to Him. I feel that I also have an obligation to you—to tell you the truth and give you a chance to know the

Lord. When I have done this, I have done all I can do for you. You and the Lord must do the rest."

Those solemn words silenced his visitors and seemed to give them something to think about. When they left shortly thereafter, they did not have what they had come for. But Zvi hoped they carried away something more in their hearts than what they had brought.

Others in Israel also work hard to stop believers from sharing their faith. One group has offices in towns throughout Israel to monitor missionary activities and oppose anything it interprets as an effort to help Jewish people find Christ.

In its view, when a Jewish person becomes a follower of Jesus, a Jewish soul has been lost. For a Jew to allow this to happen to another Jew is considered a sin of tremendous magnitude. Such a belief allows this group to justify almost any action intended to prevent Jewish people from turning to Christ. If it involves violence, so be it.

As a means toward this end, a bill was offered in the Knesset in 1985 which read, in part: "Any non-Jew, be he an Israeli citizen or not, if he . . . preaches, writes, speaks, lectures, teaches or tries to influence in whatever way . . . Jews to abandon their faith and accept principles contrary to Judaism," even if they do so *"of their own free will and without being solicited* [italics added for emphasis] . . . will be expelled from the country . . . and their citizenship will be taken away. Any person born Jewish who does one of these things . . . will be sentenced to 5 years imprisonment."

The Knesset overwhelmingly rejected the legislation. However, the mere fact that it was introduced demonstrated how serious some of Zvi's countrymen were in their quest to expunge the name of Jesus from Israel.

Their anxiety was heightened by the fact that in the aftermath of the Yom Kippur War, many Israelis began seeking personal peace and fulfillment. Some sought it in a return to Orthodox Judaism. Others pursued it through the cults. Still others found it by embracing Jesus as Messiah and Lord.

This growing shift in attitude reflected a perceptible change to be found among many second-generation Israelis, and it frightened the opponents of believers in Jesus. The post-World War II immigrants to Israel had extremely deep feelings toward anything called *Christian.* The Holocaust, they were convinced, was but the crowning atrocity of two thousand years of humiliation at the hand of "the Christians." To their minds, Hitler's Germany was the theological center of Christendom, and the Nazis who had "processed" their loved ones through the gas chambers were perceived as Christians. Those in "Christian" Europe, who were not themselves actually involved in the Holocaust, nevertheless had ignored the stench of burning bodies and refused to help dying Jewry. Even Hitler, the archmaniac himself, was perceived as a Christian.

Such feelings drove Jewish immigrants to respond with the kind of hostility Zvi had witnessed toward the Swiss woman distributing Bibles in Talpiyot immediately after the War of Independence. After he had become a believer, he too had tasted the bile of their bitterness. Believers were traitors who had joined their most hated enemy—the "Christians." They had denied their own people and desecrated the memory of the six million who had perished at the hands of the Nazis. Worse than turncoats, these traitors were no longer acknowledged as Jews.

The perception was, of course, terribly inaccurate and devastatingly unfortunate. True believers were more closely associated with the names gracing the plaques along the Street of Righteous Gentiles at Yad Vashem than they were with the Nazis, whom they despised. People such as Corrie ten Boom, whose name is inscribed on one of those plaques, illustrated the Christ-like compassion of genuine believers.

And while many have labored untiringly to keep the horrors of the "Christian" Holocaust fresh in the minds of the Jewish people, second-generation Israelis have seen the other side. In their lifetime, the enemy guns have not been held by pseudo-Christians. They have been held by Muslims who have conspired to "drive the Jews into the sea." The Asaads, Nassers, Arafats, Nidals, and their infamous consorts have taken aim on Israel's innocents with the intent to kill.

Christians, on the other hand, have streamed into the Promised Land from Europe and North America by the millions for nearly four decades. Their message, almost universally, has been one of solidarity, support, and unswerving commitment to the preservation of the nation and the God-given rights of the Jewish people in their land—Eretz Yisrael. Unquestionably, the most ardent supporters of Israel in the world today are evangelical Christians who continue to say by their presence, monetary support, and encouragement, "We love you!"

In a generation that has seen nationalistic idealism reduced to a tenacious struggle for survival and a search for some semblance of purposeful meaning to life, many young Jews will no longer accept the pat answers of those who want to keep them in a religious system they feel has failed them. As a result, some are finding what they have been searching for in Jesus.

These decent, loyal Israelis, who live the secure, joyful, and fulfilling life they have found in the Lord Jesus Christ, will certainly meet opposition until the Lord comes. The good fruit that they bear for Christ, however, will never be denied the power of its appeal.

Text of "Anti-Missionary" Law
ENTICEMENT TO CHANGE OF RELIGION
Giving of 'Bonuses' as Enticement to a Change of Religion:

He who gives, or promises to give money, an equivalent (of money), or other benefit in order to entice a person to change his religion, or in order to entice a person to bring about the change of another's religion, the sentence due to him is that of five years imprisonment, or a fine of IL 50,000.

Receiving of 'Bonuses' in Exchange for a Change of Religion:

He who receives, or agrees to receive money, an equivalent (of money), or a benefit in exchange for a promise to change his religion, or to bring about the change in another's religion, the sentence due to him is that of three years imprisonment, or a fine of IL 30,000.

CHAPTER
TWENTY-NINE

THE FATHER KNOWS
OUR TROUBLE

I t was different this time—really different. Israel had launched an attack on terrorists in Lebanon. The army had been mobilized. But the men with the red cards did not come for Zvi. His duty days in the IDF had finally come to an end. It went unnoticed in the public media; but for the first time in the history of the State of Israel, the nation would go to war without Zvi Weichert.

The optimistic prospects for peace had diminished steadily despite Anwar Sadat's historic visit to Jerusalem in 1979. That trip and the Camp David Peace Accords between Egypt and Israel had cost Sadat his life. Militant Arab fanatics assassinated him.

But the most convenient and frequent object of terrorist wrath was northern Israel. Terrorism became so severe it precipitated Israel's invasion of Lebanon. Although most agreed the invasion was necessary, it was distasteful business. Before it was over, Lebanon would breed internal dissent that would accentuate factional disputes already present inside Israel.

Internal strife fanned by frustration grew progressively more pronounced and sometimes resulted in uncharacteristic violence by a small segment of Jews against Arabs and, in some cases, against other Jews.

As these problems buffeted the nation, tensions between religious and nonreligious Israelis increased steadily. Secular and semireligious Jews grew increasingly fed up with the proliferation of picayune regulations imposed by a relatively small segment of ultra-Orthodox people. Their representatives in the Knesset perpetually held the government hostage, threatening to destroy the ruling coalition by walking out unless they got their way. Such intimidation often worked but generated even more unrest and dissension between the two communities.

Then there were the Palestinian uprisings on the West Bank and in Gaza, orchestrated by Arab terrorist Yassir Arafat and his cohorts. These actions were aimed at destroying Israel's repeated attempts to reach a peace settlement with legitimate Arab leaders. Israel reacted resolutely, restrained the violence, and restored order in the territories. But the predictable condemnation by the UN plus American criticism of Israel's handling of the matter compounded the tiny nation's problems and further eroded morale among some segments of the population.

Inside Israel, there were those who likened these developments to the internal situation just before the Roman conquest of Jerusalem in A.D. 70, when party was pitted against party, and infighting destroyed national unity.

Now there was trouble in Lebanon, and it became necessary for the IDF to launch an attack on terrorist bases there. This time around, however, Zvi sat with Esther, listened to field reports on the radio, and scanned the daily papers to keep abreast of developments to the north. It was not as though his presence would not be felt, however. Zvi had watched as his three sons, each in a different branch of the service, left home to fill vital roles in the ongoing struggle to keep Israel alive and free. It was not Zvi on the battlefield this time; it was his sons.

Zvi had been marching off to war all his adult life. He knew only too well what it was like to linger for a long moment at the door, pack an automatic weapon on his back, and wonder how it would be for them while he was gone. Each time, their faces had told him what they were thinking: "Will we ever see him alive again?" It was a tough way for him to leave, and it was tough for them who were left behind. Now *he* was being left behind. As it came time for them to go, he embraced each of his boys and watched them leave for duty. He didn't say it, but he was experiencing the same quiet distress his departures had caused the family for so many years. It was, he thought, so much more difficult to stay than to go. If only they could be children again, and he could go for them all. He would feel much better about the whole affair.

When they had all gone and the house was quiet, Zvi saw a side of Esther she had never allowed him to see. She wouldn't sit down for long periods of time but paced around the room, giving unneeded attention to insignificant items. "Zvi," she said finally with a worried sigh, "what will we do if they don't come back? They seem like just children. What do they know of fighting and war?" To Esther, they were just children. But then, they would always be children to her—mothers are that way.

"Esther, sit down," Zvi said. "I understand how you feel. They are children to me too. But you must remember, they are not really children; they are men—men who are well trained for their jobs in the service. They will know what to do. You mustn't worry.

"Besides, hasn't the Lord always been faithful in answering our prayers? You know we have always trusted them to Him, and He hasn't failed us. He won't fail us now." So, as they would do many times through each long day, both silently and together in the living room every evening, Zvi and Esther prayed that the Lord would hedge the boys about with His safety and bring them home soon.

The Lord always provided the rest and assurance they sought. But still, Zvi was a father, and he didn't find much to smile about while his boys were at the front. He knew war too well. And he found his thoughts, at odd times, stealing away to the north. "I wonder where Yona and Eli are. What is Mendel doing about now?" In reality, he was a father doing a father's job: being concerned for the welfare of his children. Before many days had passed, Zvi had the opportunity to share that lesson with some people who needed it badly.

The man seemed deeply depressed when Zvi noticed him waiting for the bus. As was his custom, Zvi probed gently to see if he could offer some assistance. "Are things all right for you?" he asked.

"You ask such a question of a man who has so much trouble? No, I will tell you, things are not all right for me."

"What is wrong?"

"We are at war, and my only son is in Lebanon—I don't know where. God only knows if he is safe and if we will see him again. At times, it is almost more than I can bear.

"And, as if I didn't have enough to worry about with my boy, my wife is about to drive me crazy. She is crying day and night and asks questions I cannot answer. We end up shouting at each other almost every day. Sometimes I wonder if she will keep her sanity."

"Tell me," Zvi asked, "what does your son do in the army?"

"He drives a truck."

"Well, that should help to ease your mind. Truck driving is a very good job. There is danger, of course, but not like some other things soldiers have to do."

"I've thought of that, and I'm glad his work is not more dangerous. But that doesn't seem to help much."

"Look, my friend, before you is a man who is also a father. I know how you feel. I have not one son in the army, but three. They are all away because of the war. It is bad, yes; but my wife and I have committed them to the Lord, and we have peace because they are in God's hand."

"It might be too much to ask," the man said haltingly, "but would you have time to come to my house and talk with me and my wife?"

"I will make the time. As a matter of fact, I can go with you now, if you wish."

When they arrived at the man's home, Zvi waited in the living room while the man went to tell his wife they had company. "I have brought a friend home with me. Come out and meet him. We will have some coffee and talk." He spoke in muffled tones; she did not.

The woman was obviously agitated. "You know I am in no condition to have company!" she shouted. "Send him away!"

Zvi was ready to leave immediately—with or without the opportunity to excuse himself. But the man was talking again, this time rather insistently. "But you don't understand. This man has three sons in the war. I want him to talk to us about Moshe."

"Oh," she said. "You go put on some water. I'll be right out."

The woman talked in quick bursts as they sipped coffee and shared cake together. "I understand you have three sons in the war. I wish you would tell me your secret for staying so calm about it all," she concluded.

"You are a mother. I can understand how you feel. Quite naturally, you are troubled over your Moshe's safety. What you need is a friend to whom you can take your trouble, one who will take it as his own.

"I have such a friend. He is the Lord. I take my boys and my troubles to Him, and He gives me peace.

"I have been thinking much about this since the war. I, like your husband, am a father. But I am a father who has seen more than his share of war. When I think of my boys, I know what they are going through—I have been there before them. So they have a father who knows their troubles. In a better way, I have a Father—the Lord—who knows my troubles. And He can go where we cannot, to do for our children what no human being, not even a father or mother, can do.

"You need to learn this lesson: The Father knows our trouble."

"I've never heard it put quite that way," she said quietly. "That's a very interesting concept."

"I received it from the Bible," Zvi explained. "From Psalm 27, I learned that the Lord wanted to be my Father. 'When my father and my mother forsake me, then the LORD will take me up' [v. 10].

"When I discovered this, I found also that I could ask Him, 'Teach me thy way, O LORD, and lead me in a plain path' [Ps. 27:11]. These words caused me to want to know the Lord as my Father. You can know Him as your Father too."

For over an hour, his new friends listened as he shared a witness with them. Thereafter, Moshe and his parents became a part of Zvi and Esther's prayer concern when they prayed for those touched by the war. Later Zvi learned that the boy did return home safely. He could only hope and continue to pray that the family would turn in faith to the One who wanted to be a Father to them all.

CHAPTER
THIRTY

OPERATION PEACE
FOR GALILEE

Z vi's words to the man and woman who were anguished over their only son in Lebanon could have been directed to the entire nation. Israel did, indeed, need "the Father who knows our troubles."

The Yom Kippur War of 1973 contributed to the turmoil that eventually matured into the acute trauma known as Lebanon. It began with a series of savage incidents, then afflicted Israel's northern settlements and eventually spread like a flame throughout the entire nation. Lebanon became a quagmire that drained Israeli lifeblood, divided the nation, and cast shadows reminiscent of those that fell on the United States after Vietnam.

By the time the Israel Defense Forces penetrated southern Lebanon on the morning of June 6, 1982, Lebanon no longer existed as a viable, national entity. It had been torn to shreds by internal and external Arab factions who, for years, had systematically slaughtered one another in attempts to gain control of the country. By June 1982, the Palestine Liberation Organization (PLO) had achieved its goal of creating a state within a state; and PLO chairman, Yassir Arafat, and his terrorist "fighters" were doing pretty much as they pleased—a situation that proved the last straw in the destabilization of Lebanon. PLO occupation of southern Lebanon posed a threat to northern Israel that could not be ignored.

By virtue of its origin and makeup, Lebanon was a country that invited the internal strife and the bloodletting that would eventually ravage the population. The country was created by the French in 1920 during their mandatory supervision of the region. Syria, however, welcomed any opportunity to intervene as a "peacemaker" when squabbles broke out. At one time or another, Syria has sided with virtually every faction in Lebanon and has sided with the PLO several times. Syria's goal clearly was to annex Lebanon or at least install a permanent puppet government.

France granted independence to Lebanon in 1943, and a government was formed that reflected the delicate balance between the various factions. Based on the last national census taken in 1936, Maronite Christians (Catholic) had the numerical advantage over Moslem and Druze nationals. Thus the president was always a Christian, while the prime minister was chosen from the Moslem population. Other appointments were made on the basis of apportioned representation from other religious and ethnic groups. This system created a delicate and predictably suspicious working arrangement among members of the governing body.

By 1970 Moslems felt they had surpassed the Christians in number and began agitating for change. Functionally, Lebanon consisted of family fiefdoms that controlled various areas of the nation. Gemayels, Chamouns, and Franjiehs dominated the Christians; Jumblatts were chief among the Druze; Moslems (Sunni and Shiite) were segmented by a variety of family and sectarian groups. As matters deteriorated within the country, these elements turned their respective areas into armed camps.

Further complications came with the founding of the PLO. Egyptian President Nasser pressured Lebanon into granting it areas of operation beyond government control. The PLO was also granted extraterritorial rights, predominately in the refugee camps in the south. Finally, the PLO gained what amounted to a free hand to conduct operations against Israel from Lebanon.

After King Hussein deposed and expelled the PLO from Jordan in 1970—an action remembered as "Black September"—150,000 Palestinians left Jordan and moved to Lebanon by way of

Syria. About 50,000 of them were hard-core terrorists who settled in the Beruit area. Another 100,000 moved into the southern sector around Tyre and Sidon and joined another 200,000 already in the region. This placed nearly one-half million Palestinians in Lebanon, with the military arm operating out of Beruit.

A final chapter opened with the signing of the Melkart Agreement in 1973. This accord extended the PLO influence beyond what had already been granted in the Cairo Agreement and marked the formal beginning of the PLO's "mini-state."

By 1975 more than twenty major private armies were operating within Lebanon. Each had its loyalties, territorial and governmental aspirations, and each saw the destiny of Lebanon as resting on the shoulders of its particular leader. The situation was truly a prescription for disaster.

Behind it all lurked the Soviet Union and her imperialistic designs to annex territory and to humiliate and subjugate Israel. She was investing millions upon millions of dollars in weapons of war to assist her clients, mainly the PLO and Syria, in furthering her own objectives.

By the time the Israelis intervened, the morass of spheres of influence looked like this:

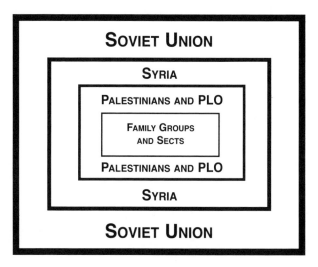

From 1970 through 1978, the PLO carried out terrorist attacks in Israel from its bases in Lebanon. Russian-made Katyusha rockets, artillery, and mortar shells rained down on the settlements. The terrorists almost never directed their assaults against military targets or personnel. Almost without exception, they chose helpless civilians. Elderly people and children seemed to be their favorite victims. An example is the 1974 attack in Ma'alot. Twenty-four civilians, mostly children, were killed. Many more were wounded in the encounter.

Such cowardly tactics are standard procedure for the terrorists whom the international press insists on calling "fighters." They turn towns and cities into vast armories of weapons, complemented by antiaircraft and artillery batteries. Storage depots, gun emplacements, and staff operational offices are routinely placed in schoolyards, among apartment houses in residential areas, and next to churches and hospitals.

In the spring of 1978, Israelis witnessed another horror when the PLO commandeered a bus on the coastal highway near the town of Zichron Ya'acov. The terrorists forced the driver to proceed to Tel Aviv where, when confronted by the military, they used hand grenades and guns to slaughter the passengers.

According to one report, between 1968 and 1982 PLO terrorists were responsible for more than 1,000 civilian deaths worldwide. Another 4,250 were wounded as a result of PLO attacks.

For more than a decade, the Jewish people in Israel led a frustrating and dangerous existence. Residents in Nahariya, Kiryat Shemona, and other northern towns lived in constant dread of whistling shells, thudding mortars, and exploding rockets. Most difficult of all was the plight of the children. The lived almost entirely in the shelters, out of harm's way. Although they did not understand the issues behind the constant bombardment, they came to know the sounds of war very well and suffered the predictable consequences.

From the end of the Yom Kippur War in 1973 until 1982, the PLO shelled northern Israeli settlements 1,548 times. The IDF answered fire with fire, but with southern Lebanon as a relatively secure base of operations, the PLO simply rolled with the punches and quickly returned to spread more death and destruction.

In March 1978, Israel decided to do more than just shoot back or chase isolated bands of terrorists. Operation Litani sent substantial numbers of Israeli troops across the border on a mission designed to sweep southern Lebanon clean of terrorists to a point on the south bank of the Litani River.

Yassir Arafat's civilian killers had no heart for facing Israeli regulars, and the vast majority beat a hasty retreat to the north. For three months, Israeli troops destroyed bunkers and removed PLO arms caches and ammunition dumps. Israel was determined to disable the PLO's ability to continue striking northern Israel from any point south of the river.

After three months, however, pressure and promises once again circumvented Israel's best interests. The United States joined the United Nations in pressing Israel to withdraw her troops. The UN agreed to provide a United Nations Interim Force (UNIFIL) to keep the peace between the Litani River and Israel's northern border.

Within two months of the arrival of UNIFIL forces in the area, the PLO decided to test their mettle. In a fight near the city of Tyre, the PLO killed three UNIFIL soldiers and wounded ten others. Clearly, the PLO was prepared to kill in order to pursue Israel on the other side of the fence. The UN and UNIFIL troops, however, were not prepared to be shot while standing in the way of Arafat's terrorists.

Within a year, Arafat had repositioned upward of 1,000 men within the UNIFIL zone, most of them in an area known as the Iron Triangle. While UN troops looked the other way, the PLO continued its activities against the Jews. In the event UN troops captured PLO personnel, they would escort them to PLO headquarters in Tyre and turn them over to their own people who, in turn, sent them out the back door so they could return to their terrorist activities. From June to December 1980, sixty-nine attacks against Israel were carried out from within the territory "secured" by UNIFIL.

To add insult to injury, when frustrated IDF forces followed infiltrators back across the border, the PLO terrorists would simply surrender to UN forces. The peacekeepers would protect them from their Israeli pursuers and take them to Tyre, where the front-door back-door routine would start all over again.

During UNIFIL's tenure in the "clean zone," it made no appreciable attempt to keep the PLO from restocking its military supply depots within the guaranteed area.

PLO gunners had returned to their old operational intensity by the spring of 1981. From May to July, 1,230 rockets and artillery shells had swooped into 26 Israeli towns. By June of 1982, the PLO had initiated 290 more attacks against Israel.

PLO intentions for southern Lebanon, however, went beyond indiscriminate shelling and harassment of the population. South Lebanon was to be a staging area for the eventual invasion and annihilation of the State of Israel. A captured PLO document states the first phase objectives: "The Supreme Military Command decided to concentrate on the *destruction* [italics added] . . . of Kiryat Shemona, Metulla, Dan, Shaar Yeshuv and its surroundings." The document went on to outline objectives on various "fronts" and closed with the words: "Revolution till victory"—the occupation of Israel.

By this time, Ariel Sharon was in charge at the defense ministry; and Sharon was ready to orchestrate an intrusion into Lebanon. Although Israel's initial plan was to push the PLO back to a point twenty-five miles from the northern border and seek a peace treaty with Lebanon, it was widely believed that Sharon had his own agenda, which ultimately was designed to accomplish two worthy objectives: (1) destroy the PLO as a fighting force; and (2) wreck Arafat and the PLO as viable political operatives.

Impetus for the invasion accelerated when terrorists (one of whom turned out to be a Syrian intelligence officer) murdered Shlomo Argov, the Israeli ambassador in London. Following

Israeli retaliatory raids the next day, PLO gunners opened a 24-hour barrage against Jewish settlements.

At 11 A.M. on June 6, 1982, the Israel Defense Forces crossed into Lebanon. "Operation Peace for Galilee" was underway.

Once inside Lebanon, the IDF found that the PLO was not its only problem. Its old foe, Syria, jumped into the fray. Consequently, the Israelis had to deal with the Syrians while rooting out the terrorists.

Predictably, the PLO terrorists did not stand to fight, and they fought poorly when they did. As Israeli forces rolled them up before their advance, PLO contingents moved north, seeking sanctuary within the city limits of Beruit. The Syrians were much better at the business of war and generally fought well in spite of the hammering they took from the IDF.

The end of June found Beruit cordoned off by Israeli troops and preparations in progress to put the city under siege. For ten grueling weeks the siege continued, with Arafat and his men bottled up in the city. PLO positions were honeycombed into residential areas, making an all-out Israeli assault too costly from the standpoint of civilian casualties.

In the end, with the world's doves crying for Israel to spare the wolves, Arafat and his PLO comrades were escorted out of the city and ferried to Arab host nations. There they licked their wounds and prepared to begin the whole dreadful cycle once again.

The war in Lebanon and subsequent occupation was a costly affair for Israel. Lebanon was an unpopular war with many Israelis. For the first time in the nation's history, some young men refused army service. Another obvious factor was the rising doubt over just how much could be accomplished by direct military intervention. Much like the Yom Kippur conflict, Lebanon was another drain on the spirit and emotions of the Jewish people.

Sharon's objectives for the PLO were partially accomplished. Arafat's military arm had been mangled, and Israel would have a considerable period of respite before the terrorist could begin to reassemble enough equipment to start over. Politically, however, objectives for victory over Arafat were not so clear-cut. He had been temporarily humbled and humiliated. He was down but far from comatose. Unfortunately, Israel would hear from him again.

The conflict clarified Syria's intentions. Regardless of what they had agreed to in the cease-fire arrangements, the Syrians had no agenda for getting out of Lebanon. Their presence in the Bekaa Valley amounted to functional annexation.

Militarily, Syria had suffered yet another whipping at the hand of the Israelis. Troop losses, dead and wounded, numbered 4,200. Three hundred thirty-four Russian-built T-62's, T-54's and T-72's, along with 140 personnel carriers, were sent to the scrapheap by the IDF. In the sky, 96 planes and helicopters were lost. Add to those figures the SAM batteries destroyed or captured (19), and they provided an impressive illustration of fact: The Syrians were far from ready to take on the army of Israel.

The big loser in the Lebanese war, however, was a "nonparticipant." Russia emerged in the aftermath of the struggle with egg on its face and questions galore for itself and a watching world. Three areas of evidence surfaced:

Russia had been humiliated. Syria's heavy losses all involved equipment requisitioned from the Russian arsenal. American and Israeli-made tanks proved clearly superior to those fielded by Syria and their Russian sponsors. (Israel's Merkava performed extremely well.) Russian-made aircraft trailed plumes of smoke into the ground with alarming regularity. The Russian "missile canopy," which had so devastated the Israeli air force during the Yom Kippur War, was almost totally nullified by Israeli technology and was of no consequence whatever during the fighting. Taking into account the disparities in the relative quality of personnel manning the equipment, the Soviet Union and her allies were given pause to wonder about the machines their men were pointing at the West.

Russia was shown to be an unreliable "friend." It was no secret that Yassir Arafat was a client of the Soviet Union. All the warm bear hugs he received in Moscow, however, turned to ice when he screamed for help as a virtual hostage in Beruit. Arafat's calls to the North found the phone off the hook in the Kremlin. That fact was not lost on Russia's other allies. For years the United States had been gleefully ridiculed as a friend not to be trusted or relied upon in a crunch. Now the "crunch" was squeezing other feet, and Soviet "friends" were discovering that it didn't feel very good. Only the international press corps, inexplicably slow to point such things out to the rest of the world, helped soften the blow.

Russian intentions were exposed. The Soviets, prime arms merchant in the Middle East, poured arms and equipment into the PLO camp in astonishing quantities. Their reasons for doing so most certainly went beyond picking up petro-dollars from Arab arms buyers.

Even seasoned military analysts were shocked at the extent of what was uncovered in Lebanon. Supplies stashed in southern Lebanon were estimated to be enough to fully equip an army of at least 100,000 troops; yet PLO strength was no more than 15,000 to 20,000.

Enormous military supply depots were discovered, concealed in air-conditioned, subterranean vaults dug into the sides of hills. The machine used to construct the vaults was a Russian-made digger, larger than anyone in the West had ever seen. One of these tunnels east of Sidon was as long as two football fields. The shaft was crammed to the doors with grenades, rockets, artillery shells, missiles, explosives, and small-arms ammunition. A single complex captured by the Israelis contained advanced Russian equipment worth 250 million dollars.

The big questions were, Why was all of the equipment there, and for whom was it intended?

There are two explanations: (1) It was placed there awaiting the advance of Arab armies on their way to invade northern Israel; or (2) it was prepositioned for Russians, in the event they opted to send a contingency for an invasion of their own. Some

Israeli experts favored the second option. Students of Bible prophecy also come down on that side of the scale. They know that the time will come when Russia will exercise the invasion option. Whether the plan was so imminent, one can only guess. Israel's intervention set that program back.

An indisputable certainty is that the Communists to the north will not rest until they find an opportunity to rectify the indignities they suffered in Lebanon.

The point closer to home is this: The wider ramifications of the war in Lebanon not only touched Zvi and his family in the immediate context of their experience but also will affect his descendants, their nation, and our world until the Lord comes.

CHAPTER
THIRTY-ONE

'TELL MY MOTHER
AND FATHER I
LOVE THEM'

Uncommon valor is a common trait among those who serve in the Israel Defense Forces. Volumes written about the military campaigns that Israelis have fought since the inception of statehood are filled with the kind of heroics, courage, and tactical ingenuity that one reads from the pages of the Old Testament.

In the brilliant array of military luminaries that Israel has depended on for its survival, none stand taller than those wearing paratroop ensignias. Jerusalem was reunited by Mordecai Gur's 55th. In far-off Africa, Uganda's tyrannical dictator, Idi Amin, and an astonished world witnessed their exploits at a place called Entebbe. Israel's "men from the sky" have paid a high price for their notoriety. Discipline, personal sacrifice, and blood mark the way for those selected to serve among the chosen few. Those tough and tenacious young men are sterling examples of the best Israel has to offer.

Since childhood, when Eli Weichert knew he would one day serve in Israel's armed forces, he dreamed of being a member of that elite corps. And if one were to write a resumé for the quintessential Israeli paratrooper, it couldn't have have been more perfect than Eli's.

Very early on, he began to practice skills in how to defend the weak against hostile aggressors. Eli was four or five when he came home one day after being roughed up by the neighborhood's little toughs. Uncle Nathan, who had dropped in for the afternoon, surveyed the damage then offered some instruction in the art of self-defense.

"Eli, listen to your Uncle Nathan. Every place you will ever go you will meet people who think they are tough and will want to push you around. You must learn to defend yourself—no one else can do it for you. When the bullies start to come after you, give them a good, hard whack. Remember two things: Hit them first and hit them hard!"

Nathan's intent student listened carefully to his uncle's words then asked to be excused and left the house to rejoin the boys outside. About fifteen minutes later, he was back inside. Eli sat quietly for the short interval before Zvi heard someone pounding on the door. It opened on a hostile mother holding the hand of a youngster who looked somewhat the worse for wear.

"What can I do for you?" Zvi inquired diplomatically.

"You can bring that little monster out here. I have a score to settle with him."

Zvi felt that, under the circumstances, a little cool-down time was preferable to delivering his youngest son into her hand. "Just what seems to be the trouble?" he asked.

"Your boy picked a fight with my son. He didn't do anything, just said something—it was nothing—and your boy hauled off and hit him in the face. What kind of children are you raising, anyway?"

Well, he was rearing good students, that's what he was doing. Eli had decided that the quickest way to test Uncle Nathan's lesson was to put it into practice. So, at the first word of provocation, he swung into action. While Zvi attempted to take care of matters at the door, Uncle Nathan began lesson two: recognition of true belligerent intent.

That was Eli, unvarnished lover of action. He was the kid in family photos who always had someone assigned to his hands, keeping the pincers closed.

He was somewhat older when he began attending church camps and retreats. Eli always enjoyed them for the people, activities, and prizes awarded for memory work, participation, punctuality, and the like. Lots of points meant lots of markers. And markers bought goodies at the camp canteen. His one problem was always conduct. The powers that be insisted on deducting points for life's little infractions. Working at point preservation became a major project for Eli during camping season.

He did pay attention to what was going on during worship services and, from his earliest memories, counted himself a believer in the Lord. He attended church, had believers as parents, and lived a clean life. Although Eli was rambunctious and loved fun, he did not get involved in "black fun," as many of his acquaintances did.

But it wasn't just worship services and Bible teachers who impacted his life; Eli witnessed everyday what it meant to be a true believer. Esther was a model of disciplined Christian motherhood. She was always aware of the dangers of the "street" and worked at providing the constructive alternatives necessary in keeping children straight. Their after-school regimen was predictable: called in at 5 P.M.; washed and presentable by 5:30; supper by 6:00; then studies, followed by "off to bed" and "lights out."

Eli saw Christ in his father and learned to adore him and follow after him. Zvi faithfully led the family in Bible reading and devotions at home. But for Eli, it wasn't only what Zvi said. It was what you learned and felt when you were with him. As Mendel had, Eli watched him talking to friends and army buddies who stopped them on the street. He admired the easy way he talked to people in the shops, asking and answering questions.

As time passed, Eli began to realize that it wasn't enough to be the son of a believing mother and father. He had lived a good life, but good living, he knew, did not wash away his sins. "Eli," he told himself one day, "you need to ask the Lord to come into your life." That conversation with himself bore eternal fruit when he sat with a friend and talked about his feelings. He already knew the right questions—and the right answers. He had known them for a long time. Now he wanted to do the right thing. As they prayed together, Eli received the Lord as His Savior and Messiah. He was seventeen. In one more year, he would enter the service.

Eli applied to become a paratrooper. For him, it was not just a matter of proving he was one rugged sabra who could make it with the toughest guys in the army. He worked hard to make the grade because he was an Israeli who loved his country with all of his heart and was willing to give everything to her and for her if necessary. But beyond this, he was a believer and viewed serving his country as a service for his Lord. And he had something to prove. Eli had seen the ultra-Orthodox hide behind their black coats to stay out of the service. Others had used their religion to became "jobniks" in the army, serving in canteens without becoming fighters.

He wanted to show them all that he was a believer, yes. And because he was a believer, he would serve the Lord in the hardest places required. Eli wanted to show his countrymen that believers in Jesus were ready to fight and willing to die for love of their country, if called on to do so.

Eli and his companions were excited as the time of their official swearing-in approached.

As with all branches of the service, the place for these ceremonies was carefully chosen to reflect the historic implications of being a defender of the State of Israel. Eli took his oath before the Western Wall in the Old City of Jerusalem. The soldiers assembled at the highest point from which the city can be entered (the gates of Jerusalem). From there they marched in quickstep toward the walls of Old Jerusalem. Once there, the route of march took them entirely around the stately walls. The place chosen for their entrance was the Lion's Gate. History leaped into the present as the young warriors passed through the gate where Gur's 55th Brigade had made its famous charge to seize the highest ground Israel could ever capture. On they went through the narrow streets until, as their paratrooper predecessors, they caught a glimpse of the ancient Wailing Wall—

the place where Jewish tears, hopes, and fears had been poured out before Jehovah for millennia.

Chills rippled along the spines of these young men and lumps came into their throats as their commander began to swear allegiance, on their behalf, to the State of Israel. "I swear to the flag of Israel to be worthy to serve her and carry out faithfully all my orders in the name of my country. . ."

All eyes were riveted on the blue and white ensign of Israel floating gently on the evening breeze. When he had finished, at a given signal, the soldiers raised their voices to shout in unison a personal pledge: "I swear!" The words echoed above the ancient walls of Old Jerusalem and seemed to linger for a moment, as if assuring Israel's brothers and sisters that their nation's safety was in good hands.

Eli enjoyed nearly everything about life as a paratrooper. He was a young man tailor-made for soldiering, right down to looking the part. The tallest of Zvi's boys, with a thick shock of black hair, Eli's rugged, tanned face and muscular body perfectly complemented the olive uniform and dark red beret he wore. He enjoyed learning military procedures, jumping out of planes, the close-knit relationships that developed among comrades dependent on one another for their very lives, and the comic relief that sometimes surfaced in scary situations.

Everybody got a big laugh over the time two brothers stood in the door of a troop transport during a training drop. Jump procedure called for a slap on the shoulder and a sharp command to jump. In a gesture of assurance to his apprehensive brother, the other brother reached up, put a hand on the other boy's back, and started to say "Everything will be okay." Before he could get a word out, the boy, much to the jump instructor's surprise, had leaped from the plane and was floating to the ground below. It would be some time before he would be allowed to forget his solo descent.

As a believer in Christ, it came naturally to Eli to do what he had experienced while growing up at home. Sharing the Lord with others was first a matter of simply living a Christian life before them. His comrades were well aware that he was a believer in Jesus as Messiah and that it made a difference—it was a lifestyle. When breaks from duty came and they were heading for questionable activities in town, they knew before they asked that Eli would decline their invitations to join them. He read his Bible faithfully; and often friends would come to him with questions about religion and the things of the Lord. He was amused when a buddy came to his bunk one day as he was reading. "Eli, two years we have been together here in the army, and you haven't finished your book yet. You must be a very slow reader!"

Lebanon was, of course, inevitable for all of them. There, all of the comradery, training, and pledges to serve faithfully by life or death, would be put to the ultimate test—combat. Eli came to know what his father had learned nearly forty years earlier in the wheat fields of Latrun. Looking into the ashen faces of soldiers much too young to die was an experience worlds away from training jumps and firing ranges. And when they are your friends, there is still another, more terrible dimension.

Eli's unit was bedded down close to the border between Israel and Lebanon. The men had been asleep for some time when gunfire shook them rudely from their slumber. "Get down! Get down!" someone was shouting in the confusion.

More shooting erupted before several helicopters swept over the scene dropping flares.

A soldier came into the tent and relayed as much as he himself knew at that point. "A dinghy has been spotted coming ashore [from the Mediterranean]; there are terrorists on the beach."

Soon the unit received orders to join the search for at least four terrorists. It was urgent they be found and dealt with before they could scatter into the darkness.

As the paratroopers were forming up for a sweep through the fields approaching the beach, Eli's officer gave instructions. "Albert, you stay here and watch the jeeps. When Yitzhak comes, send him to us."

Albert, like his friend Eli, wanted to be where the action was. Tonight the action was in combing the fields for terrorists. Albert didn't want to miss out. When Yitzhak came by, Albert insisted Yitzhak stand by the jeeps while he went on with the group.

Darkness enveloped them as they felt their way over the rocky terrain. They were deployed in the manner prescribed for searches of this kind under these conditions.

They didn't see the terrorist when he jumped up to fire a burst from his automatic weapon. The fire tore through the searchers, and several of them went down. Having betrayed their position, the terrorists were dealt with quickly. Then the Israelis concentrated on tending to wounded comrades. Eli found that Albert had been shot.

Just before he died, Albert labored for a few last breaths as his friends gathered about him. "Tell my mother and father I love them," he said. With those few words, he was gone.

It was a scene that has been reenacted in one place or another for millennia, and it is one that will certainly reemerge again and again until the Lord returns to set things right. This time it was, perhaps, made more poignant by the young soldier's parting words—one more vivid reminder of the ugly monster of war.

For Eli, it was a reaffirmation of two things. He understood more than ever the absolute necessity to fight for the survival of his beloved nation. Albert did not waste his life. He gave it to keep Israel out of the hands of ruthless killers bent on its destruction. His was the highest investment one could make for the greater good of his country.

But Eli was also sure of something else. He was certain of the rightness of having become a believer. He was making an investment that would not be terminated when he left this earth. He was serving his country, Israel, today. He will serve in that "better country" for eternity—the one his father Abraham had looked for so long ago.

"For he looked for a city which hath foundations, whose builder and maker is God" (Heb. 11:10).

CHAPTER
THIRTY-TWO

IT'S A PITY
HE'S NOT A JEW

Yona enjoyed his childhood. He was good-looking, smart, loved both play and study, and liked to keep an eye on the girls. He was aware that some people in the neighborhood took issue with the fact that he and his family were believers. For example, one day he was abruptly awakened at 6:00 in the morning by men who had come to argue loudly with his father about the Weicherts' faith in the Messiah. It was a scary experience for a small boy. But boys are boys, and no matter what parents may tell their children about being wary of the "Christian," when the Christian knows how to handle a football or basketball, he becomes a valuable commodity on the playing field.

At home, he felt a comfortable security with parents who showed him a full measure of love and consistently exhibited a lifestyle that helped shape his developing character and values. He deeply admired his mother, who could keep things together in such an orderly fashion. She was organized and predictable. Yona liked that—it was his style too. You never wondered what Esther would say or do in a given situation. Each day she was off to the market on a schedule precise enough to be the envy of the most time-conscious airline president. When she greeted her children returning from school in the evening, it was always from the kitchen, where she was immersed in her most serious enterprise: cooking for her brood. Microwave ovens and quick-fix meals never infiltrated the perimeters of her base of operation. She started from scratch and finished somewhere in the neighborhood of culinary perfection. Even in the hardest of times, there was always plenty of food on the Weichert table, food prepared with the care that demonstrated, three times each day, just how much their mother loved them.

In his private moments, when Yona thought about growing up and having his own home and family, he paid Esther the ultimate tribute by telling himself: "I want a wife who will be just like her."

From his father, he learned much about living his witness for the Lord. Zvi didn't give seminars filled with "how to" information. And he didn't march up and down hallways shouting, "Look at me and see a believer in Yeshua." That kind of ostentation doesn't go far in Israel. Of the high-pressure enthusiasts who came from abroad to shout Israelis into the family of God, Yona often heard His father say, "They bring a big wind, but very little rain."

Instead, Yona learned by watching people come to their home—folks who needed a letter or document translated; folks who were in trouble and had learned that they could find sound advice or hands to help behind Zvi's door. And by the time they left the house, they had some word of God's love and grace to take with them. Yona always saw his father weave in a witness for the Lord in ways that blended smoothly into the context of the conversation or situation. Yona was learning, in the casual offhand way children do, what it meant to allow the Lord to open doors to witness in a normal, Spirit-directed fashion.

To the children, Zvi was the eternal optimist. Everything they had was from the hand of God, and they could be glad. And what they didn't have also was in the will of God, so they could be satisfied—it was all okay! This lesson came from a man who never took the easy way out to create a "happy" situation. He worked hard at a tough job. He did it by choice, and they knew it. This knowledge gave them a kind of assurance that would later help them face tough jobs without fearing a loss of joy in the process.

When Yona entered high school, he began taking his faith seriously. Until then, he had played with "good boys" from the neighborhood who stayed pretty close to his standard of behavior. In high school, however, he was thrown together with kids who were trying their wings as young adults. Discotheques, cigarettes, and the like were fashionable with this age group and gave Yona a glimpse of what life was like on the other side of the fence. He didn't like what he saw. So he immersed himself in study and sports, areas he excelled in. Consequently, he was well thought of by teachers and respected by fellow students who knew he was different somehow but also knew that he was good at what he did.

He maintained his high standards through two years of college, and when the time came to fulfill his military commitment, Yona decided on the navy. He was accepted in officers' training school.

His choice put the men of the Weichert family into every branch of the IDF. Zvi had been regular army. Mendel was in the air force. Eli was a paratrooper. Now Yona was in the navy. As one might expect, this made for plenty of friendly rivalry when the family was together.

For some reason, most people are not well appraised of the exploits of the men of the navy. Paratroops and armored forces have dominated the public's perception of the Israeli military. Indeed, until the Yom Kippur War, Israel's navy was relegated to an auxiliary role among the fighting forces. In that bitter struggle, however, the navy came into its own and outperformed all other branches of the service in overall accomplishments. This was largely due to the fact that the navy had recognized the revolutionizing impact of missiles on warfare before the other branches of the armed services. By the beginning of the war,

Israel had built a fleet of a dozen fast missile boats, all armed with missiles (the Gabriel) designed and manufactured in Israel. On the first day of the war, Israel's Gabriels blew four Syrian craft out of the water and took charge of the sea-lanes to the north. On October 10, Israeli missile ships sunk three Egyptian vessels near Port Said, then sent four more Syrian missile boats to the bottom in subsequent engagements.

From that point on, Israel's navy commanded the entire coast from Syria to Egypt and raked enemy coastlines with the telling effects twenty-four hours a day. The 76-mm Israeli naval guns ripped up Syria's coastal oil installations, and young Israeli gunners mauled radar stations, military complexes, and supply depots in Syria and Egypt. Egypt's northernmost SAM missile sites took a pounding from the sea.

Achievements of the Yom Kippur War led the navy into a new era—one that has seen the development of a highly sophisticated military arm that is charged with the awesome responsibility of securing Israel's vulnerable coastline from enemy states and terrorist marauders.

Those aspiring to become naval officers face stiff competition and a grueling workload at the officers' school. Since it is a small branch of the IDF, the navy can afford to choose a very select group to fill its ranks. Only 30 percent of those beginning the course are still around when the commissions are distributed.

Arriving back at the barracks dog dirty and willing to trade a meal for an hour's sleep were standard fare for naval trainees. Yona's routine varied somewhat from his mates, however, and raised many questions about this guy who was "different." Before he grabbed some much-needed sleep, Yona invariably opened his Bible and spent time with the Lord.

"Why are you always reading your Bible?" he was asked. "I'm so tired, it's all I can do to stay awake."

"I read because I need what this Book has to say to me. As a believer, it gives me strength to go through all the things we are doing just now."

Yona's comrades knew he believed in Jesus as Messiah. But, as was the case in high school, his proficiency and dedication not only convinced them that "this is a guy you can count on," but also, helped Yona maintain good relationships with those around him. He couldn't help but smile one day when he overheard someone say, "You know, Yona is such a good guy. It's a pity he's not a Jew!"

His friend's comment displayed the common thread that runs among Israelis (and world Jewry, for that matter) when it comes to Jewish people who believe in Jesus as Israel's Messiah and their personal Savior. The attitude was much more subtle toward Yona, but it was, nevertheless, the same attitude his father had experienced as a demolition expert many years earlier.

"It's sad, but true," Zvi would say, "that the only time some of my own people are willing to consider me a Jew is when they find a bomb in their mailbox or trash can and need me to remove it. Any other time, because I believe in Jesus and the New Testament, I am no more a Jew."

Zvi was justly proud when his second son graduated from officers' school and received his commission. Friends and visitors to the Weichert home received the full account through pictures and lectures on just how well Yona had done on his way to becoming a naval officer.

For Yona, graduation marked a major transition in his life. Throughout all his years of education and training, he had worked hard at the business of learning and preparing. "Now," he told himself, "the true test is coming. How will I do when it comes to putting all of this into practice?"

His concern was not limited to his performance as a naval officer. He was well trained and confident that he could do his job—at least he would give it his best shot. As a believer, he knew that he had a bigger job to do.

"All these years I've been praying that God would do as He wished with my life. Now it is time to see what He will do," he thought.

His first assignment to a ship was an experience that equaled his expectations. Going on board, meeting his commander, fellow officers, and the men he would command all confirmed that this was his element. Yona was going to do his duty to the best of his ability, and in the process, he was going to enjoy it.

He decided to be forthright about his faith from the outset, so he took his Bible into the officers' room and began doing what he had done for as long as he could remember—spend time daily with God, plying the pages of His Word. Yona had long puzzled over the fact that, although he was among the "People of the Book,"—his Jewish brethren—he always saw a great look of surprise, come over them when they found him reading "the Book." Although they claimed to be God's people, they seemed to have no interest in reading His Word.

Almost as quickly as he opened his Bible, he heard the now-familiar question: "Why are you reading a Bible?"

"Because," he replied, "I believe in Jesus, and Bible reading is how I come to know Him better."

"So, you believe in Jesus. Good for you." Yona was surprised to get that response. Most of the officers, he found, were men who were ready to live and let live. He was no threat to them.

Yona's belief that the real test would come when he started his duty aboard ship was a prophecy fulfilled. As an officer, he fell under the scrutiny of all hands. His captain wanted to see what he was made of and how he would perform under fire. His fellow officers wondered about their peer's quality as a leader. His men wanted to know if the man commanding them knew his stuff and was worth following into battle. It was all on the line—and no one knew it better than Zvi's boy Yona.

His first shipboard interrogator was, quite literally, a turncoat. The man had been reared in the yeshivas of the ultra-Orthodox in Mea Shearim. His biggest decision in life had come when he decided to remove his black coat, turn from his religious prejudices, and answer his nation's call to military service.

"So you believe in Yeshu," he said, using a shortened version of Yeshua that is akin to a curse in Hasidic circles.

"Yes, I believe in Yeshua," Yona replied.

A curt "Why?" was the next question.

"Because I am a Jew."

"What do you mean, 'Because I am a Jew'?"

"You see," Yona explained, "if I were not a Jew, I would probably never read the Bible. But because I am a Jew, I read it. And when I began to read it, God showed me that Jesus is our Messiah."

"Where do you find Yeshu in the Bible?" he challenged.

"I will show you in Isaiah 53, in Jeremiah 31, in Micah. He is everywhere in the Bible."

His questioner listened intently as he read Messianic passages to him. Immediately, in a meticulously detailed manner, the former yeshiva student began answering each verse and passage with words from the rabbis. Yona had heard the same answers many times when he was on the streets with his father. In this man's eyes, the writings of the rabbis took precedence over the Word of God. To argue was futile.

"I can get you things to read, if you are interested," Yona suggested.

"No, I think I already know the facts about this matter," the man said emphatically.

In the days to follow, Yona did not attempt to say anything more. He wanted to demonstrate, through his actions, what it meant to be a believer. He showed no favoritism but exhibited the love of Christ toward the man who had no respect for his belief. Perhaps the sown seed would germinate in time.

This man turned out to be the exception among Yona's fellow officers, all of whom tended to talk freely and, for the most part, uncritically about what Yona believed. They respected him, and his faith in Jesus as Messiah did not seem to bother them. Their problem was different. Most of these men had been reared in relatively well-to-do circumstances, and their priorities weighed out on the material side of the scale. Their difficulty was the same as it has been for a generation of American Yuppies and the same that Jesus encountered in Israel two millennia ago. Having so much in the here and now makes it difficult to recognize a personal need for God.

Yona spent a good year and a half aboard ship before leaving for six more months of study. When he left, he was sure he was leaving behind the best ship in the navy.

A new station meant a new commander, which also meant interviews and sessions designed to familiarize personnel with surroundings and shipmates. At the conclusion of his initial private briefing by his commander, Yona was asked if he had anything to say or if there was anything he would like to share about himself.

"Yes, there is something I feel I should tell you. It has nothing to do with the service, but I think that as my commanding officer, you should know about it.

"I read the Bible, but not just the Old Testament. I believe that the New Testament is the fulfillment of the Old Testament. And I also believe that Jesus who was crucified is the Messiah of the Jewish people, but the Jewish people were not ready to accept Him."

His commander looked across the desk at his newest officer. Yona waited for his response, not knowing what to expect. "I find what you have said very interesting. Do you have more that you would like to tell me about it?"

Yona proceeded to touch on other points he felt were important to a conversation of this kind.

"But I am puzzled about something," the commander said. "If you are religious and believe in the Old Testament, why don't you wear a yarmulke and dress like other religious Jews?"

"Because, you see, Jesus came as a sacrifice for us, so we have a new covenant now, as it is written in Jeremiah 31. As a result, we are no longer living under the laws of *do* and *don't do* because

God, by His grace, gave us freedom from those things. All we have to do is to accept the God of the sacrifice."

After his commander had asked a few more questions, he made a request. "If you don't mind, I would like for you to speak before the other officers on board about this.

"And while you're preparing to do this, could you also spend some time explaining just what's going on with the Mormons in Jerusalem? Everybody is talking about the big fight they are having." The Mormons were in the process of constructing a study center in the city, and some religious Jews were raising a furor over the possibility of it becoming a launching pad for proselytizing.

"Something else occurs to me. Give us some information, if you will, about the Jehovah's Witnesses."

To say the least, this was not what Yona was expecting to come out of his orientation meeting with his superior. "Yes, of course, I will be happy to do it. The only thing that I'm a little concerned about is that some of the officers might construe this to be a missionary act and try to make trouble."

"No," the man replied. "This is what's happening on the streets of Israel today. There is nothing wrong with our knowing about current events. Don't worry. There won't be a problem."

Yona went to his quarters and thought it over. So this was one of the things for which the Lord had prepared him. He was going to speak, by invitation, to his commander and nine other officers on the ship. This, he knew, was not just a casual conversation—it was a full-blown lecture. He had better be prepared to deliver the goods. He had one month to get ready. Just what did he want to say to these men who were to listen to him speak of the hope that was within him?

He settled on developing four essentials during his talk: (1) why, as a believer, he was still a Jew; (2) the history of Messianic hope among the Jewish people; (3) the importance of the sacrifice to any Jewish religious system; and (4) how Messianic Jews who believe in Jesus separated from the main branches of Judaism.

Yona immediately began gathering material for his lecture. He drew on friends who were well acquainted with Jewish history and theology. He hunted down good books and any other reliable sources he could lay his hands on. By the time he was ready to speak, he had sixteen pages of information written on both sides. If he failed, it certainly would not be for lack of material. Now he faced a problem: His talk was to last for one hour. How could he possibly say all he had to say in that time?

As his talk proceeded, he managed to touch all the bases he had intended to cover, especially emphasizing the Messianic credentials of Jesus found in the Old Testament

The hour seemed to fly by, and he could not help noticing that the men seemed to be hanging on every word. Time ran out as he was discussing the vital question related to Judaism's dilemma over having no sacrifice after the destruction of the second Temple. Yona concluded by affirming from 1 Corinthians how believers in Jesus face no such problem because "Christ, our passover, is sacrificed for us" (1 Cor. 5:7).

Questions came from every angle during the brief period given to inquiries. Among the more intriguing was one about the sacrifice of a human as being contrary to Judaism. Yona took them to the Old Testament where God commanded Abraham to sacrifice Isaac. This portion of Scripture, he said, was a picture of the greater sacrifice of the Messiah. The questions provided a stimulating and challenging exchange.

When the session wrapped up to allow the next speaker to take the floor, it was evident that they were not through with Yona. "Okay," he was told, "next week, you will take the time assigned to another fellow. He can wait until the week after. We want to hear more about what you have to say."

His next lecture started in the book of Daniel and touched the ramifications of the Messianic passages found there. He then moved on to the New Testament attitude toward Jewry. In black and white, he showed from Romans 11 the love of God for His people and the future promised to the nation after its coming reconciliation to the Messiah. "You can see as plain as day that the New Testament is not anti-Semitic," he told them.

Before he finished, he explained to them about Mormons and Jehovah's Witnesses, carefully pointing out the things that distinguished their beliefs from true Christianity.

When it was time for questions, one man asked, "If I wanted to become a believer, what would I have to do to get into your group?"

"It is not like getting into some secret society," Yona explained. "Everything is out in the open, and you have to decide to accept the Lord yourself. When you do, you can come to God on your own, tell Him you want to become a believer, and receive Him as your Messiah.

"It is a wonderful thing to know that the way to God is open to us. We can come to Him."

That night, Yona spent time reflecting on the events of the past few weeks. "How foolish we are," he thought. "I was always worried about how I would act if I ever had an opportunity like the one I have just had—if I would be able to do it. But when I did it, and the Lord was in it, there was nothing to it."

He had learned valuable lessons through these encounters. First, he learned that many people are much more open than one would tend to think. Such people are willing to listen. Also, some people will reject your witness and send you away—as in the case of the ultra-Orthodox sailor. But if they do, so what! There will always be a few who will really want to hear with their hearts. The worst offense would be to deprive these people by not trying to speak for the Lord.

One can't help thinking of the response to Paul's witness on Mars Hill in Athens: "some mocked; and others said, We will hear thee again of this matter. . . . Nevertheless, certain men joined him, and believed" (Acts 17:32, 34).

Yona had taken a long stride in following in his father's footsteps.

1986

CHAPTER THIRTY-THREE

D.O.A.

JERUSALEM, FEBRUARY 27, 1987

They found him face down at a bus stop on Jaffa Road in Jerusalem. The characteristic animation that had made his eyes dance and his face crease upward in laughter was gone. Zvi Weichert was dead.

Bystanders clucked their tongues and shook their heads as ambulance attendants thumped his chest in an urgent effort to pound life back into his motionless body. Finally his heart began to flutter tentatively. They rushed him into the ambulance, and the piercing wail of the siren signaled the start of the race for Zvi's life.

Shortly after his arrival at the hospital, his heart stopped again.

"I'm sorry to have to tell you this," the hospital's chief cardiologist informed Esther, "but your husband is clinically dead. We've managed to get his heart going again, but we are convinced there is no hope for him. If we remove the life-support system, his body will cease functioning immediately.

"Even if, by some miracle, he should regain consciousness, he will never be normal again. You see, his brain has been denied oxygen for too long during the periods of cardiac arrest."

"We've done all we can for him. It's only a matter of time. You had better get the family together."

Word spread throughout the city quickly. The man who had eluded death with the agility of "a cat on the wall" was fresh out of lives.

Esther and the children sat in the small waiting room of the hospital and cried. Mendel had come from work; Yona and Eli from military service; Ruth and her husband, David, had arrived from Eilat.

Esther's face betrayed her worry as she began issuing directives. Zvi's children were accustomed to their mother's worried looks. As a matter of fact, she seemed to do all the worrying for the entire Weichert family. Their father didn't have the capacity to worry, or at least it never showed. And if they had heard him say it once, they had heard it a thousand times: "So, Okay! Don't worry. What will be, will be."

They wouldn't follow Abba's advice today; today they would worry.

"Children," Esther began, "we don't know how long we will be here. You must remember to eat and keep up your strength. You may not feel like it now, but you must do as I tell you.

"Yona, call people from the church. Ask them to pray for your father. Mendel, call The Friends of Israel in America. Tell them what has happened and ask them to have believers there pray."

Ruth had been praying hard already. On the four-hour trip up from Eilat, she had scarcely noticed the barren landscape rushing past the car window. Her thoughts were absorbed by Abba.

"It just isn't fair," she told herself. "All my father has known is war, sacrifice, and doing for others. He's only 58. He deserves some good years for himself."

The more she thought about it, the more emotional she became until, in an intemperate surge of audacity, she flung a command heavenward. "My father cannot die!" she cried. "He must have another chance to live!" Later, after she had some time to think about it, Ruth realized that God had been very patient with an overwrought child. At the moment, however, her only priority was her father's life.

Long, dreary hours drifted laboriously into days as the Weichert family began a bedside vigil that seemed to last forever. Each day, when they returned to the hospital, Zvi's children asked the same question: "Is Abba any better?"

Each time the reply was the same: "No. Nothing has changed." Briefings from the doctors were equally depressing. "We don't see any change. Keep your courage up. We are hoping for the best."

His body was barely recognizable as it lay connected to the various life-support systems that were sustaining his fragile form of existence—not quite alive; not quite dead. Tubes protruded everywhere, and a multitude of sensors enveloped him, giving a robot-like appearance to the pale form lying motionless on the bed. The family could only look and wonder how much longer things could go on this way.

As believers, they clung tenaciously to their faith in God and to the knowledge that God is merciful and just and hears the supplications of His children, who were praying fervently. They themselves were praying; believers in Israel were praying; friends in America were praying. Only the Lord could bring Zvi back to them. But then, the Lord had been bringing Zvi back to them all of their lives. In war, he had faced certain death many times. Was this so different? If God could protect their father in battle, why not from this sickness?

———————

Bedside vigils give people much opportunity to talk, to say things they sometimes are too busy to say otherwise. Reminiscing about childhood, church, good times and bad, all receive a fair measure of attention. And, although it is difficult to recognize at the time or to admit later, when we are reduced to helpless onlookers, we often experience the greatest spiritual growth. Wise people stop to take stock of where they have been, where they are, and where they are going. The Weicherts were no exception.

This was particularly true of Ruthi. As Zvi's only daughter, she had known and cherished the wonderful relationship that such an exclusive position gave her. In the early days, Abba was her special playmate, marvelously animated and always ready to entertain her by joining in whatever games her fancy dictated. At another stage, she became his teacher, correcting grammatical indiscretions and laboring mightily to keep him on key during songfests.

As the oldest of the children, she considered herself the strong one—the supreme protector of the boys and also of Zvi. But now, sitting in the hospital late at night, Ruthi was chilled by her vulnerability. Now *she* was the one who needed a strong one. And God provided for her need. She had Esther, her brothers, and her husband, David. God had been so wonderful in bringing her such a good husband, one who was now a believer and could pray with her and help her through this time. She couldn't do without him—or any of them, for that matter. She knew what the doctors were saying—that even if her father lived, he would never be normal again. Her Abba would be gone, and without him, a huge part of her world was passing from her.

Like Zvi, Ruthi had always asked questions. They were not always easy questions, and sometimes the answers produced even more perplexing queries. When she was old enough to look beyond the walls of home and church, she began to question some of the rules the family lived by. She was musical and artistic. Why couldn't she attend dances and movies with the rest of the children in the neighborhood?

These questions were not addressed exclusively to her parents or the Christian establishment. Ruthi was asking herself some of these questions. It was something she had picked up from her father.

"All I can do for you," she could hear him say, "is tell you the right way, and show you what you should do. But I want you to learn to think for yourself and make the right choices because you *want* to make the right choices." For several years, she struggled deeply within herself over making "the right choices."

Her desire to be like everyone else caused her to do some dabbling in the world. It was never anything bad—never "black fun"—but Ruthi was looking for the real Ruth, the person she would choose to become.

Over a period of time, she began to feel separated from the family. Although they treated her as they always had, she somehow began to feel like an outsider. Not that she questioned being a believer. Jesus was her Savior, and she prayed to Him; but she wasn't at peace. Too many things were unsettled in her mind.

Sometimes, when she was at home and everyone was taking part in discussions about the Bible and spiritual things, Ruthi felt estranged from it all—a feeling not unlike what the prodigal must have experienced.

As the date for her induction into the military drew near (all Israeli girls must serve two years of active duty), she began to relish thoughts of being away. Adventure (maybe she could drive a tank!) and the excitement of being far from home were seductive lures for a girl with a lot to learn. Best of all, she would be on her own! No more family curfews. No more house rules or inspections of new friends. Esther would not be playing "Detective Columbo" about her comings and goings. She would be free!

Predictably, the "freedom" afforded by the army was something far different than what she had anticipated. For Ruthi, who had never spent any appreciable time away from home, it was the rudest of awakenings.

Bedding, kit bag, towels, and uniforms (which she thought must have been worn by the British) were among her first favors. Then she was crammed into a tent with eleven other girls. Her opinion of service life deteriorated further when she gently placed a hand on the shoulder of an officer to ask a question and was barked at and told, in no uncertain terms, to keep a respectable distance. Her initial appraisal didn't change much after she was roused from sleep at 4:30 A.M. to do strenuous calisthenics in heat so oppressive that sweat-soaked uniforms practically stood on their own by day's end.

It seemed like a lifetime before she could get back to Jerusalem and register her complaints at the office of the High Command. The commander was in when she arrived, and he listened intently as she spilled everything. Her high commander, of course, was Abba, a man who knew exactly where she was coming from.

"You must remember, Ruthi," he said softly, "you are not the first one who has gone through this. Everyone is going through exactly the same thing. Many girls in the army feel just as you do. Don't take it too hard. It will be over before too long. Try to enjoy yourself and learn from this experience." Before the talk was over, Zvi prayed for her.

She was, in fact, learning from her experiences. Ruthi was going through a personal, spiritual evolution. Some lessons she learned the hard way. But she learned.

The entire subject of suffering puzzled her and provided rungs on her ladder of spiritual growth. Often she had wondered why God allowed some people to suffer so much while others, like her, suffered very little. She knew she was not better than they; so why were they afflicted whereas she was not?

Then she encountered a man who had lost three sons to the war in one day. In spite of the agony he obviously felt, he nevertheless said: "I bless your name, O Lord. You know what you are doing." God was competent, she concluded. He is bigger than all of us or anything that happens to us. And Ruthi began to see that God's competence could be her confidence.

So, ever so slowly, she began to sort things out. When the call came informing her of her father's heart attack, Ruthi came full circle. During those long, arduous days of waiting in the hospital, she experienced an intimacy with the Lord in prayer that she had never known before. Now she was praying with an absolute recognition that God must work a miracle if her father were to survive. Zvi's life, she concluded, was not in the hands of the physicians; it was in the hand of God.

There in the hospital, she knew she was no longer a nominal believer trying to straddle two worlds. Now she was totally committed to the Lord.

Mendel, too, had gone through a spiritual evolution. He was an exceptionally bright young man, and as he matured, it became obvious that he had the capacity to attain whatever goals he set for himself. His time in the service and subsequent experience in industry demonstrated that he could handle leadership capably and well. His vigil in the hospital sharpened his focus and helped him set his priorities in order.

For years Mendel had attended church because he was expected to. He was in a family of believers who went to church—it was that simple. There was no problem; he couldn't remember when he didn't believe. But the time came when he began attending because he wanted to go. And there was a vast difference between "expected to" and "want to."

For Mendel, a major adjustment in spiritual perception occurred when he was about twenty. Until then, he had viewed walking with the Lord as a type of willing servitude—a sort of "bondslave of Christ" idea. There was certainly nothing wrong with that concept; it was a perfectly biblical understanding of what it means to give yourself to the Lord. But Mendel had missed a dimension—the joy in serving God. Those who have received the gift of eternal life in the Lord Jesus have every reason to want to present their "bodies a living sacrifice" to God (Rom. 12:1). But that presentation and the subsequent life of grace should bring a settled joy, because God has accepted us and privileged us to return our lives to Him in service. Grasping these facts or, rather, being grasped by them, profoundly influenced Mendel's life.

He reached another milestone as a result of an experience at a party one night. It was a church function, and among the guests was a young woman who was not a believer. During the course of the evening, she approached Mendel.

"I hear these people always talking about being a believer. What does it mean to be a believer?"

He swallowed hard, thought for a moment, then answered haltingly. "I think you should speak to one of the elders about this. I can arrange it if you like."

It was as though a fist had been jammed deep into the pit of his stomach. He had been presented with a golden opportunity to speak for the Lord, but he wasn't able to defend his faith. The deficiency kept slamming its way back into his mind: he couldn't adequately articulate his faith in the Lord. He felt humiliated and decided then and there that he would never be unprepared again.

Mendel immediately launched a spiritual self-development program. He was in the air force at the time, and he took every spare moment to study the foundations of his faith. For eight months he studied with the intensity of a man obsessed. Before he was through, he had produced a carefully written, 40-page document that set forth his theological beliefs and personal commitment to the Lord. All of his effort quickly paid off. He soon began to encounter opportunities to make amends for dropping the ball the first time around.

When he had finished the program, he found he had a hunger to dig deeper in Bible study. But as he was prospecting for himself, Mendel found that other believers also were interested in discovering the treasures contained in the Word. Consequently, he found himself leading a Bible study for young adults and helping them in their desire to dig deeper.

Among the people who attended the study was a young woman who was not a believer. She became deeply interested in what she was hearing and told her teacher she wanted to know more. Mendel found himself faced with a situation that almost exactly duplicated the one at the church social. But this time things were different.

"I am working in a jewelry store in town," she told him. "Why don't you come by, and you can answer my questions and teach me more when I am not busy."

Mendel began going to the store routinely for one-on-one studies. She, in turn, fired questions at him when business was slack. He had the answers now, and in time, it became evident that the Lord was speaking to the woman in a powerful way.

One afternoon Mendel's subject was "Jesus as the Son of God." Up to this time, she had agreed with everything he had told her. Now, however, they both knew that this issue demanded a decision. If Jesus were truly the Son of God and she acknowledged that fact as truth, she had only one acceptable option: to receive Him and commit her life to the Lord.

"I cannot accept this," she said after a long moment's reflection.

"You cannot accept what?" he asked.

"I just cannot accept what you are saying to me now."

"I am very sorry you feel that way," he replied, obviously disappointed. "But we both know this is something you must decide completely on your own. I can tell you what the Bible says; you must make the decisions related to its truths."

The girl slowly shook her head then said, "I think it would probably be better if we didn't have any more talks on this subject."

He agreed, and the two did not get together again. But even though she refused to proceed and stopped short of faith in the Lord, Mendel had several things to be grateful for. She had heard the truth. He had not failed the Lord or her. She understood exactly what the real issue was and what she must do about it—it was her decision to make. The Lord was working in her heart and mind. Mendel was sure he could rest in the competence of God to bring her, in His time, to life in the Lord.

The military was another place where opportunities persisted in coming to him. His personal routine paralleled that of his father and brothers—the Bible was in evidence wherever he was stationed. He was doing strategic and sensitive work for the air force and firmly believed that good performance brought respect and contributed to a credible witness. Mendel had done some exceptional work in a difficult field (he won several prestigious awards for his performance) and was, as a result, highly regarded by his peers.

Eventually he became known as the resident expert on theology and religious matters for those in his group. A controller who came in from time to time happened to be one of the rare Hasidics in military service. The man's favorite pastime was to start conversations with the soldiers about the Mishna and Gemara. "Why are you talking to me?" they would complain. "Mendel is the expert on religion. Go bust his head with your questions."

Mormonism was a subject that often came up, and Mendel was forced to face an old issue among Jewish people. They believed that because he was a believer—a "Christian"—he was the same as a Mormon. Sometimes the questions almost became too much, and he would say, "But I am not a Mormon!"

This misconception arises from the situation Israelis have in contemporary Judaism. In Israel, there are essentially three branches of Judaism: Conservative, Orthodox, and ultra-Orthodox. Although they differ somewhat and are often at odds with one another, they are all a part of Judaism. Thus the Jewish people extend that concept to Christianity: Christianity has many sects; so if you call yourself a Methodist or Mormon, conservative or cultist, what difference does it make? To them, all are "Christian." This misconception is common and poses the most difficult and persistent questions asked of believers in Israel. Mendel patiently sorted out the distinctions for his confused questioners. In spite of all the good-natured digs he got about what the Mormons were doing in building their study center in Jerusalem and about whether he had ties with the project, he was grateful to be God's man in the right place, at the right time, with the right answers.

———◆———

"We have seen some improvement in your husband's condition," the doctor told Esther. "His heart seems to be stabilizing.

"I must caution you again, however, not to be too optimistic. We cannot yet interpret this as a sign of significant improvement."

Significant or not, it was a far cry from what they had come to expect from the doctor's visits to the waiting room. Even a small speck of improvement was more than they had been told they could anticipate.

More good news. "His breathing has improved considerably. If this trend continues, we will remove him from the life-support system and see how he does on his own." It was like a word from Heaven! Zvi hadn't come back to them yet, but things were certainly looking up.

Then it happened. The eyes flickered; the eyelids blinked open. Tears were streaming down their faces as, for the first time since his attack, Zvi regained consciousness. Attending physicians were amazed to see their patient rolling his head back and forth while his eyes swept the ceiling.

"It is something we are at a loss to explain," the doctors said, mystified.

"This is something that almost never happens—for one who has been unconscious for so long, with such severe damage to his heart, to improve like this.

"I can only tell you that we are not the ones who can take credit for what is happening. Someone beyond us is doing something."

But bad news soon tempered their joy. "If this is not just a temporary phase, you cannot hope for him to be as he was mentally. Don't be surprised if he doesn't recognize any of you. We are virtually certain that his memory will be gone, and he will probably never be able to look after himself again."

When Zvi finally began to attempt conversation, it was as the doctors had warned. Mendel came close to the bed. "Abba, do you know who I am?" he asked tentatively.

"Yes, I know who you are. You are an Arab!"

"Eli," Mendel said. "You come over. See if he will recognize you."

Eli walked to the bed and bent over his father. "Look at me Abba. It's Eli, your son."

"Don't say you are my son. You are not my son."

They stood in stunned silence. They wept again, but this time it was not for joy. Although they had been told what to expect, it was just too much to see him like this after all they had been through.

Ruthi and Esther sat by Zvi's bed, talking about what the future held for them now.

"Well," Ruthi said, "I am sure God has answered our prayers and brought him this far. If he is to be like a baby, we will take care of him. I will teach him from the beginning, just as I would a child."

She didn't have to wait long to start the lessons, because Zvi started asking questions almost from the moment he awoke.

"What is that?" he asked.

"That is a door," his teacher responded.

How far they could go or how long it would take were two big questions. But at least he had, in some fashion, survived. They would do whatever was necessary to make the best of things.

CHAPTER THIRTY-FOUR

LAZARUS MEETS SHAKESPEARE

The voices sounded as though they were coming from far away—like echoes reverberating off corridors of stone. He couldn't figure out what they were saying; he just knew he recognized the sound of voices, and his mind struggled to decipher their meaning,

For the first time in six days, Zvi recognized what he was seeing. It was all new to him. Where was he? The last thing he remembered was standing at the bus stop on Jaffa Road. He surveyed the tubes trailing from his body and answered his own question at once. This was a hospital, and something serious had obviously befallen him. Like Lazarus, whom Christ had raised from the dead, Zvi was beginning to emerge from the shadows.

He was in a small room. Hospital personnel had moved him from the cardiac intensive care unit. On the other side of the room, he could see a woman sitting by another bed. He was thinking how far away they looked as his eyes slid closed and he drifted off to sleep again.

It was evening when he began to reemerge into the world of consciousness. Again he could hear voices before he opened his eyes. This time the words were discernable instead of disorganized jumbles. His roommate's wife and several other people were at the man's bedside, speaking to one another in German. Before long, Zvi could hear that he was the topic of their conversation.

"So, I see they have brought someone else to your room," the man's wife said. "I had hoped that you could be alone."

"This is not a hotel," he replied. "When you come here, you can't pick your accommodations or choose your roommates."

"Do you know who he is?" she continued.

"No, they just brought him in a short time ago. He hasn't been awake since he's been in the room. I do know he's a very sick man."

With some effort, Zvi lifted his head slightly and raised a hand in greeting. The man's wife turned to him and began speaking in Hebrew. Her appearance and manner told him a great deal about her and the occupant of the other bed. They were upper-register Israelis. Speaking another language was "in" in certain circles where Hebrew was considered the common tongue of the less enlightened. In fact, Max turned out to be a person of some stature. He was a successful writer. At the moment, however, he was a man reduced to the "common" level by a common problem—a bad heart.

"May I ask what kind of work you do?" the woman inquired.

Zvi caught the condescending tone in her voice, one that didn't set well with a man who had just returned from the brink of eternity. Her question, addressed as it was to someone she had been told was "a very sick man," instantly revealed her values with respect to the *here* and the *hereafter*. Rather than inquire sensitively about Zvi's health, she inquired about his status. Instinctively, the first coherent words that Zvi uttered when God virtually raised him from the dead gave these people a Bible lesson on just how their priorities should be scaled.

"I am a carpenter by trade," he said.

"Max, did you hear? Your new roommate is a carpenter."

Max, who didn't seem to be overly interested in the conversation, grunted an acknowledgment.

Zvi had already seen the small Bible Ruth had placed on the bedside table. She thought it would help if he found his copy of the Scriptures in the same place it had always been at home. "When Abba opens his eyes, I want this to be the first thing he sees," she had said.

"I would like to read something to you from the Bible," he said, thumbing through the pages until he arrived at Psalm 49. Deliberately, Zvi began to read. "For when he dieth he shall carry nothing away; his glory shall not descend after him, Though while he lived he blessed his soul; and men will praise thee, when thou doest well to thyself. He shall go to the generation of his fathers; they shall never see light. Man that is in honor, and understandeth not, is like the beasts that perish" (vv. 17–20).

Zvi suspected correctly that he was addressing people who may have known much about books, philosophy, and the like; but when they heard him reading from the Bible, he was taking them onto unfamiliar terrain.

"Here," he began, "the psalmist tells us something very important, something to which we should listen carefully. When it comes time for us to leave this world, as we all will, He will not ask us what we have done in life or whether we were important people or not. Writer or carpenter—it will mean nothing when we stand before God. Your relationship to the Lord is what will count at that time. Then you will answer for how you have invested your life—what you have done for Him and other people. This is the most important thing in life, because to live here and not know the Lord is to be lost forever when you die."

His line of conversation was far removed from the level of their interest, and they seemed anxious to change the subject. He obliged them by carrying on a conversation in German.

Max congratulated him. "You handle German very well. How long have you been in the county?"

"Nearly forty years," Zvi answered.

"It is amazing that you speak so well after being away from Europe for so long."

Their talk was cut short when a young doctor entered making his evening rounds. He had exchanged only a few casual remarks with Zvi before he realized that his patient was no longer disoriented but seemed to be making intelligent conversation. His discovery caused him to exit the room abruptly and return in an equal hurry in the company of a bevy of hospital staff members who immediately began probes and inquiries designed to test Zvi's memory and reasoning ability.

Zvi provided rational answers to all the preliminary queries. He was a little puzzled when he saw them looking at one another in amazement and exchanging astonished nods as the questioning proceeded. When they were through, Zvi had some questions for them. The physician in charge did a mental walk-through of all that had occurred over the past six days.

"Well, my friend," he concluded, "you have proven us all wrong. When they brought you in here, we didn't give you one chance in a million. When you regained consciousness, it was like a miracle. But we were sure you would live only as a vegetable—without a rational mind. But we are very happy that you fooled us."

"It wasn't I who fooled you," Zvi corrected. "You see, for most of my life, I have placed my trust in the Lord. I am sure if He had not help me, I could not have survived. I know you did the best you could, and I thank you for that. But I know that it was by His hand that I have come back to where I am now. I suppose we could use the old saying, 'God does the healing; the doctors get the fee!'"

That was good for a hearty laugh all around. But everyone at his bedside knew full well the consummate truth of those words as they reflected on what had transpired over the last few days.

No one had to tell Esther and the children whose hand was at work in bringing Zvi back to them. They had seen a prominent TV personality come to the hospital with what appeared to be a comparatively minor problem. Within a few days he was dead. Zvi came in clinically dead; now he was alive. It was like a dream come true—too good to be true. Suddenly, those desperate days when death seemed a certainty and the dark days afterward when he had awakened with no memory seemed almost as though they had never happened. Today they woke up to find everything just as it had always been. Again the mighty hand of God had performed a miracle—something He delights in doing for those who love Him. Zvi was back.

Each time hospital personnel came to his room, they were treated to vintage Zvi—good humor, lots to say, and an eagerness to witness to his faith.

Several doctors were at his bedside when one of them said, "You talk about faith so much. You must be a very religious man."

"Not religious," he quickly responded. His faith was not like the religion of many who came to this hospital, which was very Orthodox in orientation. "A man can have religion but not know God. My faith is in the Lord, not a religious system. I believe as it says in Isaiah 12:2: 'Behold, God is my salvation; I will trust, and not be afraid; for the LORD, even the LORD, is my strength and my song; he also is become my salvation.'"

One of the doctors had picked up Zvi's Bible while he was talking. "I see your Bible contains the New Testament. The faith you are talking about must be the Christian faith. It is not the belief of the Jews."

"Is it forbidden for a Jew to bring the whole Bible into this hospital?" Zvi questioned.

"No, of course, it is not strictly forbidden. But I can certainly tell you it is not well thought of by the people here."

"My friend, I can tell you that I did not receive my faith to believe in the Lord from the New Testament alone, but according to the entire Bible. If you will take the time to read Isaiah 53 and many other passages I can show you from the Old Testament, you will find that this is also the message of the New Testament."

"But Zvi, can you, as a Jew, really believe in the New Testament?"

"Yes, I can. And I can show you how the faith of the New Testament parallels the faith we find in the Old Testament."

He took the Bible from the young doctor's hand and turned to Hebrews 11. "Here it talks about the faith of our fathers. 'By faith Noah . . . By faith Abraham . . . the prophets.' It was all by faith. Abraham offered up his son Isaac by faith. Isaac was a picture of the sacrifice to be made for us all. So it is not faith in one or the other; it is faith in the one God of both Testaments."

"You quote a lot of verses and seem to know much about the Bible. Did you go to a school and study to learn this?"

"No, I did not learn this in school. I went to school only three years—elementary school. But when I came to the Lord, the Bible became my life. I cannot tell you how many times I have read it through. I suppose you would say it is my hobby. If it is so, it is the only hobby I have in my life.

"And if you want to know why I think I have been spared from death, it can be found in the Bible also. It says in Psalm 118:17, 'I shall not die, but live, and declare the works of the LORD.' He saved my life so I can show people the way to life."

The doctors left his room with valuable information, both medically and spiritually. They were interested in monitoring his ability to remember. So they engaged their patient in extended conversations that not only confirmed the health of his memory but the health of his faith as well.

Over the remainder of his stay in the hospital, the doctors listened intently to his conversations with the staff and received reports on his talks with other patients. In the process, the Holy Spirit had a magnificent opportunity to give a clear witness for Christ.

In the end, everyone agreed that Zvi's expressions of faith in Jesus as Messiah were not the evidence of a Jewish mind out of touch with reality. Quite the contrary. Jesus was the supreme reality to their cheerful patient whose lifestyle soon became such a powerful witness that the doctors and nurses developed an out-of-the-ordinary relationship with this extraordinary patient.

One morning Zvi was resting in bed when he looked across the room to find Max, the writer, reading a copy of Shakespeare's works. "Hey, Mr. Max," Zvi called cheerfully. "I see you are reading Shakespeare."

"Yes," Max thundered. "Do you know about Shakespeare?"

"Sure. He was a big writer. You also are a big writer. But even big writers sometimes don't understand the true meaning of their own words."

"And what do you mean by that?"

"I mean, Shakespeare wrote, 'To be or not to be? That is the question.' What he wrote about is not the big question. The real question is only 'To be.'"

"And how is that?" Max wanted to know.

"My Book tells us how 'to be.' And it was not written by a man, like Shakespeare. My Book was written by the prophets; and they wrote by the Holy Spirit.

"The Bible tells us how to know the Lord—'to be.' It also tells us what will become of us if we don't know the Lord—'not to be.'

"Shakespeare had many good things to say, and we can enjoy reading them. But only the Bible can give us the true meaning of life and death."

Max was listening, and his estimate of the "common" man was undergoing a transition. Even the writer's wife was now lingering at Zvi's bed, offering him generous slices of the cakes sent by friends.

Before they parted, the writer and the carpenter were sitting together discussing profound things—things as profound as eternity. It was good to see.

It was good also—profoundly good—to see Zvi leave the hospital to resume his life and ministry as God's man in Jerusalem.

CHAPTER THIRTY-FIVE

TRINA

Mendel met Ellen at church. She was a lovely girl who had come to live in Israel with her mother. Among Ellen's deepest desires was to show the Lord's love to the Chosen People. Little did she suspect when she arrived in Israel that she would become the Lord's chosen one for Zvi's eldest son.

Zvi and Esther were intrigued counselors as they watched the relationship between Ellen and Mendel progress from friendship to love. They were even more interested when the announcement came that the two were making wedding plans.

It was a beautiful wedding, and the happy newlyweds settled into a home not far from Zvi and Esther.

After a while, the couple began to hear the inevitable question: "How long are you going to wait before you have your first child?" The query was of more than academic interest to Zvi and his wife, of course who could hardly wait for grandchildren to augment the family circle and carry the Weichert name into the third generation. When the news finally came that Ellen was expecting, Zvi reacted with a restrained smile—he was under control. Esther, however, began to make plans—she was going to be ready.

In due course, Mendel and Ellen presented grandfather and grandmother with a round-faced little girl bursting with good health. To Zvi and Esther, Trina was the picture of what grandparents have a way of believing they have a right to expect—the most beautiful child ever born!

When Zvi looked down into the soft face of baby Trina, he witnessed a double miracle. He had a grandchild, yes. But after thousands of years, God was still at work fulfilling His promise that Abraham's posterity would never perish from the earth. All the plans of evil men will never extinguish the existence of the Jewish people. This little "seed" was proof enough. In an even more significant way, she also was prophetic evidence of the Lord's promise of a spiritual seed in those who believe. She would be reared in the nurture and admonition of the Lord.

With Trina's birth, Zvi's story continues into the third generation. All of Zvi's children eventually married. Today Zvi and Esther have fourteen grandchildren; and all are living reminders of the eminent perfection of a faithful God who will bring His people and program through whatever trials may lie before them. What He began in a teenaged Polish Jew who found his Messiah will continue to bear fruit to the glory of God until Jesus comes again.

Mendel, his brothers, sister, and others who make up the Lord's precious remnant in Israel are the visible life and breath of this magnificent realization. Together they are bringing the message of life in the Lord Jesus Christ to the next generations.

These young people are faithfully taking the torch from Zvi, Joseph Davidson, Uncle Nathan, and other courageous people who stood for Him in the hardest of places, and are carrying it to God's ancient people, Israel. God has sovereignly opened the way and continues to open new doors of ministry every day for His honor and glory. And we can all rejoice in the assurance that what He began through a believing handful at the birth of the modern State of Israel will continue until that nation turns to God and calls for the Messiah.

"And I will pour upon the house of David, and upon the inhabitants of Jerusalem, the Spirit of grace and of supplications; and they shall look upon me whom they have pierced, and they shall mourn for him, as one mourneth for his only son" (Zech. 12:10).

 POSTSCRIPT

When I first took up the pen to write Zvi's story those many years ago, we started in Poland with a bewildered ten-year-old boy who was clenched in the brutal vise of Hitler's determination to make him just one more dead Jew. Together we have watched in suspense as fifty-eight astounding years unfolded in the life of this extraordinary man of God.

In 1997, for the first time since his days as a child during the Holocaust, Zvi returned to his boyhood home in Warsaw. It was the only pre-World War II home still standing on the street. To see him enter the house that held so many memories for him was a deeply moving experience. As he walked through its rooms and hallways, he retraced where he had eaten, slept, and played with his sister and brothers.

Many thousands of people have taken the journey with him by way of the award-winning video, *ZVI: The Return*. This film version of Zvi's escape from the Nazis and emigration to Israel is now being viewed in English, Russian, and Spanish, and plans are underway to release it soon in German.

The story of the life of this courageous son of Abraham on the battlefields of Israel and on the streets of Jerusalem, faithfully witnessing for the Messiah, is one that will endure for generations to come. Above all, it is the story of God's sovereign ability to raise up those who will leave an enduring legacy of His power and grace.

ABOUT THE AUTHOR

Elwood McQuaid is a former executive director and editor-in-chief of The Friends of Israel Gospel Ministry, Inc., and its world-renowned magazine, *Israel My Glory*. An internationally known broadcaster and expert on Israel in the Middle East, he is the author of numerous books and was the voice of Friends of Israel radio for almost 20 years. He is currently consulting editor of *Israel My Glory*, where his articles appear regularly, and a frequent contributor to *The Jerusalem Post*.

MORE BOOKS BY ELWOOD MCQUAID

Zvi's story is also available in Spanish in two volumes:

ZVI
ISBN-10: 0-915540-62-2, #B01S
ISBN-13: 978-0-915540-62-4

ZVI Y LA GENERACION SIGUIENTE
ISBN-10: 0-915540-63-0, B28S
ISBN-13: 978-0-915540-63-1

COME, WALK WITH ME
From the award-winning "One Nation Under God" to the celebrated "Death Meets the Master," this inspiring assortment of poems, mini-biographies, delightful anecdotes, and devotionals will take you for a memorable stroll through time, through countrysides, and through the streets of Jerusalem.
ISBN-10: 0-915540-47-9, #B37
ISBN-13: 978-0-915540-47-1

IT IS NO DREAM
Said Theodor Herzl, the father of Zionism, "If you will it, it is no dream." This amazing book scans the entire biblical prophetic program and shows how a faithful, promise-keeping God molded historical events to make the modern state of Israel a "dream come true."
ISBN-10: 0-915540-21-5, #B02
ISBN-13: 978-0-915540-21-1

Not to the Strong

Journey to the time of the judges as Elwood McQuaid examines four "heroes of the faith" whom God chose to turn the tide and deliver Israel. Their frailties mirror our own—and what God did for them, He can do for us as well.

ISBN-10: 0-915540-45-2, #B42
ISBN-13: 978-0-915540-45-7

II Peter: Standing Fast in the Last Days

- How can we live for God during these climatic days before the Lord returns?
- How can we identify false teachers and charlatans?
- How can we understand what eternity holds?

This excellent volume provides answers to these all important questions from the little but powerful Bible book of 2 Peter. Its timely message will become an invaluable addition to your life as well as your personal library.

ISBN-10: 0-915540-65-7, #B79
ISBN-13: 978-0-915540-65-5

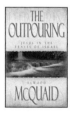

The Outpouring

This superb book will immeasurably enhance your understanding of how God certified the credentials of the Jewish Messiah among Abraham's seed in connection with the great, festive commemorations of the Jewish nation. John's Gospel will come alive as you discover the magnificant relationship between the feasts of Israel and the Lord Jesus Christ.

Also available in Russian.

ISBN 0-915540-49-5, #B35 [ENGLISH], #B35R [RUSSIAN]
ISBN-13: 978-0-915540-49-5

THE ZION CONNECTON

Elwood McQuaid takes a thoughtful, sensitive look at relations between Jewish people and evangelical Christians, including the controversial issues of anti-Semitism, the rise of Islam, the right of Jewry to a homeland in the Middle East, and whether Christians should try to reach Jewish people with the gospel message—and how.
ISBN-10: 0-915540-40-1, # B61
ISBN-13: 978-0-915540-40-2

THERE IS HOPE!

A Celebration of Scripture About the Rapture
What's ahead for the church? Learn how the church (1) is programmed for a sudden departure, (2) is going where death has no domain, (3) has no reason to fear the Antichrist, and (4) should look beyond His "Coming with Clouds."
ISBN 0-915540-11-8, # B62 *[ENGLISH]*.
ISBN-13: 978-0-915540-11-2

Also available in Spanish by the title of **Hay Esperanza.**
ISBN-10: 0-915540-64-9, # B62S *[SPANISH]*.
ISBN-13: 978-0-915540-64-8

to be more instant in prayer about particular concerns

To order by credit card or obtain a complete catalog of all the resources available from The Friends of Israel, call us at **800-345-8461**; visit our Web store at **www.foi.org**; or write us at **P.O. Box 908, Bellmawr, NJ 08099.**